Power
and the
Soviet
Elite

POWER
and the
SOVIET
ELITE

"The Letter of an Old Bolshevik"
and Other Essays by

BORIS I. NICOLAEVSKY

EDITED BY JANET D. ZAGORIA

Ann Arbor Paperbacks
The University of Michigan Press

c C

First edition as an Ann Arbor Paperback 1975
Copyright © 1965 by Boris I. Nicolaevsky
All rights reserved
ISBN 0-472-09196-4 (clothbound)
ISBN 0-472-06196-8 (paperbound)
Published in the United States of America by
The University of Michigan Press and simultaneously
in Don Mills, Canada, by Longman Canada Limited
Manufactured in the United States of America

Originally published for the Hoover Institution on War,
Revolution, and Peace by Frederick A. Praeger, Publishers

Editor's Note

The articles collected here have been written during the past twenty-five years. They have been selected for republication now not only to make them available to an English-speaking audience, but in the conviction that, while some of the arguments advanced by the author may be controversial, he addresses himself to fundamental issues of the Soviet system. The information and the insights contained in these articles provide invaluable background to an understanding of the Soviet scene, especially during the Stalin era. At the same time, so long as terror is a weapon that can be wielded by the Soviet leadership, Mr. Nicolaevsky's comments will have relevance to Soviet political life.

The articles were originally conceived of essentially as historical essays. I have tried to aid the reader with explanations, and the author himself has helped considerably with notes.

I would like to thank the following for permission to use articles originally published by them: *The New Leader, Novoye Russkoye*

Editor's Note

Slovo, Sotsialistichesky Vestnik, and, finally Allen & Unwin for their translation of "The Letter of an Old Bolshevik." I would also like to thank Seweryn Bialer and my husband, Donald, without whose foresight and generous help this volume would never have been possible; Barry Rubin for his role in translating the essays; Max Hayward for the care and keenness with which he went over the manuscript; and Jean Steinberg for labors beyond the call of her editorial duties. Editorial responsibility, of course, is mine alone.

J. D. Z.

New York City
May, 1965

Foreword

The articles in this collection deal with a single subject: the history of the complicated struggle in the higher reaches and secret recesses of the Communist Party apparatus, a struggle that in the past and still today determines the basic political line of the Kremlin. And in order to understand this political line, we must scrutinize the groups involved in the inner-Party conflict. Through the years, it has varied in intensity. In the early years of its history, the Communist dictatorship used terror only against its non-Communist enemies; it did not use violence against Communists who opposed official policy. True, in Lenin's time and for some years after his death, oppositional Communists were silenced: they were assigned to jobs in outlying provinces or foreign countries; they were arrested, exiled, sent to internment camps, etc., but they were not killed. Lenin's immediate successors felt bound to respect his "testament," in which he enjoined his followers not to shed the blood of their Party comrades. Stalin did not observe Lenin's testament, and when it came to the extermination of enemies, he made no distinction between Communists and non-Communists. The terror of the Stalin period, beginning with the murder of Kirov, differs from the terror of the pre-Stalin period in that during the years of the Great Purge and subsequently, Communists and non-Communists alike were "stood against the wall." The story of the inner-Party struggle during this period is closely bound up with the story of Stalinist terror.

In the post-Stalin years, many interesting facts about the history of the terror have come to light for the first time. In gathering and analyzing these facts, I have tried to illuminate the political implications of the various stages of the terror. These essays, written in the post-Stalin era, obviously cannot give a complete picture of the years of Stalin's bloody rule, but it is hoped that the diverse events examined in them will help to shed light on some abiding aspects of the inner-Party struggle for power.

The initiative for the republication of these articles came from a group of American students of Soviet affairs, among them Mrs. Janet Zagoria, the editor of this volume, who selected the articles and helped to prepare them for publication. Most of them first appeared in *Sotsialistichesky Vestnik* (Berlin, Paris, New York); two appeared in *Novoye Russkoye Slovo* (New York), and some have appeared in English in the *New Leader*. They are reproduced here without substantial changes, except for some additional footnotes by the editor and by myself. I would like to express my sincere thanks to Mrs. Zagoria; Mr. Seweryn Bialer, Columbia University; and Professor Robert C. Tucker, Princeton University.

BORIS I. NICOLAEVSKY

Menlo Park, California
June, 1965

Remember, I pray thee, who ever perished, being innocent? or where were the righteous cut off?

Even as I have seen, they that plow iniquity, and sow wickedness, reap the same.

By the blast of God they perish, and by the breath of his nostrils are they consumed.

The roaring of the lion, and the voice of the fierce lion, and the teeth of the young lions, are broken.

The old lion perisheth for lack of prey, and the stout lion's whelps are scattered abroad.

Job 4:7-11

Contents

Contents

Introduction

The Russian Revolution, as a concept taken to include the entire revolutionary process from the fall of Czardom to the end of the Civil War of 1918–20, had the effect of transferring a theoretical and actual monopoly of power from the person of the Czar to a small and rather ill-defined group of men, leaders of the Bolshevik faction of what had been known for some fifteen years as the Russian Social-Democratic Party. In theory, of course, these men were responsible to the occasional congresses, and through them to the rank and file, of this political faction, which they soon transformed into a separate party under the name of "Communist." In practice, however, this state of accountability never had reality, even at the start; and it was soon to be even formally deprived of meaning by Party statutes that gave to senior permanent bodies, throughout the Party hierarchy, the power of veto over elections or appointments to more junior ones. Thus Bolshevik leaders, in addition to asserting and exercising a right of absolute dictatorship over the population at large, became effectively supreme—self-appointed, removable, and replaceable only by themselves—even within that body to which they professed a specious theoretical accountability.

Now situations of this nature are not new in human history; but there were certain features of this one which differed from almost all other contemporary patterns and were destined to have profound effect on the development of Soviet power in future years.

First of all, there was the fact that the formal procedures by which this process of self-renewal might take place within the ruling group were never entirely clear or effective. Theoretically, the Central Committee, or later the Central Committee and the Central Control Commission sitting together as a Plenum, were regarded as competent to decide who should and who should not belong to their own senior permanent organs: the Politburo, the Orgburo, and the Secretariat. But it soon became apparent that membership on the Central Committee itself was something controlled in reality not by the periodic congresses of the Party (as it was supposed to be) or even by the majority of the Committee itself (which would have made it a truly self-perpetuating body), but by a small circle of persons—never formally identified and frequently changing members of these same senior permanent bodies. This obviously reversed in actuality the formal lines of authority, relegated the true power of personnel decision to the shadows of personal ingratiation, and opened the way for every sort of manipulation and intrigue.

This, in turn, might have been less dangerous had there existed at least a clear code of personal and collegial ethics to which, as among these senior figures, appeal could be taken. But here, too, what existed was inadequate. These, it must be remembered, were all men who had renounced, as a matter of ideological conviction, the view that there were any absolute standards of personal morality to which one owed obedience. Usefulness to the cause of social transformation, as defined by themselves, was the supreme determinant of right and wrong in all human conduct, including their own. With relation to people outside the Party itself, this was indeed the only criterion. Here, dishonesty, trickery, persecution, murder, torture were all in order, if considered to be useful and important, at the moment, to the cause. Within the Party itself, and within its higher ranks in particular, things were more complicated. An ethical code of sorts had indeed existed, in the prerevolutionary period, for the governance of relations among members of the Bolshevik faction and even to some extent (but more dubiously) among revolutionary socialists in general. Certain kinds of loyalty were expected; certain forms of betrayal were deplored; certain manifestations of personal consideration, sympathy, and even tenderness were permitted. All of this was overlaid, of course, on a substructure of what might be called bourgeois mannerisms and pretenses, inherited from the decidedly nonproletarian homes out of which, in great majority, these revolutionary intellectuals had emerged.

But as a code of mutual relations for the men in power after 1917, these traditional rules of revolutionary ethics were deficient. They were deficient, above all, by virtue of the very fact that these men *were* in power. The rules had been devised for men associated in an unequal struggle against a well-installed enemy, disposing over all the instruments of the power of the state. In the main, this enemy had now disappeared. To a certain extent, of course, his continued existence could be, and still was, argued: in the form of remnants of the possessing classes within Russia, of conscious and unconscious agents of the encircling capitalism, etc. But after the end of the Civil War, the main task of the Party no longer lay in the destruction of this Goliath, but rather in the building of socialism which his destruction was supposed to make possible. Could an ethical code designed for conspiratorial struggle against a more powerful adversary be successfully applied to relationships between men now themselves possessed of power, confronted primarily with the peaceful tasks of socialist construction?

The implications of this question cut deep. For it must be remembered: these rules, adequate or not, were all these men had to go on. There was nothing else to fall back on, no other set of restraints to contain the powerful impulses of personal ambition and the multitudinous abrasions, frictions, misunderstandings, and jealousies that affect the mutual relations of men associated in a political undertaking. Nor, in the absence of effective arrangements for political accountability, was there any elaborate, any legislative branch, any supreme constitutional authority, to which appeal could be taken in the event of disagreement. The Bolsheviks had themselves destroyed everything of that sort when they suppressed and wrecked, by force of arms, Russia's first and only constitutional convention, in January, 1918. The Bolshevik leaders thus lived, from the time of the Revolution, in something very close to a complete moral vacuum—a vacuum tenuously filled only by an earlier code of comradely loyalties, designed for a militant struggle now rapidly receding into history.

The breakdown of this code, as an effective guide to action, began at an early date. It began with the outlawing of the other revolutionary socialist parties, the Mensheviks and the Socialist-Revolutionaries, and finally the persecution of their members; for the code, after all, was one that initially had had relevance to other socialists and to other revolutionaries. But the breakdown could not stop at this point. There was too much fluidity, at that early date, among the memberships of these various socialist groupings. If the Socialist-Revolutionary deserved death, what did the Bolshevik deserve who leaned to Socialist-Revolutionary, or Menshevik, or other unacceptable views? The task of governing a great country was bound to open up abundant disagreements and bones of contention among members of a ruling elite. To an extent these were, inevitably, matters of temperament. They could not fail to be affected by personal attachments or antipathies. What consequences were to be drawn from such divisions? What place was to be assigned to the leading Bolshevik who could not support with conviction the current postulates of the Party line and—even worse —could not feel entire confidence in the motives of the sponsors of postulates with which he did not agree? It was easy enough to say that those whose views had been rejected should fall silent or give lip service to party policies in which they did not really believe. But this was not easy for men of deep intellectual convictions and polemic temperament. And when doubts arose as to motive, and when personal rivalries and jealousies and suspicions intervened as well, as they were bound to do in the presence of egos such as those of Trotsky and Stalin, what rules were then to prevail? What were the limits of action in personal rivalry? To what code of behavior could appeal be taken?

Introduction

Lenin was well aware of the importance of this question. Though he had himself·taken leadership in pressing for the execution of the Socialist-Revolutionaries, thus restricting the operation of the old rules to the Bolshevik faction alone, he had never doubted that within this narrower circle, at least, the rules could be, and ought to be, effective and adequate. It was not accidental that his deathbed quarrel with Stalin was primarily not over issues of political policy (although there were some of these, too) but rather over just this problem of personal ethics in relations among leading figures of the Party. It was precisely for lack of loyalty, of courtesy, of consideration for comrades, etc., that Lenin, in his political testament, urged Stalin's removal from the post of Secretary General of the Party.

Lenin scarcely appreciated the extent to which he, by his own ruthlessness, intolerance, and lack of scruple in the conduct of Party affairs in earlier years, had contributed to the creation of the problem with which, on his deathbed, he saw the Party faced. So long as he lived, his personality was sufficiently powerful to contain and conceal the problem, even though he had helped to create it. But with his death, and with Stalin (to whose darkly mistrustful mind no political issue was ever without its personal implications) in the dominant position within the Party, nothing could prevent these weaknesses from coming to· the fore.

Through the remaining years of the twenties, the agony grew. Ten years after Lenin's death, the problem of whether it was permissible and proper to apply the death penalty to leading Party comrades, as a punishment for opposition and "factionalism," loomed, with dread immediacy, as the great unspoken issue behind the debates of the Seventeenth Party Congress. At the end of 1934, this issue was settled, disastrously, in the wake of the murder of Kirov: settled in favor of the death penalty, and settled—significantly—not by consensus within the leading group (the consensus would unquestionably have run the other way) but by the simple fact that Stalin succeeded in creating a situation where anything but the pretense of liveliest agreement with *his* views had become mortally dangerous.

For nearly two decades thereafter, the terror of the personality of a single man was the main arbiter not only of relationships between the regime and the people but also of personal and political relationships within the ruling group. The results are too well known to require mention here. Even the vague pretenses of a constitutionality within the Party, which had marked its inner life in the early periods, were now largely discarded. Bodies which should formally have met at regular intervals failed, finally, to come together for years on end. The machinations of Stalin's personal chancery and of the secret police now mocked the formalities of consultation and collective decision within the highest organs of the Party, just as in the past these highest organs had mocked the will of the Party rank and file, and the Party itself had mocked the will of the populace at large. The corruption inherent in this situation unavoidably affected not only the dictator himself and those who were the intimate instruments of his intrigues and persecutions but also those more dignified and independent political figures who had contrived to survive, however unhappily, in his political entourage. And when, in 1953, he died, and his system of personal terror died with him, this left an entourage dazed, bewildered, disoriented by the long, degrading experience; anxious to restore something of constitutionality in the procedures of the Party and something like decency to the atmosphere of their own mutual relations; tending to grope, with this in view, back into the Lenin era for precedents; but not too sure, any longer, in the understanding of these precedents; unable, in the wake of their own extensive involvement, to repudiate or even to understand fully the very evils that had been the source of their discomfort.

How, in a moral vacuum of this nature, do men behave? How, specifically, did the men around Stalin behave in the midst of such vicissitudes? How did they come to permit the establishment of this regime of personal terrorism in the first place? And how, in the case of those who survived it, did they react as it approached its end, and when it was gone? These are the questions to which, in large part, the various articles contained in this volume are addressed; and speculative as many of these discussions are, unsatisfactory as is much of the evidence on which, unavoidably, their judgments rest, they do, in their entirety, give some idea of the answers to these questions.

Boris Nicolaevsky, Russian Social-Democrat of Menshevik persuasion, collaborator of the Marx-Engels Institute in Moscow, historian of the Marxist movement, long-time Director of the Paris Branch of the International Institute of Social History, and as such custodian of the important collections of the Second International, is one of the great surviving figures of the socialist segment of the Russian revolutionary movement of Czarist times. Like so many other educated Russian youngsters of his day, he was reared in its spirit; its ideals have dominated his life; its tragedy has been his tragedy. He has been, at various times, the prisoner of both the Czarist and the Soviet regimes. In the long, lonely years of his present exiled existence, the sources with which he has had to work have become thinner. Memories have lost some of their relevance to present conditions. The generation of his comrades in the movement—those within the Soviet Union, and those who, like himself, were obliged to seek refuge outside—has been steadily decimated. The bright ideals of a humane Marxism, to which he and many of the other Russian Social-Democrats were committed, have met, over these years, with fearful abuse at the hands of Stalin; and they have been tarnished in Western understanding by semantic association with the methods of Stalin's regime. In the face of all these discouragements, Mr. Nicolaevsky has carried on as a student and commentator of Soviet political life, applying to it the unfailing intensity of his interest, the wealth of his experience, the extraordinary capacity of his own memory, and, by implication, the discipline of his own conscience as a Russian Marxist and (in terms of Czarist Russia) revolutionary.

The general picture that emerges from the sketches contained in this volume is a strange one for the Western reader. Mr. Nicolaevsky has carried over into the treatment of his subject that austere impersonality—that rigorous outward subordination of the personal individuality to the political one—which has marked the Russian revolutionary movement even from its Populist days. The result is that the actors in his studies seem to have no flesh and blood, no physical appearances, no personal lives, no homes, no loves, no recreations. They are only names, algebraic symbols, representing certain values, here and there, in the abstract problem of total politics. As such they flit, ghostlike, across his pages, tilting at each other with ideas and with organizational chess-moves, not

entirely devoid of interest, it would seem, in the welfare of the state
or the movement, but never forgetting the jungle-like quality of a
political environment in which the penalties of political failure
either are, at the particular moment, mortal or have recently been,
and could easily become so again.

Mr. Nicolaevsky's most important service to the historiography
of the Stalin era has been his bringing to light, in the form of the
"Letter of an Old Bolshevik," of Bukharin's views, as of the spring
of 1936, on the situation then prevailing in Stalin's political entourage. This document, despite its indirect quality (it represents
not Bukharin's actual words, but Nicolaevsky's memory of them,
somewhat disguised to protect Bukharin's position), is the most
authoritative and important single bit of source material we have
on the background of the Purges. Its credibility and importance
are heightened by the interesting account (published for the first
time in this volume) of the manner in which Bukharin's views
came to Nicolaevsky's knowledge. It is largely to this "letter" and
to Nicolaevsky's other researches that we owe our present knowledge of the formidable internal-Party opposition with which Stalin
was faced in the period between 1932 and 1934, of the political
background of the Kirov murder, and of the significance of Kirov's
disappearance from the scene. All of this is illuminating, in a most
important way, for the motives of the Purges that were soon to
follow. Not only Western scholars, but future generations of
Russians as well, will be grateful for the industry and the interest
that brought all this to light.

The remaining articles of the volume are all ones that appeared
(mostly in Russian-language periodicals) in the period after Stalin's death. With the exception of two that deal, retrospectively,
with the Kirov murder, all are concerned primarily with the events
of the post-Stalin period. This being so, they are necessarily tenta-
tive and speculative. They represent attempts to break through the
various veils of official reticence or prevarication and to evoke
some idea of what was occurring at given moments, behind the
scenes, in the highest circles of the Soviet Communist Party. The
argumentation is sometimes involved, the evidence in some cases
unavoidably tenuous or obscure. But enough is both demonstrable
and demonstrated here to make it plain that the basic dilemma,

arising from the lack of a valid system of political restraints and ethical rules, still plagues the senior figures of the Party, and that they are still far from having discovered the solutions.

In concluding these observations, I may give it as my personal conviction that the leaders of the Communist Party of the Soviet Union will not find the answer to this problem within the framework of their Party alone. A constitutionality and an ethical code capable of supporting over long periods the personal strains of political association in the higher echelons of a ruling regime can be effectively derived only from institutions that embrace and protect the entire society subject to the regime's authority. Over the long run, men in power can expect no greater protection from injustice and cruelty at the hands of their peers than they are themselves willing to extend to the humblest of their subjects. When the Soviet leaders bring themselves to recognize that there are certain indispensable restraints on the manner in which men may be permitted to treat other men, anywhere, and that the observance of these restraints, as a matter of methodological principle having relation to common people as well as to Party members, is more important to the progress of a society than any specifically conceived goals of political action, then, and then only, will they create an atmosphere in which the rivalries that politics inevitably engenders can be borne without shame or danger; only then will they be able to unfold their full powers as individuals and to unleash the full constructive potential of the ideology they believe in, such as it may be. Until then, they will have to continue to cope in semidarkness, in anxiety and suspicion, with the problems of personal relations engendered by their mutual association; and until then, men who share Mr. Nicolaevsky's dedication will have to continue, in the interests of historical truth, their efforts to penetrate the veils behind which people will always try to obscure the sordid and unhappy process of political rivalry that inevitably ensues.

GEORGE F. KENNAN

Princeton, New Jersey
May, 1965

ONE

Bukharin on the
Opposition to Stalin

Furthermore, during my last trip abroad in 1936, after the conversation with Rykov, I established contact with the Menshevik Nikolaevsky, who is very close to the leading circles of the Menshevik party. From the conversation with Nikolaevsky, I ascertained that he knew about the agreements between the Rightists, Zinovievites and Kamenevites, and the Trotskyites, and that, in general, he was in the know on all that was going on, including the Riutin platform.

From BUKHARIN'S *testimony*
at his trial, March, 1938.

An Interview with
Boris Nicolaevsky*

INTERVIEWER: You have said that "The Letter of an Old Bolshevik" was largely based on your conversations with Bukharin in 1936. Would you tell us first, Mr. Nicolaevsky, how you came to meet him then?

NICOLAEVSKY: This is a very long story, interesting in itself. I will tell it as briefly as possible. My meetings with Bukharin concerned certain German archives I had taken out of Germany, along with the Russian Social Democratic archive, when I left Berlin in May, 1933. I had taken these materials out at the request of Otto Wells, chairman of the executive committee of the German Social Democratic Party, whose property they were. The German archives, together with the Russian archive, were shipped to Paris, where I acted as their curator.

* This interview between Mr. Nicolaevsky, on the one hand, and Seweryn Bialer and myself, on the other, took place in New York on January 30, 1964.—J.D.Z.

The Bolsheviks were extremely anxious to obtain the German archives for their collection in Moscow, which, in addition to the archive of Bebel, Liebknecht, and others, included the archive of Marx and Engels. In 1935, they sent a representative of the Marx-Engels Institute to ask me if I would agree to conduct negotiations for their sale to the Russians. I said that I could only transmit their offer to the German Social Democrats. I did so, and the negotiations were begun.

The main stage of the negotiations took place when a delegation was sent to Paris. This delegation consisted of Bukharin, who was then a member of the Central Committee, V. V. Adoratsky, who was director of the Marx-Engels-Lenin Institute, and Arosev, a well-known Soviet writer, who was chairman of VOKS, the All-Union Society for Cultural Relations with Foreign Countries. Bukharin came as an expert on Marx, and apparently at his own request.

The negotiations lasted from February to the end of April, 1936. The Bolsheviks made an offer of 10 million francs, but this enormous sum was rejected because the Germans did not want to relinquish the material on Marx.

It was in this connection that Bukharin and the other members of the delegation came to see me on the day they arrived in Paris.

INTERVIEWER: Then the conversation was of a purely official character?

NICOLAEVSKY: No, there was an unofficial side as well to my talks with Bukharin. Bukharin and I had never met before. But he was almost the same age as I, and he had had many of the same experiences as I. I was arrested for the first time in January, 1904; he was arrested for the first time in 1908. But he had been in the same place of exile as I, in Onega, in Archangel province. We had mutual acquaintances, and we had occasion to reminisce about them.

Moreover, Bukharin tried to give a more personal character to our dealings. When he came to my place that first evening, for example, his first words were, "Regards from Vladimir" (my brother). Later, when Bukharin and I had occasion to talk alone, he said, "Regards from Aleksei" (Rykov).* My brother had married Rykov's sister, and they lived together with Rykov, at whose place Bukharin often was a guest. In the presence of the other members of the commission, Bukharin had given me regards only from my brother, who was a Menshevik, although not politically active. Only when we were alone did he convey Rykov's greetings. Thus he set the tone for our subsequent conversations.

INTERVIEWER: Why do you think Bukharin was interested in lending this unofficial aura to your talks with him?

NICOLAEVSKY: I had a definite impression that he wanted to acquaint someone from the outside world whom he regarded with trust with his position on certain matters. For example, concerning the trial of the Socialist Revolutionaries in 1922, he asked me, "Do you know my *real* role in this trial?" I replied that I knew that behind the scenes he had opposed the execution of the defendants. There had been a fierce battle over the trial, on whether or not to execute the defendants. Bukharin had committed himself against the executions, but the Central Committee did not recognize this commitment, and forced by Party discipline, Bukharin then came out officially with the most violent anti-SR speeches.

I had the impression that Bukharin deliberately wanted to set the record straight on this and other points, so that his real views might be known outside of the Soviet Union. But clearly his desire to talk conflicted with his fear of telling too much.

I recall that Arosev, who for a long time had lived abroad, was present at one of our conversations. He interrupted our talk and practically cut Bukharin off with a remark to me: "Well, we're going and you'll write down some interesting recollections." I felt that he was apprehensive. And so I answered: "Let's make an agreement: The last one from among us here to be alive will write about our meetings." As it happens, I am the last.

* Rykov succeeded Lenin as the Chairman of the Council of People's Commissars. He became part of the Rightist group which opposed Stalin, and at the Sixteenth Congress he was forced to admit his errors abjectly. At the time of Bukharin's visit to Nicolaevsky, Rykov was still a member of the Central Committee, but very much in disfavor with Stalin.—Ed.

INTERVIEWER: How did Bukharin seem during the period covered by your talks? What was his mood?

NICOLAEVSKY: Bukharin strongly seemed to desire a rest from the strain of life in Moscow. He was tired. He wanted to rest for a few months, perhaps to swim in the sea, not to think or argue. This seemed his mood when one day he said to me: "Boris Ivanovich, why do we spend all our time haggling? Let's go down someplace to the Mediterranean. You will write to your people that I am not agreed. I'll write that you're not agreed. And we'll take a rest for a month or two." Of course, the remark was made jokingly, but there was a serious undertone. At this moment his young wife approached. She was a student awaiting their first child. Bukharin introduced me to her. She also very much needed a vacation and she smiled sympathetically when her husband spoke of a trip to the sea.

At the same time, it appears that Bukharin would not have wanted to leave Russia for good. He said as much in a conversation with a certain Communist woman—Fanny Yezerskaya—who came to see him in Paris and who later reported their talks to me. She, the former secretary of Rosa Luxemburg, was on very good terms with Bukharin, having worked under him in the Comintern. And she tried to persuade him to remain abroad. She said that it was necessary to set up an opposition paper abroad, one which would be really informed about what was going on in Russia and which might exert a great influence there. She claimed that Bukharin was unique in being able to fill that role. But, she told me, Bukharin said to her in reply: "I don't think that I should be able to live without Russia. We are all accustomed to things there and to the tenseness of life."

He would say such things as this. When we were in Copenhagen, Bukharin recalled that Trotsky lived relatively close by, in Oslo. With a wink, he said, "Suppose we took this trunk [containing manuscripts by Marx] and went to see Trotsky for a day." And he continued, "Needless to say, he and I had bitter fights, but this does not prevent me from regarding him with great respect."

He was capable of talking in this way, of the difficult life at home, of his respect for Trotsky. But this was as far as he went.

Interview with Boris Nicolaevsky

INTERVIEWER: Did he speak freely of the situation in the Soviet Union at the time and of the struggles inside the Party?

NICOLAEVSKY: Because I knew of the resolution of the Communist Party forbidding Communists from speaking to non-Party members about intra-Party relations, I never raised the subject. However, we had many conversations about the situation within the Party. Bukharin clearly wanted to talk about it. And I understood his mood.

Another Bolshevik—also important, though not so important as Bukharin—once said to me, upon arriving abroad: "Back there we have forgotten how to be frank. Only when one goes abroad and speaks with someone like you, about whom one knows everything from our secret archives and upon whom one can also rely, then one can speak frankly." In my opinion, this was also Bukharin's feeling, although he tried to restrain himself.

Usually Bukharin and I passed to general political questions from remembrances of the past and from stories about mutual acquaintances, of whom we had many. And the transition from the past to the present was very easy. Thus our conversations had a discursive character. He did not speak directly about the situation in the U.S.S.R.; he would often counter difficult questions with one of his own. And to this day I am not sure why. Was it that he did not want to confide completely in a man who was not also a believer in Communism? Or was it that he feared to draw certain conclusions even in his own mind? Yet from certain remarks, from his silences or his questions, I could get some idea of his attitudes on various matters, even though he did not define them.

INTERVIEWER: These conversations of yours figured in Bukharin's trial, I know. What were the charges against him in this respect?

NICOLAEVSKY: At his trial, Bukharin made the following statement in connection with our talks:

> The concrete and new element of our conversation was that in the event of the exposure of the Rightist center or the contact center or the upper organization of the conspiracy generally, there would be, through Nikolaevsky, an understanding with the leaders of the Second International that they would launch a suitable campaign in the press. . . .

7

"I forgot to say that my meeting with Nikolaevsky was facilitated for me, and camouflaged, by the fact that I had to meet with this Nikolaevsky by virtue of my official business. Thus I had a quite legitimate cover behind which I could carry on counterrevolutionary conversations and make agreements of one kind or another."*

In other words, Bukharin was accused of having made an agreement with me to alert the Socialist Second International in the event of his arrest, so that it might come to his defense.

I must add that these assertions in the indictment of Bukharin have no basis whatsoever in reality. Of course, no agreement was concluded between Bukharin and me. We did not even discuss such an agreement. I recall, however, that at the time of the 1938 trial, I detected in Bukharin's testimony a desire to vindicate himself in the eyes of Socialist public opinion in the West, that is, to demonstrate that he and his friends were now becoming proponents of a *rapprochement* with democratic socialism. But I believe this feeling developed only after our meeting in Paris.

INTERVIEWER: One more question before we get to the substance of the "Letter," Mr. Nicolaevsky: Can you tell us something about the manner in which you composed it?

NICOLAEVSKY: I wrote "The Letter of an Old Bolshevik" without having any sort of notes on my talks with Bukharin. I had made a number of such notes but had thought it necessary to get rid of them after the August, 1936, Chekist raid on the premises of the Paris section of the Amsterdam International Institute of Social History, of which I was then director. At the time of this raid, thirty or forty packages were stolen. These contained materials from the Trotsky archive which his son had just given to the section for custody. There is no doubt that the Chekists were searching for materials for prospective trials, that they considered the Bukharin-Rykov trial one of the most important, and that they were investigating Bukharin's meetings abroad. Because the circumstances of the theft of the Trotsky archive indicated the existence of an inside

* "The Case of the Anti-Soviet 'Bloc of Rightists and Trotskyites,'" Report of the Court Proceedings Heard before the Military Collegium of the Supreme Court of the U.S.S.R., Moscow, March 2–13, 1938 (Moscow: People's Commissariat of the U.S.S.R., 1938, English ed.), p. 426.

source of information—it is now clear that Zbarovsky, the confidential secretary of Trotsky's son, was an agent of Stalin—I decided to destroy all of my notes on Bukharin's political conversations. But I still remember the contents of these conversations, and several portions were set forth in the "Letter."

I should explain that the "Letter" was originally written not as the reflections of an Old Bolshevik, but as an account of my conversations with Bukharin. F. I. Dan, then editor of the *Sotsialisti-chesky Vestnik,* asked me to rewrite what I had done because he felt a simple account by the Bolshevik himself would be better. Thus the document appeared without annotation, as though it were a verbatim report.

I must also add that Bukharin's accounts went up only to 1936. Our meetings took place in the spring of that year. For facts about the rest of the year I relied on information from other sources, above all Charles Rappoport, a well-known French-Russian Communist who, because of the Zinoviev-Kamenev trial, had begun to retreat from Communism and who readily shared with me his extensive information.

Rereading the "Letter" now, I see that I omitted many of the stories that Bukharin told me, especially those relating to him personally. I did this for various reasons, chiefly to avoid giving any clue as to the identity of my informant. Yet all that Bukharin told me was very strongly colored by personal overtones. For he was a man completely immersed in politics who did not speak of politics in isolation from the details of his own life. On the contrary, Bukharin described the political struggle then being waged in the Soviet leadership through the prism of his personal experience. As I have already said, I felt at the time that he was telling me everything so that later someone might correctly explain the motives behind his conduct. Now, three decades later, in the light of all that has happened, I am convinced that my suspicion was correct. There was much that Bukharin did not talk about at all, there was much he did not explain fully, but what he did tell me, he told me with his obituary in mind.

In fact, this was the main source of difficulty in composing the "Letter." I had, on the one hand, to extract the substance of his remarks as they related to political events; on the other, I had to preserve the general mood he conveyed of the Old Bolsheviks, who found themselves in a new, Stalinist environment and who were dying in it.

INTERVIEWER: Turning now to the content of your talks with Bukharin, you said that he mentioned the trial of the Socialist Revolutionaries in 1922. Did he have anything further to say about his role in this affair?

NICOLAEVSKY: Bukharin was a member of the Comintern delegation which, in March and April, 1922, negotiated with the Socialist International for a united front. You may remember that at that time, meetings of the three Internationals were being held in Berlin: the Second International, the so-called Vienna Union, and the Third Communist International. Bukharin told me that in the negotiations he, Radek, and the other members of the Comintern delegation were conducting with the Socialists, the latter declared that it would be possible to create a united front on the condition that the Bolsheviks establish a minimum of democracy in Russia. They demanded that, as a first step, the death penalty not be applied in the case of the Socialist Revolutionaries, whose trial was then being prepared in Moscow.

The SR's had been put under arrest when they fought for the reconvening of the Constituent Assembly, which had been dispersed by the Bolsheviks. They were to be tried in the summer of 1922 as enemies of the Soviet regime. The foreign Socialists wished to make sure that the Socialist Revolutionaries would not be executed. Bukharin indicated to me that he and the other members of the delegation agreed to this, backing it up with their personal guarantees. At the same time, there was begun in Russia, on the initiative of Trotsky, a campaign to prosecute relentlessly all "counterrevolutionaries." In support of this campaign, the Central Committee of the CPSU refused to recognize the guarantee given by Bukharin and the others in Berlin, and all principal defendants in the SR trial were subsequently sentenced to death.

In his talks with me on this question, Bukharin twice explained his position by saying: "Yes, it must be admitted, you Socialists were able in the early twenties to put all of Europe on its feet and to make execution of the sentence against the Socialist Revolutionaries impossible."

INTERVIEWER: I understand that "The Letter of an Old Bolshevik" contains the first account of the so-called Riutin platform. Did you learn about this from Bukharin?

NICOLAEVSKY: I had, of course, known about the platform of Riutin, whom I had met personally in 1918 in Irkutsk, when he was still a Menshevik. I knew that in 1928 he was one of the pillars of the right-wing opposition in the Moscow Committee, which Stalin broke up, and that after he was removed from his post as editor of *Krasnaya Zvezda* he wrote a long program, the bulk of which dealt with an analysis of the role of Stalin in the life of the Communist Party.

But Bukharin acquainted me to some extent with the specifics of Riutin's attack on Stalin. He said that Riutin had claimed the Soviet leader was "in his way the evil genius of the Russian Revolution, who, motivated by a personal desire for power and revenge, brought the Revolution to the verge of ruin," and that he argued that "without the elimination of Stalin, it is impossible to restore the health of either the Party or the country." Stalin said that the platform was an appeal for his assassination. In fact, however, it contained no such direct appeal, although it did hold that it was necessary to remove Stalin from his post as General Secretary.

INTERVIEWER: Did you discuss any people with Bukharin—Lenin, Stalin, or others?

NICOLAEVSKY: Yes. His remarks about Lenin were particularly interesting, too, because Bukharin was so devoted to him. Even when he spoke about their disagreements—over the Malinovsky case,* for example—he did so in a tone of warmth and friendship.

---

* The affair of Roman Malinovsky, deputy of the Fourth State Duma and member of the Bolshevik Central Committee, was one of the most disgraceful chapters in Lenin's biography. Malinovsky had been an agent of the Czarist police for a number of years and had betrayed hundreds of Party workers. But his activity was advantageous to Lenin for factional reasons; for the Czarist police, in order to safeguard its agent Malinovsky, supported Lenin's policy of promoting schism in the ranks of the Social Democratic Party and the workers' movement. Lenin had been warned about Malinovsky by a number of people, including many prominent Bolsheviks, among

11

Bukharin on Opposition to Stalin

This is what he told me about the final period of Lenin's illness. From various details in Bukharin's account, I gathered that he meant the early fall of 1922. "Lenin would summon me to come and see him," Bukharin said. "The doctors had forbidden him to speak lest he become upset. But when I arrived, he would immediately take me by the hand and lead me into the garden. He would begin to speak: 'They don't want me to think about this. They say that this upsets me. But why don't they understand that I have lived my whole life this way? If I cannot speak about this, I become more upset than when I do speak. I calm down when I am able to talk about these matters with people like you.'"

I asked Bukharin what the conversations had been about. He replied that he and Lenin spoke mostly about "leaderology," as we called it—that is, the problem of succession, of who was fit to be leader of the Party after Lenin was gone. "This," said Bukharin, "is what worried and upset Lenin the most."

In this connection, he told me that the last articles of Lenin's, *Better Less but Better,* about cooperatives and so forth, were only part of what Lenin had planned to do. He had wanted to put out another series of approximately the same number of articles which would give a complete picture of the future policy to be pursued. This was his principal goal.

Lenin's testament consisted of two parts, a small part about the leaders, and a bigger one about policies. I asked Bukharin what the principle of Lenin's policy was. He said to me: "I have written two things about this policy, *The Road to Socialism and the Worker-Peasant Alliance* and *Lenin's Political Testament.* The first

---

them Bukharin. He had had occasion to deal with Malinovsky in Moscow in 1911, and at that time became convinced that Malinovsky was a police agent. From the first he warned Lenin of the known facts, but Lenin not only did not heed his warning, he even threatened Bukharin—in the name of the Central Committee—with exclusion from the Party if he did not cease to "slander" Malinovsky.

I learned about the struggle at the top of the Bolshevik Party over the Malinovsky affair from A. A. Troyanovsky, who in 1913–14 was a member of the Bolshevik Central Committee. But Bukharin filled in some of the details, including his arguments with Lenin, whose position he could not understand. In 1936, Bukharin attributed Lenin's failure to act on this matter to an "obsession" of his.—B. N.

is a pamphlet, which came out in 1925, the second was published in 1929." Bukharin asked me, "Do you remember those pamphlets?" I replied, "I confess I don't at present remember *The Road to Socialism.*"

"That is the more interesting one," he said. "When I wrote it, I included my conversations with Lenin about the articles already published and those not yet published. I tried in that pamphlet to keep to only what Lenin thought, to what he told me. Of course, they were not quotations; my understanding of what he meant was reflected in what I wrote. But it was my outline of Lenin's ideas as he expounded them to me. The main point of his testament was that it is possible to arrive at Socialism without applying more force against the peasantry." The question concerned, of course, the treatment of the peasantry, which constituted 80 per cent of the population of Russia. In the opinion of Lenin and of all Communists in general, it was possible to apply force against the peasantry at a given moment, yet this was not to be made a permanent method of treatment. This was the point of *The Road to Socialism.*

With *Lenin's Political Testament,* Bukharin said, it was a different matter. "There were big arguments about it, and I had to write only about what Lenin had already published. It was fundamentally the same thing. But the first pamphlet went further and the ideas in it were more crystallized; it did not stop at what he had already written." •

I have reread these pamphlets and I see that Bukharin was quite right in presenting Lenin's ideas in this way. This was the way Lenin thought. And Lenin considered Bukharin the one most able to convey his thoughts. He spoke with him so that Bukharin would write what he himself had left unsaid.

I should add here that when Bukharin told me about what Lenin said to him, I replied, "You know, in telling you these things, Lenin in essence was returning to Struve." At the end of the 1890's, Struve wrote a long article that discussed the question of the use of force after the Socialist revolution, maintaining that a Socialist system of production must not be built on force as a permanent factor. Bukharin was interested in this article. He said that he would without fail find it and look at it.

13

INTERVIEWER: And Stalin? Did he comment on Stalin?

NICOLAEVSKY: If you are speaking of personal meetings between them, then only in the most cursory fashion. One day at my place he saw an edition of *Knight in a Leopard Skin,* the great Georgian national epic poem by Rustaveli. It was a de-luxe anniversary edition with some illustrations, published by the Georgian Government. When Bukharin saw it, he said: "I saw that at Stalin's house the last time I visited him. He showed it to me." That was all.

Fanny Yezerskaya told me, however, that she asked him directly, "What is your relationship with Stalin?" And Bukharin replied, "Three minus," . . . the very lowest.*

For the most part, Bukharin hardly mentioned Stalin's name and said almost nothing about their personal relations. I gained the impression that he knew of the "Caucasian vengefulness" of Stalin, about which people talked even in the pre-Revolutionary period, and that he had already come into conflict with Stalin because of it. For this reason he was very restrained in his remarks to me.

INTERVIEWER: Did he talk of any other people?

NICOLAEVSKY: Yes, he told me an interesting story about his first meeting with Ivan Pavlov, the famous Russian scientist. Bukharin had been elected to the Academy of Sciences. When his name came up for election—it was, if I'm not mistaken, in 1926–27, perhaps even earlier—Bukharin said that Pavlov made a speech against his election, calling him a "person who is up to his knees in blood." This happened in Bukharin's absence. Bukharin, upon learning of Pavlov's remark, decided to have it out with him. "I respected him very much," he told me. "Of course, I was not in agreement with him on a number of points, but I respected him as a scholar, a scientist, and most of all as a person. I went to see him and said, 'I want to have a talk with you.' Pavlov received me more than coldly. But, since he had led me into his apartment, he had to converse. We spoke for several hours. Lunchtime came and, already faintly embarrassed, Pavlov said: 'Well, there's nothing to be done about it. Let's go. I invite you to have lunch with me.' We went into the dining room and, as we entered, I noticed that on the walls were cases of butterflies. Pavlov was a collector of butterflies, as

* In Russian schools, this mark denotes a failing grade.—Ed.

was I.* I had already sat down at the table when, directly across from me, over the door, I saw a case with an exceedingly rare type of butterfly. And I exclaimed to Pavlov, 'What? You have *this*?' 'So . . . ,' Pavlov replied, 'he even knows this.' I inquired where it had been caught, and so on, and he became convinced that I did indeed know it. Thus began our friendship."

INTERVIEWER: How did Bukharin affect Pavlov? What was it that impressed him?

NICOLAEVSKY: It had to do with Bukharin's humanist ideas. Bukharin discussed with Pavlov his belief that the intelligentsia must—as Gorky later did—help the Bolsheviks to change the general atmosphere in Russia. As Bukharin explained to me: "They are all good people, ready for any sacrifice. If they are acting badly now, it is not because they are bad, but because the situation is bad. They must be persuaded that the country is not against them, but only that a change of policy is necessary."

He once asked me to get him Trotsky's bulletin so that he could read the latest issues. I got him not only Trotsky's *Bulletin Oppositsy,* but also Socialist publications, including the *Sotsialistichesky Vestnik.* He regarded the *Vestnik* rather critically, but one thing attracted his attention. One article in the latest issue that had appeared before his arrival in Paris—that of February, 1936—contained a discussion of Gorky's plan to unite the intelligentsia into a separate party to take part in elections. On this, Bukharin said: "Some second party is necessary. If there is only one election slate and there is no contest, it is the same as Nazism. In order to differentiate ourselves in the minds of the peoples of both Russia and the West, we must institute a system of two electoral slates as opposed to the one-party system."

His idea was that the second party, composed of the intelli-

---

* Bukharin greatly loved butterflies. When we were in Amsterdam, he simply had to go to the Museum of Natural History, which had displays on the ethnography and natural history of all Dutch colonies and was quite exceptional—perhaps the foremost museum in the world—for its extensive collection of butterflies. Bukharin fell hungrily upon this collection and could not be pulled away. I left him there busying himself and examining everything with a magnifying glass, while I looked at other things. When I returned, he told me, "This was the passion of my childhood."—B. N.

gentsia, would not be a force opposed in principle to the regime, but one making proposals for changes and remedies.

INTERVIEWER: And Pavlov agreed with him in this?

NICOLAEVSKY: Yes, Pavlov as well as several other outstanding scholars. This was the basis of Bukharin's friendship with Pavlov. Pavlov had died just before my talks with Bukharin, and Bukharin remarked one day that this was a tremendous loss, because Pavlov had agreed to support him on this issue.

The idea was, to a considerable extent, Utopian, because the country had just gone through collectivization and was on the threshold of the Great Purge. But Bukharin and others obviously believed that their plan could be realized.

INTERVIEWER: How, precisely, did Bukharin believe that humanism might be used to fight the Nazis?

NICOLAEVSKY: When Bukharin passed through Germany en route to Paris, he stopped in Berlin for a day, ran around to all the bookstores, and bought a pile of theoretical pamphlets about Fascism. They lay on the table in his hotel room and he constantly studied them.

He felt that Hitler had posed this question to the Soviet leaders: Is what is going on in Germany a rapid deterioration of the social fabric? Bukharin concluded that it was necessary not only to prevent such a deterioration in the Soviet Union, but also to create a slogan under which the international movement could unite in the struggle against Nazism.

"It is impossible to fight them," he said to me, "without setting some idea of our own against theirs. Their idea is violence. You remember that pseudo-philosophical aphorism that was widely used by them, 'Killing affirms the strength of man.' In the end, this is the idea of violence, of coercion as a permanent method of exercising power over society, over individuals, over man's personality. And this idea must be fought. Their idea includes the suppression of other nations and peoples.

"Throughout the history of mankind," Bukharin went on, "many evil deeds have been committed in the name of humanism. We must resolutely dissociate ourselves from such abuses. For this reason, we must stress that our humanism is different and original, a proletarian humanism. We must conduct the struggle against anti-humanist Nazism under the banner of this new humanism."

I remember that this idea of humanism was set forth by Bukharin in very elementary terms, but with great fervor. He insisted always on the importance of this approach and it soon became clear to me that the humanist struggle against "permanent coercion" was for him a struggle not only against the external enemy, Nazism, but also against an internal enemy, against attempts within the Bolshevik Party to revise Communist theory, to dehumanize it. I myself was interested in this theme and because I wanted to understand Bukharin's conclusions, I said to him: "Nikolai Ivanovich, what you are now saying is nothing other than a return to the Ten Commandments. And this is nothing new." He answered, "Do you think the Commandments of Moses are obsolete?" I said: "I am not saying they are obsolete. I'm saying that they have existed for 5,000 years. Have we arrived at the point where Moses' Commandments have to be rediscovered as a new truth?" Bukharin did not reply.

On another occasion in Paris, he was to deliver a speech on the goals of Communism. In this speech, which was never published in Russian, he emphasized the humanist idea even more forcefully. I happened to go to see him while he was finishing his preparation of this speech. "If you like," he said, "I'll read you what I've been writing just now. It has a direct relation to our conversations." I said that of course I wanted to hear it, and he read some passages to me. When he finished, I said to him, "Nikolai Ivanovich, that's what we've been talking about—humanism, the return to humanism." He replied that in the early days they had rebelled against humanism. And indeed, if we take the literature of 1917–20, this was a revolt against humanism, and not only by Bukharin, not only by Gorky, but also by the poet Alexander Blok and many others. Bukharin went on to say that everything passes through difficult stages. Earlier, destructiveness was necessary and the struggle against humanism inevitable. But now we have entered a different period, he said, when we are faced by tasks of construction. They demand the reorganization of our entire outlook. Not only our Communism but also your Socialism must, he continued, become rooted in this humanist base, like the Communism of Marx.

I made no objection to these ideas. I myself had arrived at them before, during Hitler's attack on German democracy. In February, 1933, on the eve of Hitler's accession to power, a friend and I put out a book about the young Marx, the main idea of which was that he was a humanist. Bukharin read my little book and I think that to a certain extent he shared my feelings. This was why he could become close to Pavlov.

INTERVIEWER: You speak of an internal enemy against whom Bukharin struggled. Can you elaborate on this?

NICOLAEVSKY: Bukharin's humanism was in large part produced by the cruelty of forced collectivization and the struggle within the Party connected with it. Once I mentioned to Bukharin that much was known abroad about the horrors of collectivization. He became angry with me and retorted sharply that everything that had been written gave only the faintest picture of what really happened at the time. He was literally overflowing with impressions gained by direct participants in the collectivization campaign, who were shaken by what they saw. Several Communists committed suicide, some went mad, and many threw in the towel and withdrew completely.

"I saw many things even before collectivization," Bukharin told me. "In 1919, when I proposed restricting the Cheka's rights of execution, Vladimir Ilyich put through a decision appointing me as a representative of the Politburo to the Collegium of the Cheka with the right of veto. 'Let him go there himself,' said Lenin, 'and let him try to keep the terror within limits, if it is possible. We all will be very glad if he succeeds.' And as a matter of fact, I saw things that I would not want even my enemies to see. Yet 1919 cannot even be compared with what happened between 1930 and 1932. In 1919, we were fighting for our lives. We executed people, but we also risked our lives in the process. In the later period, however, we were conducting a mass annihilation of completely defenseless men, together with their wives and children."

Nonetheless, the worst development, in Bukharin's opinion, was not the horrors of collectivization. It was deep changes in the psychological outlook of those Communists who participated in this campaign and, instead of going mad, became professional bureaucrats for whom terror was henceforth a normal method of administration, and obedience to any order from above a high virtue. "They are no longer human beings," Bukharin said of them. "They are really cogs in some terrible machine." There is taking place, he went on, a real dehumanization of the people working in the Soviet apparatus, a process of transforming Soviet power into an empire of the "iron heel."* This process, more than anything else, frightened Bukharin, arousing in him a desire to recall certain elementary human truths. In his "proletarian humanism," the first word was only an adjective. The essence of the phrase was "humanism," fear for man, for his survival as a human being.

INTERVIEWER: Didn't Stalin know of Bukharin's ideas? If so, why didn't he take measures against him?

NICOLAEVSKY: Bukharin was not physically molested at this time. He was only worked over, so to speak, in the press and at all sorts of meetings. The Communist Academy was even forced to conduct a special discussion devoted to unmasking his deviation, and the Politburo forbade his participation in the discussion. On this occasion the real views of Bukharin were slanderously distorted. He was, for example, accused of being in favor of war. But no action was taken against him.

This was not true of his closest disciples and associates, whom Bukharin had painstakingly selected over a decade and many of whom were very talented. Stalin bore down on them. Almost every member of this group, whom Stalin later termed Bukharin's "little school"—Aikhenvald, Ostrov, Maretsky, Slepkov, etc.—was sent to the provinces, then arrested, and finally liquidated. It was with difficulty that Bukharin bore these blows, especially the extermination of his young students, for whose future he felt personally responsible.

INTERVIEWER: You mentioned earlier that you went to Amsterdam and Copenhagen with Bukharin. This was to look at some materials of Marx, wasn't it?

NICOLAEVSKY: Yes. A portion of the German materials—chiefly the major manuscripts of Marx and Engels—had been sent out

---

* The title of a novel by Jack London, with whose works he was thoroughly familiar.—B. N.

separately from Germany via the Danish Embassy. They were kept in the Danish Social Democratic Party archive in Copenhagen. The members of the delegation wanted to be sure of seeing them, so we agreed to go there.

Arriving in Copenhagen we went to the Party archive, where they got out for us the trunk containing Marx's manuscript of *Das Kapital*. Bukharin scanned the pile of notebooks that contained the results of Marx's successive attempts to analyze the complicated, changing structure of human society, built on the basis of private economic relations. Then he began to leaf through the manuscripts, trying to make out individual phrases upon which his eyes would fall. This was fruitless work, and, turning to me, he said, "Surely you can find the place where Marx writes on classes."

I knew the passage very well and quickly found it for him. Bukharin carefully took from me the pages written by Marx, held his head with both hands, and began to read those well-known lines in which Marx had first attempted to formulate his ideas on this question. They had been jotted down in a very uneven way, in what seemed a hurried handwriting, as though Marx's pen could barely keep pace with his quickly unfolding thoughts. But the ideas had not been finished; they had been broken off, almost as if someone had come in and interrupted Marx at his work.

Bukharin read the passage through to the end and then turned the pages, glancing at one side and then the other. He was clearly checking to see if the draft might not contain some clue to the omission which would throw new light on the course of Marx's thought . . . and he did not find it. He began to read the passage once again, but having satisfied himself that nothing new would be found, he broke off, sighing, "Ah, Karlyusha, Karlyusha,* why didn't you finish? It was difficult for you, but how you would have helped us!"

I remember exchanging glances with Adoratsky, who had come with us. He was also an expert on Marx, but of an entirely different kind. As a youth, Bukharin was in love with the great ideas of Marx, and in these ideas Marx continued to live for him; with these ideas Bukharin could converse, even argue. Adoratsky, on the

---

* Russian diminutive of Karl (Marx).—Ed.

other hand, was a dry dogmatist, a product of the Kazar seminaries, without a hint of Bukharin's sense of the romantic. To Adoratsky, Marx's ideas were scattered in notebooks, systematized, and spread out on bookshelves. He knew all of the necessary and even the unnecessary quotations, he knew what to think of them, where to find them. But he was not interested in applying them to changing times. Bukharin lived precisely for this projection of Marx's ideas into the present, and for this reason he sought to discern the unstated thoughts of Marx and to resolve unresolved problems.

Adoratsky sat for another two hours with the manuscripts, cataloguing them and reading many which had not yet been published. Bukharin began instead to look at the Danish archives, to make inquiries about them and about the Danish workers' movement as well. Then, for the rest of the day, he dragged us through museums and bought up a full briefcase of photographs of old masters, and led us for several hours through the colonial museum, studying its unique collection of butterflies. He had to see everything with his own eyes. Several times during the course of the day he returned to Marx's remarks on classes.

Bukharin was one among a group of outstanding Russian Marxist theoreticians. In 1893, Plekhanov had affirmed that Russia must go through a stage of capitalist development before it could enter into socialism. Bukharin rejected this idea and asserted the possibility of one revolution profound enough to permit a direct jump into socialism. Bukharin had to deal not only with the old arguments of Plekhanov, but also with those of A. A. Bogdanov, who in the early days of the Bolshevik Revolution foresaw the growth of a dictatorship of a new class of economic managers. An original thinker and, during the 1905 Revolution, the second most influential Bolshevik, Bogdanov played a significant role in Bukharin's education. Bogdanov's ideas on the new class made a tremendously great impression on him. Bukharin did not agree with Bogdanov's conclusions, but he understood that the great danger of "rapid socialism," which the Bolsheviks were undertaking, lay in its probable creation of a new class of dictators.

Bukharin and I spoke at some length about this question. Later, I dug up many of his articles. They leave no doubt that he greatly feared the degeneration of the Bolshevik Party into a new ruling class.

INTERVIEWER: Bukharin is rumored to have been largely responsible for the Constitution of 1936. Did he have anything to say about it?

NICOLAEVSKY: It was already clear from various signs that Bukharin had played a major role in drawing up the Constitution. He was secretary of the commission that worked out the draft Constitution. Back in 1930, he had come out with a draft for universal suffrage and fought for the elimination of all special privileges for the Communist Party, two points that were reflected in this Constitution. In addition, in his talk with me about the group of Gorky, Pavlov, and others, Bukharin gave the impression that the idea of the Constitution had originated with them.

Then, one day, while we were discussing "proletarian humanism," Bukharin took his fountain pen from his pocket and, showing it to me, he said: "Look carefully. With this, the entire new Soviet Constitution was written, from first word to last. And I bore the work alone; only Karlyusha [Radek]* helped a little. I could come to Paris only because I had completed this work. All of the important decisions have already been taken. Now they are printing the text. And in this Constitution the people will have more room. They can no longer be pushed aside!"

Bukharin was very proud of this Constitution. Not only did it introduce universal and equal suffrage, it also established the equality of all citizens before the law. In general, it was a well-thought-out framework for the peaceful transition of the country from the dictatorship of one party to a genuine people's democracy. Bukharin said that the commission for drawing up the Constitution had even raised the question of having several candidates compete at elections.

But Bukharin underestimated his opponent and did not foresee how cunningly Stalin would apply these principles, perverting equality of all before the law into the equality of Communists and non-Communists before the absolute dictatorship of Stalin. Stalin

* Radek was also a member of the commission established to draw up the Constitution.—Ed.

not only went so far as to have the very author of the Constitution executed, but he also ruthlessly dealt with all others in the Party who subscribed to Bukharin's humanist ideas.

INTERVIEWER: Do you think that Bukharin had any premonition of his later fate, that he would stand trial for opposition to the Stalinist regime?

NICOLAEVSKY: I pondered this question at the time of the trial in 1938. I think that deep in his heart Bukharin had misgivings when we met in Paris.

He told me, for example, a very interesting story of a trip he had made to Soviet Central Asia after Stalin purged the group Bukharin had assembled around him. This trip remained an important landmark in Bukharin's life. I sensed this in his conversations, and I was convinced of it later, when I had occasion to study his biographical materials. Several times in our conversations, he returned to this trip, showing signs of different moods and a deep reserve. He spoke of flying in some plane which fell into an air pocket from which they barely got out . . . of a meeting with bandits* from which he was lucky to get away, etc. These various details merely lifted the edge of the curtain before which Bukharin hesitated.

It was on his trip to Central Asia that Bukharin went to the Pamir Mountains, "which are unequaled in the world"; he spoke of being on the very "roof of the world" there, where the borders of the Soviet Union, China, India, and Afghanistan meet. People had persistently tried to dissuade him from going—the roads were washed away, the times were unsettled, gangs of bandits roamed about, and in general, they said, there was nothing of interest in the Pamirs. "This only urged me on," Bukharin said. "I have always loved the uncharted paths in the mountains, as in science I prefer the unsolved problems." He had his own way in the matter.

They gave him a guide—a border-guard who knew those parts well, a man of endurance and courage. "You must have seen a film they made about his dog 'Wolf,' " Bukharin said. "It was shown not long ago in Paris." I had seen the film with the border-guard, his intelligent dog, and especially the mountains. "For several days, the

* The reference was to *basmachi,* members of a counterrevolutionary robber band in Central Asia at the time of the collectivization.—B. N.

two of us wandered through the mountains, through the most difficult places. Wolf invariably went ahead, carrying himself with an enormous dignity that I had never before seen in a dog. Thus we arrived at a fork in the road. My guide led his horse a little ahead. 'This one is shorter,' he said, pointing to one path, 'but to take it now would be certain suicide. The rain has washed portions of the path away, and there have been landslides. Even a goat could not make it.' He took the other path. "But I," continued Bukharin, "led my horse to the washed-out path and went that way. When the paths joined again, my guard was already waiting. And he looked angrier than his Wolf. 'You were lucky,' he scolded me severely. 'But don't play such tricks on me again. I may forget you are a member of the Central Committee.' "

"But I wanted to see what the road was like," Bukharin shrugged it off.

"Don't stand and talk!" the guide retorted. "Of course I was right. The road was completely impassable. That horse had his work cut out for him!"

Bukharin spoke a great deal about this guard, who, evidently, was a very colorful figure. He was, of course, a Communist, but with an independent philosophy of life, with great sensitivity, personal dignity, and a sense of social responsibility. As Bukharin spoke of him, it was clear that he did not see in him simply a clear-thinking man, acquainted with untrodden paths, but also a representative of the new people who, under Soviet rule, were being drawn into low-level positions.

Bukharin suggested indirectly to me that he had been overcome by a great pessimism in Central Asia and that he lost his desire to live. However, he did not want to commit suicide. This would have been an admission of defeat. He wished to die without taking his own life, and so he tempted fate by taking the washed-out path. Death did not come, but not because he did not try.

The incident of the two paths somewhat lifted Bukharin's spirit. He developed a belief in man, not man in general, but a new man, adjusted to Soviet dictatorship who yet remains a human being, not merely a cog in the monstrous machine. In connection with this episode, Bukharin developed a whole theory, which I would call the theory of a "human stream."

"It is difficult for us to live," he told me. "And you, for example, could not accustom yourself to it. Even for some of us, with our experience during these decades, it is often impossible. But one is saved by a faith that development is always going forward. It is like a stream that is running to the shore. If one leans out of the stream, one is ejected completely." Here Bukharin made a scissor-like gesture with his two fingers. "The stream goes through the most difficult places. But it still goes forward in the direction in which it must. And the people grow, become stronger in it, and they build a new society."

Thus, I would say that Bukharin had doubts about his future. He must have known his relations with Stalin boded ill for him. Yet he felt he had to remain in Russia, and he refused to believe that a better future was not in store.

There is one footnote to this tragic period. In his memoirs, R. V. Ivanov-Razumnik,* the well-known Russian literary historian, tells of meeting Bukharin's guide from the Pamirs in prison. The latter had been imprisoned, doubtless because of his association with Bukharin. But when, during the trial, they accused him of having worked for foreign intelligence, he wore out both the interrogator and the Chekists who had hastened to the interrogator's aid. They could get something on him only after a real battle. In revenge, they arranged it so that he would never again see his beloved mountains.

* R. V. Ivanov-Razumnik, *Tyurniy i Ssylki* (New York, 1953).

The Letter of an Old Bolshevik

HERE in Russia, the Zinoviev-Kamenev-Smirnov trial came upon us like a thunderbolt. Recent events and present occurrences almost beggar description. Of course, what is being said in this letter does not apply to the mood of the Soviet "public" in general. It is utterly sick of politics and asks for nothing but to be left in peace and to be able to live in peace. I speak here of the state of mind of those elements who, until recently, had considered themselves the sole possessors of the right to occupy themselves with politics—of what might be called the *"officers' corps" of the Communist Party.*

During the previous spring and summer, there was a feeling of calm and confidence among these political elite, such as they had not felt for a long time. Looking back today, one recognizes certain symptoms that might have given ground for concern. But that is being wise after the event. In reality, everyone had been convinced that the worst had passed and that a period of economic and political improvement had begun, which, though slow, would, nevertheless, be certain. The importance of the new constitution was not overestimated. It was known that the constitution had been proposed mainly out of political considerations arising from the fear of war. But the feeling prevailed that these very considerations would militate, for a time at least, against any extreme revival of the terror, and help stabilize the situation to some extent. All this resulted in a feeling of confidence as regards the immediate future, and it was in this confident frame of mind that we set off on our summer holidays. (Greater importance is being attached nowadays to summer holidays than ever before. In Russia we say that the right to summer hunting is about the only right achieved by the Revolution, which even Stalin dare not take from government and Party dignitaries.) At the beginning of August, it was known that several members of the Politburo had gone away, that Stalin himself would shortly leave on a holiday, and that the "dead season" had set in, during which, as a rule, no important decisions are taken and no events of major significance are to be expected.

However, instead of the expected political calm, there came the trial, a trial utterly unprecedented. It is only gradually that we are recovering from the shock. We are beginning to take stock of what has happened and how it happened. Slowly, it is becoming apparent that what occurred was no mere accident: In general, things happen much less accidentally here than might appear to an outsider.

Among the last testaments left by Lenin there is none to which our "Party leadership" had clung more tenaciously than his imperative advice not to repeat the mistake of the Jacobins—to eschew the road of mutual extermination. It was considered an axiom that in the fight against the Party Opposition any methods save the death penalty should be resorted to. True, there had been occasional lapses from this rule: Blumkin and a few other Trotskyites had been shot for infiltrating, on instructions of their organization, the secret recesses of the GPU and warning their comrades against betrayal and impending arrest. These executions were generally regarded as exceptional measures, imposed not for participation in the struggle within the Party, but for betrayal of official duties. Misdemeanors of this kind were always severely punished in the U.S.S.R. In 1924–25, a Menshevik was shot who had forced his way into the Secretariat of the Central Control Committee and had taken certain documents in order to send them to the *Socialisti-chesky Vestnik*. Even during the "Menshevik Trial" (1931), re-course to the death penalty had never been seriously considered, however.

The first time the death penalty for participation in oppositionist activity in internal Party politics was discussed was in connection with the Riutin affair. This was at the end of 1932, when the situa-tion in the country was similar to 1921—the time of the Kronstadt rebellion. In 1932, it is true, there were no actual revolts, but many believed that it would have been better if the government had had to deal with actual revolts. Half of the country was stricken with famine. The workers were on short rations. Labor productivity had greatly fallen and there was no way of raising it, for it was not a question of unwillingness on the part of the workers, but of physical incapability of working productively on an empty stomach. The predominant view in Party circles was that Stalin had led the coun-try into an impasse by his policy, that he had roused the peas-ants against the Party, and that the situation could be saved only by his removal from Party domination. Many influential mem-bers of the Central Committee were of this opinion. It was said that an anti-Stalin majority was being formed in the Politburo as well. Wherever Party officials met, the subject of discussion was: What program was to be substituted for Stalin's "general line." It is obvious that, in the process, various proposed programs and declarations were being passed from hand to hand. Among them, Riutin's program was specially noteworthy. It was definitely pro-peasant in character. It demanded the abolition of the collectives and the granting of economic self-determination to the peasants. But this was not all that differentiated this program from others. At that time, the program of the right-wing Bolsheviks, such as that of Slepkov, was emphatically pro-peasant, but so was that of the former left-wing Trotskyists, who had been, in fact, politically re-sponsible for Stalin's "general line," since it was they who had been its original ideologists. Riutin's program was remarkable chiefly for its *severe criticism of Stalin*. It was 200 pages long, 50 of which were devoted to Stalin's personal characteristics, to a con-sideration of the part he had played in the Party, and to the reasons for the basic contention that unless Stalin was removed from Party domination, there could be no recovery in the Party or in the country. These views were expressed with remarkable vigor and made a deep impression. Stalin was depicted as the evil genius of the Russian Revolution, who, motivated by vindictiveness and lust for power, had brought the Revolution to the verge of ruin.

This section of the program, for which the author was to pay a heavy penalty, was largely responsible for its success. The program aroused a great deal of discussion, and it was not surprising, therefore, that a copy was soon brought to Stalin's desk. This, naturally, led to arrests and house searches. As a result, not only were all those who had circulated Riutin's program arrested, but also those who had distributed other declarations. Riutin, who at that time was in exile or in an "isolator," where he had worked out his plan, was brought to Moscow. Upon examination, he admitted the authorship. As an old Party leader who had rendered eminent service to the Party, he came within the classification of those who, in accordance with Lenin's commandment, could not possibly receive the death penalty. The question was, therefore, considered by the Politburo, because the OGPU (naturally, at Stalin's wish) had demanded his execution.

The discussions in the Politburo were heated. Stalin was in favor of granting the OGPU's demand. His strongest argument was a reference to the growth of *terrorist sentiment among young people,* particularly in the Komsomol (Young Communist League). Reports of the OGPU were replete with stories of terroristic talk among *young workers and students.* Moreover, quite a number of terroristic acts against minor Soviet officials and Party officers had become known. Against such terrorists the Party did not shrink from resorting to the "supreme penalty," even when it was a question of members of the Komsomol, Stalin maintaining that it was politically illogical and unjust to administer such severe punishment to those who performed terroristic acts while sparing those whose political propaganda had inspired these acts. He recommended that no undue attention be given to the small fry, but that the Politburo go straight to the root and cause of the matter. Riutin's program, Stalin said, was a direct justification of and an apology for the necessity of murdering him.

I can no longer recall the actual division of opinion in the Polit-

29

buro when this question was being considered. I know only that Kirov spoke with particular force against recourse to the death penalty. Moreover, he succeeded in winning over the Politburo to this view. Stalin was prudent enough not to push matters to an open conflict. Riutin's life was thus spared. He was sentenced to a long term in an isolator where a particularly severe regime was in force. It became clear to everybody, however, that the Politburo would be compelled again to take up the big questions which had arisen, in one form or another, out of this affair. And, indeed, they soon made themselves manifest, but under quite different circumstances than those of the winter of 1932–33. Both as regards home and foreign policy, *the summer and autumn of 1933* was a significant period for the Soviet Union. The harvest was unexpectedly good. Hardly anyone had dared to hope that, in the prevailing economic disorder, it would be possible to complete the work in the fields and bring in the grain. This achievement was undoubtedly due to Stalin, who had evinced even more than his usual extraordinary energy, compelling everyone to work to the point of exhaustion. He unquestionably perceived that that summer would determine his fate; that unless the economic situation improved, the rebellious feeling against him would find an outlet in one way or another. However, as it became apparent that the achievements of the summer were good, a psychological change ensued in the attitude of Party circles. For the first time, wide circles of the membership came to believe that the "general line" could be really successful, and, having acquired this faith, altered their attitude toward Stalin, with whose name this line was inextricably bound. "Stalin has conquered," said even those who only yesterday had been trying to obtain a copy of Riutin's platform. The question of how this improvement in the economic situation would be reflected politically became all the more emphatic. The situation was further complicated by the fact that, at the same time, most important questions of *foreign policy* were pressing for solution. In the first few months after Hitler's seizure of power, it seemed to us in Russia that the Third Reich would be merely a *passing phase in Germany's history,* that Hitler would be able to remain in the saddle only a few months, to be followed quickly by a severe crash and revolution. That the "imperialists" of England and France would permit

Germany, their "hereditary foe," to carry out her rearmament plans was generally regarded as impossible; neither were Hitler's mouthings about a campaign against Russia taken seriously. Gradually, however, we began to realize that the situation was far more serious than we had thought, that no preventive measures against Hitler by the Western powers could be expected, and that preparations for a campaign against Russia were in full swing. A big stir was produced by the investigations into and the disclosures regarding German propaganda in the Ukraine, and particularly with regard to the so-called *homosexual conspiracy*. The particulars of that conspiracy, which was discovered at the end of 1933, were as follows: An assistant of the German military attaché, a friend and follower of the notorious Captain Roehm, managed to enter the homosexual circles in Moscow, and, under cover of a homosexual "organization" (homosexuality was still legal in Russia at that time), started a whole network of National-Socialist propaganda. Its threads extended into the provinces, to Leningrad, Kharkov, Kiev, etc. A number of persons in literary and artistic circles were involved: the private secretary of a very prominent actor, known for his homosexual inclinations, an important scientific collaborator of the Lenin Institute, etc. These connections were utilized by the Germans not only to procure military information, but also to sow dissent in government and Party circles. The aims of those directing this conspiracy were so far-reaching that the leaders of Soviet policy were compelled to intervene. Thus, there gradually ensued the change in foreign policy that soon led to Russia's entry into the League of Nations, and to the creation of the "Popular Front" in France. Naturally, this change did not take place without a great deal of discussion. It was not easy to overcome the old, deeply rooted orientation for an alliance with Germany, even with a reactionary Germany, for the purpose of bringing about an explosion in the victorious countries. This was all the more difficult because it was clear that a new orientation in the direction of the democratic parties of Western Europe would inevitably lead to considerable changes in the *internal policy* of the Soviet Union. It was at this time that Kirov began to gain great influence.

Kirov played an important part in the Politburo. He was a 100 per cent supporter of the general line, and distinguished himself during its operation by great energy and inflexibility. This caused Stalin to value him highly. But there was always a certain independence in Kirov's attitude that annoyed Stalin. The story is told that Stalin had prevented Kirov from attending the meetings of the Politburo in Moscow for several months under the pretext that his presence in Leningrad was indispensable. However, Stalin could never make up his mind to take strong measures against Kirov. It would have been folly to add to the already large number of dissidents an important Party leader such as Kirov, especially since he had succeeded in surrounding himself in Leningrad with reliable and devoted aides. A new conflict with the Leningrad Party might have been more fatal now than in Zinoviev's day. In the winter of 1933–34, Kirov had so strengthened his position that he could afford to follow his own line. He aimed not only at a "Western orientation" in foreign policy, but also at the conclusions that would follow logically from this new orientation as far as domestic policy was concerned.

The task, therefore, was not only that of creating a mighty army in preparation for the impending military conflict, a conflict that appeared inevitable, but also, politically speaking, of creating the proper psychological frame of mind on the home front. There were two alternatives: to pursue the former policy of crushing all dissenters, with the administrative pressure ruthlessly tightened and the terror intensified, or to try "reconciliation with the people," to gain their voluntary cooperation in the political preparation of the country for the coming war. The most convinced and most prominent advocates of the *second alternative* were Kirov and Gorki. It would be worth-while to describe in greater detail Gorki's influence in the life of the Party, particularly as it is now possible to speak more openly since his death. But that is another matter, and would take us too far afield. Gorki had exercised a great and beneficent influence upon Stalin. But, despite all his influence, Gorki was *not a member* of the Politburo and had no direct part in the making of its decisions. Kirov's part became therefore all the more important.

Kirov stood for the idea of *abolition of the terror,* both in general and inside the Party. We do not desire to exaggerate the importance of his proposals. It must not be forgotten that when the first Five-

Year Plan was being put into effect, Kirov was one of the heads of the Party, that he was among those who inspired and carried through the notoriously ruthless measures against the peasants and the wiping out of the kulaks. The Kem and Murmansk coasts, with their prison camps, etc., were under his jurisdiction. Furthermore, he was in charge of the construction of the Baltic–White Sea Canal. This is enough to make it clear that Kirov could not be accused of undue tenderness in the manner in which he disposed of human lives. But this very fact added to his strength in the official circles in which he had to defend his point of view. That he had so large a share of responsibility in the horrors of the First Five-Year Plan made it possible for him to come forward as a leader and protagonist of the policy of moderating the terror during the Second Five-Year Plan. Kirov's line of thought ran as follows: The period of destruction, which was necessary to extirpate the small proprietor elements in the villages, was now at an end; the economic position of the collectives was consolidated and made secure for the future. This constituted a firm basis for future development, and as the economic situation continued to improve, the broad masses of the population would become more and more reconciled to the government; the number of "internal foes" would diminish. It was now the task of the Party to rally those forces which would support it in the new phase of economic development, and thus to broaden the foundation upon which Soviet power was based. Kirov, therefore, strongly advocated reconciliation with those Party elements who, during the period of the First Five-Year Plan, had gone over to the Opposition, but who might be induced to cooperate on the new basis, now that the "destructive" phase was over.

In one of his speeches, Kirov is said to have stated that there were now "no more irreconcilable foes of any importance." The old groups and parties had melted away during the fighting period of the First Five-Year Plan and they were now no longer a factor of consequence. As far as new foes were concerned, there were, with few exceptions, none with whom an understanding could not be attained by a policy of reconciliation.

Kirov's viewpoint (put forward even more emphatically by Gorki) gained considerable influence among *those at the head of the Party*. The period of struggle for the Five-Year Plan had been no easy one for them. The horrors which accompanied the transformation in the villages, and of which you have only a faint idea, beggar description. Those in charge of the Party knew all this, and for many of them the knowledge was hard to bear. One event during this period is very characteristic. At the end of 1932, some young people in Leningrad organized a literary function at which Kalinin was a guest. This was in connection with some anniversary of the OGPU (I believe it was the fifteenth anniversary of the founding of the Cheka, its predecessor). Poems about the Cheka were recited, the main tenor of which was "may the Cheka continue to exterminate our foes with even greater ruthlessness." The unkind maintain that on that evening Kalinin had had too much to drink. Be that as it may, it would only prove that alcohol broke down his restraint and made it possible for him to express his true feelings. Those who were present at that meeting say that Kalinin's speech was like the cry of a wounded heart. After a particularly bloodthirsty poem had been read, Kalinin got up and said: "We are often obliged to resort to terror, but it must never be glorified. It is our tragedy that we are obliged to have recourse to such terrible measures, but there is nothing for which we all yearn more than abolition of the terror. For that reason, we should not glorify the mercilessness of the Cheka, but hope that the time may come when we may dispense with the 'punishing hand.' "

It was said that this speech caused a considerable stir. It was discussed not only in Leningrad, but also in Moscow. Kalinin is said to have been reprimanded. Such occurrences as Kalinin's speech show that those who had to carry through the First Five-Year Plan had become inclined to embrace a policy of moderating the terror as soon as conditions would permit. Hence, Kirov met with great success, especially since Stalin did not directly oppose his line, but tried merely to limit the practical consequences arising from it. This attitude on Stalin's part is said to have been due particularly to Gorki's influence, which had reached its zenith at that time.

Hence, early in the summer of 1933, when it became certain that the harvest would be good, Kamenev, Zinoviev, and a number of other former members of the Opposition were once again readmitted as members of the Party. They were even permitted to

34

choose their spheres of work, and some of them actually received invitations to the Party Congress (February, 1934).

At that Congress, Kirov appeared in triumph. Previously, his election in Leningrad had been celebrated as was no other. At district conferences in various parts of the city, all of which he toured on the same day, he had been received with wild cheers. "Long live our Mironich!" the delegates shouted; it had been an exceedingly impressive demonstration and it showed that the entire Leningrad proletariat was behind Kirov. At the Party Congress, too, Kirov received an extraordinarily enthusiastic reception. He was cheered, the entire assembly rising to its feet on hearing his report. During the recesses there was discussion as to who had had the more tumultuous reception, Kirov or Stalin. This very comparison shows how strong Kirov's influence had already become.

Not only was Kirov re-elected to the Politburo, but he was also chosen a secretary of the Central Committee, making it necessary for him to move to Moscow within a short time to take over direction of a whole group of departments which had heretofore been under Postyshev and Kaganovich. This was to ensure putting into effect the new line that Kirov had inspired. His removal to Moscow was delayed, however. The official reason given was that his presence in Leningrad was indispensable; a substitute was supposedly being sought in Leningrad, but until someone could be found fit to take his place, his transfer to Moscow had to be postponed. In spite of this, he took part in the work of the Politburo, and his influence there continued to grow.

At a meeting of the Politburo—early in 1934—a question arose that may be regarded as a continuation of the previous discussion with regard to the Riutin affair. Certain Komsomol groups—youths and students—had been discovered debating the problem of terrorism. These groups had not actually committed any acts of terror; had they done so, there would hardly have been any question as to their fate. Ever since the period of the civil war, the principle that groups committing terroristic acts were to be physically annihilated was regarded as unalterable. The members of these groups, however, had not gone further than mere discussion of the necessity for terrorism. Their general argument ran as follows:

In view of the complete lack of democracy within the Party, and with the Soviet constitution being disregarded by the government, there was nothing left for the Opposition to do but to resort to terror.

In the past, the "supreme penalty" had been imposed in such cases, but since the new course, the OGPU had to obtain special instructions before proceeding. A comprehensive report on these groups was presented. In retrospect, it appears that there were other reasons for the reappearance of this question in the Politburo. Stalin and his immediate circle sought to test the degree of effectiveness of the new course and to determine how far the Politburo would go in its "liberalism." The instructions issued by the Politburo were very flexible. No firm, general decision was taken: it was simply recommended that each case be considered on its merits. However, the tenor of the instructions was that it was considered desirable to apply the "supreme penalty" only in extreme cases, in cases of proven incorrigibility of any given member of the insurgent groups. As a result, members of these groups received relatively light sentences. They were sent to isolators, prison camps, or banished, in some cases, to not too distant places. Thus, the affair of the Leningrad "terrorists" was brought to a close in very mild fashion. The news of the new course soon spread through Party circles. Under its influence, a number of prominent members of the Opposition abandoned their implacability, including men like Rakovski, Sosnovski, etc. This, too, was regarded as a great success for the policy of reconciliation. Those who "repented" were immediately given permission to live in Moscow and to take up responsible work. Rakovski was even welcomed by Kaganovich personally. Sosnovski was able to resume his journalistic work, if not on *Pravda,* at least in *Izvestia;* and further examples could be given. Kirov's success reached its zenith at the plenary session of the Central Committee in November, 1934. This session discussed a number of concrete measures which were to be taken in accordance with the new course. Kirov presented the report on the question and was the hero of the hour. His transfer to Moscow was again discussed and it was definitely decided that it would occur very shortly.

All those sections of the Party secretariat having to do with "ideology" were to be under his direction. He was to return to

Leningrad for only a short time to transfer his duties to his successor. All the more shocking, therefore, was the news by telephonogram telling of his assassination.

More could be said about Kirov's murder that would undoubtedly make very interesting reading, for this unfortunate shot ushered in a new period in the history of the Soviet Union. But such a report would take me too far afield, and my letter has already become too voluminous. For this reason, I will only touch on factors particularly important for understanding the subsequent developments inside the Party.

The very first telephone messages informing Moscow of Kirov's murder made it clear that the murder was a political one. A declaration giving the motives for this deed was found on the assassin Nikolaev. But in the light of the conciliatory mood which had marked inner Party policy during the months preceding the murder, it was psychologically impossible for most of us to interpret the shot of December 1, 1934, as an act of terror emanating from the conflicts within the Party. It was hard to believe that none other than the chief advocate of the policy of reconciliation should fall by the bullet of a member of the Opposition, and particularly at the moment when victory for that policy seemed assured. Moreover, the very consequences that could be expected to flow from such an act of terror in its effect on the further course of internal Party politics militated against such an interpretation. Hence, the mood of those early December days, in which most people tried to depict the murder as the result of *the machinations of a foreign power* (it was not felt necessary to mention which), of whom Nikolaev was supposed to have become the blind tool. From this it was concluded that the murder was of no significance so far as political conditions in the U.S.S.R. itself were concerned, and that the line as proposed in Kirov's report to the plenum of the Central Committee shortly before would remain unchanged as the definite guide for Party policy. All those who had at any time been connected in any way with the Opposition and who were now, and not without cause, concerned for their personal safety, were particularly assiduous in propagating this interpretation. The major responsibility for presenting this viewpoint fell to Radek. *If only he could have guessed that this very version of the "hand of the Gestapo" would later be used against all the former members of the Opposition and against him personally!*

But it was not the former members of the Opposition alone who inclined to this interpretation of Nikolaev's shot. It was generally accepted, and, apparently, the leaders of the People's Commissariat for Home Affairs were inclined at first to make it their own. If the first list of executions which followed as an answer to Nikolaev's shot be recalled, it will be found that this included, in the main, individuals suspected (rightly or wrongly) of relations with some foreign secret service. In Russia, the Germans were generally considered as being responsible for the separatist propaganda in the Ukraine. The order for these shootings came from Moscow, under the initial impact of the telephone reports from Leningrad.

The version that the hand of a foreign power was behind the Kirov assassination was not, however, the official version of the government. At first, Stalin issued no instructions. While leaving it to others to seek explanations for what had occurred, he himself concentrated his attention on the energetic organization of the inquiry. Together with Voroshilov and Ordjonikidze, whose support in the Politburo was particularly important to him, Stalin immediately went to Leningrad and there prescribed the scope and direction which the work of the committee of investigation was to take. He was present in person at certain of the more important interrogations, notably at the examination of Nikolaev himself. He also took charge of all measures for a shake-up in the Leningrad section of the People's Commissariat for Home Affairs. Agranov, who, of late years, has enjoyed the special personal confidence of Stalin, was given charge of the actual conduct of the investigation. Stalin knew well that Yasha (for so Stalin addresses Agranov, sometimes even at official gatherings) would always remain the zealous and obedient executor of his orders and that he would never allow himself to be influenced by others. Stalin was by no means so sure of other officials of the commissariat.

A number of interesting facts developed at the very beginning of the investigation. Nikolaev's diary contained certain important data regarding the motives for his act. Extracts from this diary, even though brief ones, were included in the report of which I shall speak later. Varying rumors of all descriptions were current in connection with this diary. On one point, regarding Nikolaev's general character, they all agreed, however. So fatal did his shot prove to be, both for the Party and the country as a whole, that it is, admittedly, very difficult to remain completely objective with respect to him. However, one is bound to recognize that in Nikolaev we have a typical representative of that younger generation which was driven into the Party by the civil war, which, in the years that followed, had to go through fire and water, and to adapt itself to various phases of radical change, emerging finally from it all with nerves shattered, health broken, and soul deeply seared.

Nikolaev's career had been as follows: At the age of sixteen, during General Yudenich's uprising, he went to the front as a volunteer and remained there throughout the rest of the civil war. At the front he became a member of the Komsomol. A dark spot in his history is his connection with the Cheka. He never played a leading part in these organizations, but there can be no doubt that he belonged to them, although, for understandable reasons, this fact was kept secret even in documents dealing with the investigation circulated for inner-Party use. Nikolaev was never very active in the Party, although he had been affiliated with it since 1920, beginning as a member of the Viborg section of the Komsomol. He did not take part in the Opposition of 1925, with the exception of participating in the voting at certain meetings of that period, when 90 per cent of the members of the Leningrad organization supported Zinoviev's line. At all events, at the time of the general "clean-up" of the Zinoviev organization after the Fourteenth Party Congress, he was not subjected to any punitive measures. Nor was he transferred to another town (at that time the mildest form of punishment imposed upon any "Leningradist" who could be regarded as in any way connected with the Opposition). The years 1929–33 he spent in various towns, notably in Murmansk, where he was sent by the Party to occupy a minor post as supervisor of a forced-labor group. Later, upon his return, he was again associated with the GPU and, apparently (this was kept especially secret), as a member of the guard at Smolny. This, in brief, is the formal story of Nikolaev's career. The notes in his diary, which cover the last two years, the period since his return from Murmansk, cast light upon the ideological content of the outward aspects of his life. Everything seemed to point to the fact that his mind was preoccupied principally with personal conflicts with the Party machine, which was becoming increasingly bureaucratic. The diary is full of references of this kind and of complaints at the disappearance of the old friendly relationships that had made life in the Party so pleasant in the years following the revolution. He turned back again and again to the memories of those days, which appeared to him very simple and rosy, the days of a sort of "blood brotherhood." The formality he now found oppressed and irritated him. In this connection he became involved in a number of conflicts, which led to his expulsion from the Party early in 1934. Shortly afterward his expulsion was rescinded. It was stated that he was suffering from nervous fatigue because of his exhausting work in Murmansk, that he was ailing, and that, therefore, one could not expect too much from him.

His complaints about the bureaucratism that had developed inside the Party were the starting point of Nikolaev's critical attitude. But farther than this he did not go. The striking thing is the disproportion between the gravity of his act and the absence of any more profound criticism on his part—a certain superficiality in his manner of looking at things. Nothing existed for Nikolaev outside of the Party; but even Party life did not interest him in a general political sense. He was interested exclusively in the question of inner-Party relationships. To the condition of inner-Party relationships he began to react with a growing intensity, and gradually he came to regard the situation as a veritable betrayal of the fine Party traditions of the past, as a betrayal of the Revolution itself.

At the same time, he developed a mounting urge for martyrdom. More and more frequently he asserted that someone must sacrifice himself to draw attention of the Party to this fatal development. This, he believed, could be accomplished only by a terrorist act against an outstanding representative of the group of "usurpers" who had seized power in the Party and in the country as a whole. The reading of Russian revolutionary literature of earlier periods had exerted a profound effect upon him. It is clear from his diary that he had read deeply of this material. He had read everything he could lay hands on of the memoirs of the terrorists—the Narodovoltsi and the Social–Revolutionaries. He regarded his own act as the *continuation of the terrorist activity* of the Russian revolutionaries of the past. The story is told that when Stalin asked him why he had committed the murder and pointed out that he was now a lost man, Nikolaev replied: "What does it matter? Many are going under now. But in the days to come my name will be coupled with those of Zheliabov and Balmashev." Other details of the Nikolaev case also speak for this desire on his part to establish a link with the terrorist acts of the Russian revolutionaries of previous epochs.

When these motives of Nikolaev's act were made clear, the committee of investigation directed its attention to the two following points: on the one hand, the discovery of "accomplices" and "instigators," and, on the other, ascertainment of the degree to which the chiefs of the Leningrad section of the Commissariat for Home Affairs were to blame for not having prevented the assassination.

The reply to the first question was, in the main, simple. In his statement Nikolaev had emphasized the fact that his act was definitely an individual one, and that there were *no accomplices whatsoever*. This assertion was supported by the contents of the diary. *There was not a single reference in it to support the assumption of the existence of any secret organization of which Nikolaev might have been a member, or on whose behalf he might have acted.* At all events, the report on the Nikolaev case already mentioned does not contain a single reference to that effect. Doubtlessly, the investigation officials would have included any notations to that effect in their report had such been present in the diary. The general nature of the diary makes it impossible to assume that Nikolaev would consistently have remained silent about anything connected with a secret organization of which he was a member, had any such organization existed. For in his diary he had made note, and very incautiously, too, of all conversations that strengthened his views.

We are, however, long past the days when only those actually involved, directly or indirectly, in an act of terrorism are treated as "accomplices" or "instigators." Today, those who support or encourage sentiments that may impel anyone to commit such acts are condemned as accomplices or instigators. To find such ac-

41

complices and instigators in the Kirov assassination was not difficult. From Nikolaev's diary it was obvious that there were many
dissatisfied elements in and about the Leningrad Party organization who made no secret of their critical attitude toward those in
power in the Party and in the country. These were, in the main,
former members of the Opposition who had recently been subjected
to various punishments and who had just come back to Leningrad
from their places of exile. Since they had held, in the past, better
posts in the Party and had been accustomed to political activity
and to being politically of some importance, they found it hard
to put up with their present modest lot. They were always ready to
rail against the new order and to compare it with the "good old
days." They had no secret organization, but maintained mutual
friendly relations, which, in some cases, had been of long standing.
At their gatherings they exchanged information about Party affairs
and the fate of comrades still in prison or in exile. They took up
collections on their behalf, and heartily abused opponents they
particularly disliked. *This was, however, the limit of their political
activity.* They did not attempt any *public* activity. Occasionally,
one would read a paper before some society on such subjects as
"Reminiscences of Historical Events."

The existence of such groups of "ideologically undisarmed Oppositionists" was no secret. The People's Commissariat for Home
Affairs was aware of it and tolerated it, just as Czarism of old had
tolerated colonies of former political exiles united in their own
communities and who, looked upon as "alien elements," had not
mixed with the society around them. Agranov, who had been assigned the task of investigating this group, now began to seek information as to the "capacities for mischief" of those composing it
and as to who and what they were.

The second part of Agranov's work was a more delicate matter.
From his investigation of the Leningrad section of the People's
Commissariat for Home Affairs, it was discovered that the heads
of this section had been well informed as to Nikolaev's state of
mind, and even as to his inclination to terrorism. A nervous and un-
disciplined individual, Nikolaev frequently spoke quite openly on
this fatal subject, even in the presence of people he hardly knew.
Moreover, our spy system functions so well nowadays that oppo-

sitionist remarks, uttered even in the presence of only two or three persons, are bound soon to reach the ears of those "who are supposed to know all about it." If we take into consideration how carefully our "leaders" are guarded, it becomes *incomprehensible* that Nikolaev should have been allowed to come so close to Kirov's person. It became necessary, therefore, to tackle the question from a different angle. The motives that had actuated Nikolaev were clear from his written statements. It was necessary, however, to determine whether there had been negligence on the part of those whose duty it was to prevent an attempt at assassination. *Who had an interest in getting rid of Kirov before he was to have moved to Moscow? Were there any threads connecting such interested persons with this or that chief of the Leningrad section of the People's Commissariat for Home Affairs? It is probable that an investigation along these lines would have brought to light much interesting material.* I did not hear any conversations on the subject. Of late, people are very sparing of talk in general, particularly on such dangerous subjects. One does, however, hear hints of these questions. In December, 1934, an increased interest suddenly began to be manifest in the assassination of Stolypin, which bore many points of resemblance to the murder of Kirov.

The investigation did not concern itself, however, with any of these questions. It was concentrated mainly on a different aspect. The investigation as to "accomplices" immediately transformed itself into an investigation of the Leningrad Opposition circles, while the investigation on the subject of the role and responsibility of officials of the Leningrad section of the People's Commissariat for Home Affairs became an investigation of the reasons for their negligence vis-à-vis the Oppositionists, i.e., of why they had allowed them to live in Leningrad, to collaborate in the press, to speak at meetings, etc. In self-exoneration, the accused officials cited the verbal and written orders of Kirov, who, in accordance with his general political conception, had insisted on easing the situation of former Oppositionists and ordered the commissariat not to torment them by petty annoyances.

This attempt at justification on the part of the officials was in accordance with the facts. Of recent years, Kirov had been at great pains to restore the old Zinoviev tradition and to transform Lenin-

grad into an independent literary and scientific center able to compete with Moscow in both these respects. He therefore facilitated
publishing activities in Leningrad, helped create favorable financial
and censorship conditions for the publishing of periodicals, gave
support to the activities of scientific societies, etc. In all this, *Kirov
had encouraged the pressing into service of former Oppositionists,*
just as, in Czarist days, liberal-minded governors would invite
political exiles to collaborate in scientific studies and investigations
in Siberia. This analogy with the aforementioned "alien elements"
held good also in this respect. Kirov's "liberalism" went so far that
in the autumn of 1934 he permitted even so hardened a sinner as
Riazanov, former head of the Marx-Engels Institute, to reside in
Leningrad.

The heads of the Leningrad section of the People's Commissariat
for Home Affairs had thus received orders as to their conduct from
their immediate chief, a most influential member of the Politburo,
who had had an entirely free hand in Leningrad. What could they
do under the circumstances?

By the middle of December, the investigation had reached a
point at which it was possible to present a report to the Politburo.
This report was considered jointly with the question as to what
political conclusions were to be drawn from Nikolaev's shot. What
interested me most was Stalin's attitude in this investigation.

The struggle that had been going on since the autumn of 1933
in the ranks of the Party leaders differed very greatly from similar
conflicts in the past. Whereas formerly all forms of opposition had
been opposition *against* Stalin and for his removal from the post of
Party chief, there was now no longer any question of such removal.
The groupings were now not for or against Stalin. Everyone emphasized tirelessly his devotion to Stalin. It was rather *a fight for
influence over Stalin,* a fight for his soul, so to speak. The question
as to the group for which he would ultimately declare himself at
the decisive moment remained open, and since the direction of
policy in the immediate future depended on Stalin's decision, each
group tried to win him over to its side. Until Kirov's murder, Stalin's
attitude was very reserved; at times he supported the advocates of
the new line, and at other times he tried to stop it. Without identi-
fying himself with the representatives of the new line, he refrained

at the same time from expressing himself against it. He now reduced the number of daily reports presented by officials to the very minimum, frequently locking himself in his study, where he would spend hours pacing the room and smoking his pipe. On such days it was said in his immediate secretariat that Stalin was thinking, that he was working out a new line. And when Stalin was thinking, absolute silence was incumbent upon everybody.

Gorki exercised great influence upon Stalin. As already indicated, these were the months in which Gorki's influence had reached its zenith. He was a keen supporter of the necessity of reconciling the non-Party intelligentsia with the Soviet Government and shared fully Kirov's ideas of a preliminary policy of reconciliation within the Party. He believed such reconciliation was bound to strengthen and tighten the ranks of the Party, thus improving the prospect of exerting a moral influence on large sections of the intelligentsia in the Soviet Union. Gorki well understood Stalin's fundamental characteristics, his truly Oriental mistrust of those around him, and tried to make him see that the attitude toward him was now quite different from the one that had prevailed in the days of former fights against the Oppositionists. He tried to convince Stalin that everyone had finally come to recognize the genius of his basic line, that no one wanted to dispute his position as leader. In these circumstances, Gorki argued, generosity to his opponents of yesterday would in no way undermine his position, but would serve only to strengthen his moral authority.

I do not know Stalin well enough to say whether his response was only a pose or whether he was really hesitating whether to accept or reject Gorki's arguments. To one argument of Gorki's, at all events, Stalin was quite susceptible: the thought of what this or that of his measures would mean so far as the verdict of his future biographers was concerned.

For some time now, Stalin has been concerned not only with making his biography, but also with the desire that it be written in the future in favorable colors. He would like to be depicted not only as strong and ruthless in battle against irreconcilable foes, but also as simple and generous on occasions when the present hard-boiled era makes it possible for him to show himself as he believes himself really to be in the depths of his soul. Hence his efforts to play Haroun-al-Rashid, for was not the latter also from the East, and quite as primitive? At any rate, Gorki knew well how to play upon this string and tried to make use of it for good ends—to diminish Stalin's mistrust, to soften his vindictiveness, etc. It may also be that Stalin was guided by other considerations. Everyone was utterly exhausted by the strain of the past ten years and resistance to this mood and Gorki's counsels could only lead to new conflicts. Be that as it may, there can be no doubt that in 1934, Stalin suddenly became milder, more affable, more yielding; he took pleasure in the society of writers, artists, and painters, in listening to their conversation and in stimulating them to frank discussion.

This mood soon found its reflection in Stalin's attitude with respect to the former Oppositionists. Particularly significant in this connection was the reinstatement of Bukharin, who had been in disfavor for some years, as editor of *Izvestia*. More characteristic still was Stalin's new attitude toward Kamenev. If I am not mistaken, Kamenev had been expelled from the Party three times and had as many times repented. His last sideslip had occurred in the winter of 1932–33, when he was discovered "reading and not reporting" Riutin's program, a document Stalin hated with particular force. This time it seemed as though Kamenev was in for serious and protracted trouble. But Gorki, who greatly esteemed Kamenev, succeeded in softening Stalin's heart. He arranged a meeting between Stalin and Kamenev at which Kamenev is said to have made some declaration of love toward Stalin.

No one knows the details of this meeting, which took place in strictest privacy, but its outcome was received with approval in Party circles. Stalin, as he almost publicly declared, had "come to believe Kamenev." At the interview Kamenev is said to have spoken quite openly of his entire oppositional activity, explaining why he had formerly opposed Stalin and why he had now ceased his opposition. It was said that Kamenev gave Stalin his "word of honor" not to engage in any more oppositional activity. In return he was given wide powers in the management of the Academia publishing house and was promised important political work in the near future.

As something on account, so to speak, he was allowed to speak at the Seventeenth Party Congress, where his appearance was a great success. In his speech Kamenev presented a "theoretical" justification for the need of dictatorship, not just for a party or a class dictatorship, but for a *personal* dictatorship. Democracy, according to Kamenev, both inside a class and inside a party, was only practical in periods of peaceful development, when there was sufficient time for discussion and for convincing the other fellow. But in times of crisis, the situation was different. At such times the country required a leader, a man who could take responsibility for decisions upon his own shoulders. Happy, indeed, were a party and a country possessing at such moments a leader gifted with intuition, which made it possible to overcome most difficult situations. But woe to them if at the helm stood a man unfit for leadership, for then destruction became certain.

Kamenev's speech was so formulated and delivered that no doubt could remain in the minds of the audience that the speaker regarded Stalin as a leader of first rank. The congress gave Kamenev an ovation, which turned into an ovation for Stalin. Not until much later was it observed that the speech was rather Machiavellian, and that, carefully read, it was likely to produce an impression opposite to the one apparently intended. This was what Vyshinsky meant when, at the Kamenev-Zinoviev trial, he referred to Kamenev as a hypocritical disciple of Machiavelli.

If one may assume that, for a time, Stalin had been in favor of a complete change in the Party course and of a policy of reconciliation inside the Party, his immediate circle, his working staff, was always completely against it. This was not because the members of this staff were in principle opposed to a change in the *general policy* of the Party, as expressed in the projects of Kirov and his friends, but because questions of general policy were more or less a matter of indifference to this group. In this respect, as was later demonstrated, they were prepared to accept even more striking changes than those proposed by Kirov. *What they emphatically opposed was any change in internal Party policy.* They realized that while many were ready to overlook the negative aspects of Stalin's character because of his outstanding positive features, his immediate assistants (who knew precisely how to take advantage of the negative aspects of his character) could expect no mercy in the event of a change in the inner-Party regime. For, to repeat,

47

the fight being waged was no longer for or against Stalin, but for priority of influence over him. In the language of the Orgburo (Organization Bureau), the struggle was being waged around the proposed replacement of the existing working personnel of the Central Committee with new men seeking to introduce new ways and a new attitude toward people. It was quite natural, therefore, that this old staff resisted any changes by every means in its power.

Directing this resistance were Kaganovich and Yezhov.

Kaganovich is, without doubt, a man of parts. Without much education, he is very quick at grasping and assimilating the ideas of those around him and stands out by his remarkable capacity for work, extraordinary memory, and organizational ability. No one knows better how to direct all sorts of conferences and commissions when the presiding officer is required to steer discussion into the proper channel, to compel adherence to the points in question, and to see to it that the participants stick closely to the matters in hand. And one can only regret that so much brains is the endowment of a man of whose moral attributes there can hardly be two opinions. In Party circles he is known for his undependability. No one can rely on his word: It is as lightly given as it is broken or denied afterward. It is possible that the circumstances of the times in which he has risen to power, in which perfidy brings success, are to blame for this. On the other hand, he has contributed more than anyone else to the spread of such duplicity.

Yezhov has been right-hand man to Kaganovich. If, so far as Kaganovich is concerned, one might ask whether he would not have been able to make his way by honest means, there can be no question of any such query with respect to Yezhov. In the whole of my long life, I have never encountered a more repellent personality than Yezhov's. When I look at him I am reminded irresistibly of the wicked urchins of the courts in Rasterayeva Street, whose favorite occupation was to tie a piece of paper dipped in paraffin to a cat's tail, set fire to it, and then watch with delight how the terrified animal would tear down the street, trying desperately but in vain to escape the approaching flames. I do not doubt that in his childhood Yezhov amused himself in just such a manner and that he is now continuing to do so in different forms. It is only necessary to observe with what ecstasy he badgers any of the old Opposition-

ists, whenever he has a chance. It seems that for a long time
Yezhov had found it difficult to make his way in the Party. He was
disliked and despised. A great store of bitterness had accumulated
in his soul against all those who had formerly occupied prominent
posts in the Party—against intellectuals who were good speakers
(he himself is a poor orator), against writers whose books achieved
popularity (he himself could never write anything but informers'
reports), against old revolutionaries proud of their past (he himself
had never worked in the underground movement). No man could
be more fit to function in this period, when the persecution of old
Bolsheviks has become the official slogan of the "rejuvenated"
Bolshevist Party. The only talent with which nature has abundantly
endowed him is his talent for intrigue behind the scenes. And he
misses no opportunity to use this talent. Nearly ten years of work
in the apparatus of the Orgburo and the Central Control Committee enabled him to acquire extraordinary knowledge of the personal characteristics of the active workers in the Party machine.
He congenitally detests all those who evince the slightest measure
of independence or steadfastness in their opinions and systematically removes them from their posts, substituting instead persons
ready to execute without question any orders from above. Of
course, he is able to pursue this policy because it has the blessing
of higher-ups, but to the manner of its enforcement Yezhov adds
the stamp of his own character. As a consequence, he has managed
in the past ten years to set up a network composed of his trust-
worthy satellites. There are many of them, in all branches of the
Party apparatus, in all Soviet administrative organs, not excluding
the People's Commissariat for Home Affairs, and in the army.
These persons have proven particularly useful to him now that
he has become the chief of this commissariat, the governing staff
of which he has radically "rejuvenated." Incidentally, Yasha Agranov is the only member of this governing staff retained by
Yezhov. They are old and stanch friends!

This pair, Kaganovich and Yezhov, had opposed, from the very
beginning, the policy of internal Party reconciliation. While Kirov
was alive, they did not venture to come forward into the open.
Instead, they contented themselves with stirring up Stalin against
it, with intensifying Stalin's natural mistrust of those in whom he

surmised a foe, in sabotaging, as opportunity presented itself, Kirov's transfer to Moscow, for they knew well that this move would reopen the whole question of changes in the personnel of the Party machine which they had assembled with such painful effort. As will be recalled, this attempt at sabotage was defeated at the November plenary session; nevertheless, Kirov never came to Moscow. After Kirov's death, which the pair found very convenient, they came out into the open.

Agranov's report on the Kirov assassination was drafted in their spirit. The harmless Leningrad dissidents in the ranks of the former Oppositionists were described in the report as conspirators consistently engaged in plotting terrorist acts. A group of former Komsomol members active in the Vyborg district in the time of Zinoviev's rule, led by Rumianzev, Kotolinov, Shatzki, etc., were characterized as the center of this conspiracy. In actual fact, however, they had met fairly regularly since the autumn of 1934. The truth was that the Party Institute had contemplated the publication of the history of the Komsomol movement in Leningrad, and had organized a series of district meetings throughout the city devoted to recalling the activities of former Komsomol workers. These former workers of the Zinoviev period, including even men like Shatzki, who had completely abandoned politics, were actually dragged by force to these meetings. In the Vyborg district these meetings proved particularly lively. Very interesting, in particular, were Rumianzev's reminiscences, the very same Rumianzev who early in 1926, at the meeting of the Leningrad provincial committee of the Komsomol, had brought about the defeat of the proposal by members of the Central Committee that the provincial committee endorse the decision of the Fourteenth Party Congress, which had emphatically condemned the Zinovievites. This conduct on the part of Rumianzev was at that time bitterly assailed by the Leningrad *Pravda,* of which Skvorzov was then editor. In his reminiscences, Rumianzev touched also upon the period of the Zinoviev Opposition, and, it must be admitted, spoke in a language not in harmony with the official line. There had been widespread talk about these reminiscences, and Agranov utilized them as the basis of his conclusions, because, forsooth, Nikolaev had attended the meetings in question, which Agranov now characterized as meetings of the Oppositionists.

Anyone familiar with Agranov's work can well imagine what a yarn he was able to concoct from all this. This time he excelled even his former achievements, and, not satisfied with limiting himself to Leningrad, he extended the threads to Moscow, to Zinoviev and Kamenev, who had been careless enough to meet their former supporters when the latter visited Moscow. Thus was created the appearance of widespread conspiracy composed of the leaders of the old Opposition, at the moment when the higher circles were debating the question of inner-Party reconciliation.

With the particular purpose in mind of impressing Stalin, the report stressed testimony intended to demonstrate that Kamenev, in whom he, Stalin, had expressed faith, had not kept his word of honor, and, knowing of the oppositionist sentiments, had not only failed to report them to the Central Control Committee, but had also not denied himself the pleasure of making carefully couched but rather "disloyal" utterances in conversations with friends.

The discussion of this report in the Politburo took place in an atmosphere of extreme tension. There were two questions to be decided: First, what was to be done with the "participants" and "instigators" of the Kirov assassination as allegedly revealed by the investigation? And, second, what political conclusions were to be drawn from the unearthing of the "conspiracy" of the Oppositionists? The last question was the more important. The majority was opposed to any change of policy, as proposed at the plenum of the Central Committee, which had envisaged a series of economic reforms and promulgation of a new political constitution. On this the majority in the Politburo appeared to have won. Stalin declared categorically that all these measures must be carried through, that he, too, strongly favored them, and that the plan which had been proposed by Kirov should be altered only in one point, namely, that in view of the refusal of the Opposition to "disarm," and as a measure of self-defense, the Party undertake a new energetic "check-up" of the ranks of the former Oppositionists, particularly of the "Trotskyites," "Zinovievites," and "Kamenevites." This proposal was approved, although not without some hesitation. As regards the first question, it was decided to turn it over to the

Soviet courts as an ordinary terrorist case and to leave it to the investigating authorities to bring indictments against all those who might be implicated. *This was nothing less than surrendering the leaders of the former Opposition for trial and crucifixion.*

With the adoption of this decision, the Party machine was set in motion. The campaign was launched with simultaneous plenary sessions of the Moscow and Leningrad Party committees. These assumed a solemn character, with addresses by members of the Politburo, etc. The committee members received copies of the copious report on the Nikolaev case (the report mentioned above), with citations from Nikolaev's diary, abstracts from his testimony, and other documents. Only a limited number of copies of the report were printed, and these were distributed under the personally signed receipts of the committee members. Those who received copies were obliged to return them, under receipts, after having read them, to the secretariats of the respective committees, where they were placed in special, secret safes. But even this secret report did not contain the full text of the declaration found on Nikolaev at the time of his arrest: Knowledge of it was, apparently, forbidden even to this close circle of people. There were, of course, no discussions at these plenums. The prepared resolutions were unanimously adopted, and the following day the bloodhounds were unleashed. A furious campaign against all Oppositionists, particularly former "Trotskyists" and "Zinovievites" was let loose in the press and at meetings. This was how "public opinion" was manufactured for the crucifixion. The first trial aroused comparatively little comment. The accused were doomed from the start. No one dared to defend them. No one was admitted to the court proceedings, not even relatives. Incidentally, it would have been difficult to find relatives, especially in Leningrad, as everyone in any way connected personally with the accused, irrespective of age, sex, or Party membership, had been arrested as suspected of "complicity." Only those who had cause to be there in an official capacity were present at the trial. This explains why the trial was so little discussed. Of one thing, at any rate, there can be no doubt: it was not all plain sailing. Almost all the accused denied the crimes with which they were charged; denied, too, the evidence attributed to them, and spoke of the pressure brought to bear upon them during the investigation.

Not one of them confessed to the existence of a "conspirators' center." Naturally, their protests availed them nothing. The trial of the chiefs of the Leningrad section of the People's Commissariat for Home Affairs took place in even greater secrecy. It was held, however, in a different atmosphere. The charges were more mildly formulated. The accused admitted their guilt, but blamed it on the orders that had been issued by Kirov. The sentences were astonishingly mild, especially when it is recalled how severely mere negligence in the guarding of the persons of our "leaders" is usually punished. Balzevich, who was responsible for the guard service at Smolny, was charged only with "criminal negligence" in the exercise of his official duties, and sentenced to ten years in a concentration camp. The chiefs of the Leningrad section of the Commissariat for Home Affairs and their deputies received only two- or three-year sentences, and were, at the same time, given responsible posts in the administration of the concentration camp to which they were sent. Actually, therefore, the punishment meant nothing more than a reduction in rank.

The first trial of Zinoviev, Kamenev, and others was of a totally different nature. From the beginning it assumed the character of a "demonstration," was carried out with "full publicity," and its purpose was to "unmask," once and for all, the leaders of the Leningrad Opposition before the population of the city. The accused, who had not lived in Leningrad in recent years, were brought there from Moscow and other cities. The composition of the group of defendants made it in reality a trial of the Leningrad Party committee of the Zinoviev period, with the exception, of course, of those few who had always been loyal Stalinists. The accused were told that "the Party demanded their help" in the struggle against the terrorist tendencies that had developed as a result of extremes in the factional struggle to which they themselves had at one time gone, and that it was their duty to help by sacrificing themselves politically. They were informed that only by appearing in court as the leaders of the Opposition, taking upon themselves the responsibility for the existence of these terrorist sentiments, and condemning these sentiments, could their supporters be checked and prevented from continuing their terrorist activity. This proposal frightened and repelled many of the defendants. Kamenev, how-

53

ever, was loudest among the accused in recommending its acceptance.

Some time before his arrest, Kamenev had been summoned to appear before Stalin. This took place, apparently, immediately before the aforementioned decisive meeting of the Politburo. Stalin, it seems, wanted to make sure in personal conversation whether Kamenev had really broken the word he had once given him; whether Kamenev had actually continued to maintain relations with the Oppositionists, in spite of his promise.

The Oppositionists in Moscow did actually maintain contact by coming together from time to time at "social tea drinkings," which were marked by critical conversations, like those in Leningrad. Although he did not attend these gatherings, Kamenev knew about them and of the conversations that took place. In confidential talks with individual participants he declared that in his soul he remained what he was. These statements of Kamenev's became known to all the participants of the "tea-meetings," and some communicated them to their political friends in Leningrad, who, in turn, informed Agranov. At his meeting with Stalin, Kamenev maintained that he had been misunderstood, but, in the end, admitted his guilt, confessed, and even wept. Stalin declared, however, that he no longer believed him, and would let the matter take the "normal" course of criminal court procedure.

It must be admitted, that from the point of view of political morals, the conduct of the majority of the Oppositionists was by no means of high quality. To be sure, the conditions prevailing in the Party are intolerable. To be loyal, to do every single thing that is demanded of us is almost impossible: to do so would mean to become an informer, to run to the Central Control Committee with reports on every utterance of opposition picked up more or less accidentally, and on every Oppositionist document one comes across. A party that expects such things from its members cannot expect to be regarded as a free association of persons of like views, united for a common purpose. *We are all obliged to lie;* it is impossible to manage otherwise. Nevertheless, there are limits that should not be exceeded even in lying. Unfortunately, the Oppositionists, and particularly their leaders, often went beyond these limits.

Letter of an Old Bolshevik

In former times we "politicals" used to observe a definite moral code in our relations with the rulers. It was regarded as a crime to petition for clemency. Anyone who did this was finished politically. When we were in jail or in exile, we refrained from giving the authorities any promise not to attempt to escape. We always adhered to this rule, even in instances where to have given such a pledge would have meant alleviation of our lot. We were their prisoners. It was their business to guard us, ours to try to escape. But whenever it became necessary, under exceptional circumstances, to give such pledges, they were rigidly observed. To take advantage of alleviations granted in return for one's "word of honor" and to escape was looked upon as unworthy, and the exiles of old took strict note of the names of all who brought the name of a "political" into disrepute by committing such offenses.

There is quite a different psychology nowadays. To plead for pardon has become a common phenomenon, on the assumption that since the party in power was "my party," the rules which applied in the Czarist days are no longer valid. One hears this argument everywhere. At the same time, it is considered quite proper to consistently deceive "my party," since it does not fight its intellectual opponents by trying to convince them but by the use of force. This has given rise to a special type of morality, which allows one to accept any conditions, to sign any undertakings, with the premeditated intention not to observe them. This morality is particularly widespread among the representatives of the older generation of Party comrades. Only now, and with great difficulty, is the young generation beginning to break with it.

This new morality has had a very demoralizing effect inside the ranks of the Oppositionists. The border line between what is and what is not admissible has become completely obliterated, and many have fallen to downright treachery and disloyalty. At the same time, the new morality has furnished a convincing argument to those opposed to any *rapprochement* with the former Oppositionists, the argument being that it is impossible to believe them because they recognize in principle the permissibility of telling lies. How is one to determine when they speak the truth and when they lie? The only proper attitude to take is to believe none of them at any time, no matter what they say or swear. This was precisely the point of view taken by Yezhov, and now he was to garner a decisive victory.

Kamenev was completely crushed by his arrest. He tried desperately to win credence for his new professions of repentance, but could not move all of the defendants in "the case of the Leningrad Party committee" (for this would be the proper way of characterizing this trial) to plead guilty. For this reason, the original plan of making this a "show trial" failed. To carry through at that juncture a trial at which one-half of the accused would dispute what the other half maintained appeared out of the question. The trial was, therefore, held behind closed doors, and its results satisfied no one. Yezhov demanded the death penalty, and the campaign, in press and meetings, was in that direction. Many old Bolsheviks were unable to reconcile themselves to this idea. Petitions against the application of the death penalty were presented to Stalin by individual, highly influential members of the Party. The Society of Old Bolsheviks was openly collecting signatures for a petition addressed to the Politburo, in which attention was drawn to Lenin's chief testament: "Let not blood flow between you." Apparently, the ground was not yet sufficiently prepared for the application of the "supreme penalty," and Stalin himself proposed in the Politburo that it should not be resorted to in this instance. For the time being he was satisfied with the fact that the question had now been brought into the open. However, the process of "cleaning up" the Party was pursued with even greater vigor. In the circumstances that now prevailed, the rapid rise of Yezhov was a matter of course. Not only was he made a member of the Politburo, but he was also given the post of fifth secretary of the Central Committee, the post to which Kirov had originally been appointed and on account of which he was to have moved to Moscow. Yezhov was now given charge of all the departments that were to have come under Kirov's jurisdiction. The balance of forces in the Politburo shifted decisively. The two posts that had become vacant after the deaths of Kirov and Kuibishev (both advocates of the policy of reconciliation) were filled with outspoken opponents of this policy.

Once equipped with full powers, Yezhov began an energetic clean-up of the machine. The Society of Former Political Exiles (political prisoners who, under the Czar, had drawn sentences of imprisonment at hard labor) was ordered closed. It was from the publications of the society (memoirs, etc.) that Nikolaev had acquired his terroristic sympathies. *The Society of Old Bolsheviks* was also dissolved. This had been the home of the "fault-finding old men" who were unable to grasp the "needs of the times." Furthermore, the Communist Academy, in which the "theoreticians" had entrenched themselves, was liquidated. Stetski made himself responsible for an energetic clean-up of the editorial staffs of the press in the capitals and the provinces.

In the spring of 1935, the "second Kamenev trial," in connection with a terroristic conspiracy against the life of Stalin, was held. In this trial a number of members of the Kremlin guard were involved. Apparently there was a grain of truth in the case: It was hushed up with a care customarily exercised only in trials of opponents who are anything but broken. Kamenev was also implicated, naturally without cause. He had nothing to do with it, but his name had to appear in the case, this being necessary to further discredit the Opposition. Stalin's personal attitude toward him was such that the accusers could find it only profitable to accentuate their zeal. But, I repeat, there was a grain of truth at the bottom of this affair. Those involved had at least engaged in discussion as to the necessity of following the same path in Moscow as had been taken by Nikolaev in Leningrad. But the guard service in the Kremlin was more efficient than in Smolny.

The most important result of this trial was the fall of Yenukidze, on one hand, the first warning to Gorki, on the other.

Yenukidze was one of the closest and oldest of Stalin's personal friends. Stalin undoubtedly loved him and maintained close personal relations with him to the last. Yenukidze was one of the few people whom Stalin occasionally visited and one who was invited to all social gatherings at which Stalin was present. Yenukidze had been a great friend of Stalin's dead wife, whom he had known as a child, and Stalin treasures every memory of his wife with a tenderness little in accord with his nature. Furthermore, Stalin felt certain that Yenukidze had never tried to undermine him. Nevertheless, he fell, because he had ventured to extend some assistance to those found guilty in the Leningrad trial and their families.

It must be stated that Yenukidze had always tried to help political prisoners and exiles. This fact was known in Party circles, and among the exiles and prisoners themselves. Stalin, too, knew of this personally, not only from the reports of the OGPU, but also from Yenukidze himself. The latter, as was generally known, had Stalin's unofficial permission for this; without it, such action on his part would have been impossible.

But times had changed. Yezhov declared that Yenukidze's kindness weakened the machine, and that Yenukidze must be removed in order to strengthen its driving force. Up to a point, Stalin tried to defend Yenukidze, but perhaps insufficiently, for, finally, Yenukidze was removed from all his posts. The only thing Stalin granted him was immunity from additional punishment and a quiet job of no influence. He was made director of convalescent homes and health resorts in Northern Caucasus. Members of Yezhov's circle tried to picture Stalin's conduct as noble, pointing out that when it was a question of the needs and interests of the Party and the country, Stalin did not hesitate to suppress his personal feelings. In reality, the situation was quite different. To the extent that Stalin knew of and sanctioned Yenukidze's activities, it was simply a case of betrayal.

Gorki's case was a more complicated one. After the murder of Kirov, Gorki became furious and demanded energetic action against the terrorists. But as soon as it became apparent, however, that efforts were under way to utilize Nikolaev's shot for political purposes, in order to alter the line embarked upon in 1934, in support of which Gorki himself had spent so much energy, he tried desperately to stop Stalin from taking the road of revenge. Gorki's dissatisfaction became particularly acute at the time of the second Kamenev trial, when the latter's life was seriously in danger.

All Gorki's efforts were unsuccessful, however. Stalin stopped visiting him and did not accept telephone calls from him. Things went so far that an article by Zaslavski against Gorki appeared in *Pravda*, a thing hitherto impossible. The initiated knew that Zaslavski had written this article on direct instructions of Yezhov and Stetski. Zaslavski is usually employed for jobs of this kind. He can write well but has no moral principles. Gorki was furious, and things reached such a pitch that he demanded a passport to go abroad. That was categorically refused him. No severer measures were taken; he was, after all, Gorki, whom one could not simply remove from a job or cast aside.

All these measures of internal Party terrorism, which followed the first Kamenev-Zinoviev trial, remained unknown to the uninitiated. Even inside the Party they were not learned until much later. They took place behind the scenes. For the outside world, the beginning of 1935 was the period of the real "Soviet spring." One reform followed another, and they all tended in one direction: reconciliation with the non-Party intelligentsia, extension of the government's base by attracting all those who by their work in any department of Soviet development gave practical proof of their abilities and of their devotion to the Soviet State.

All those who had formerly supported Kirov's plans welcomed Stalin's measures, for they were similar to those that had been planned by Kirov. For Gorki, however, the reconciliation of the Soviet Government with the non-Party intelligentsia was the greatest dream of his life—the justification of the compromise he had made with himself when he returned to Moscow from Sorrento.

In these circumstances, it looked at first as though the continued terror inside the Party was only an unpleasant accident, a belated and exaggerated aftermath of Nikolaev's shot, and not a symptom of the impending radical change in the entire policy of the Party. All were convinced that the logic of the policy of reconciliation with the intelligentsia would ultimately be bound to induce the Party leadership to take the path of internal Party reconciliation as well. All that was necessary (it was believed) was for Stalin's acute crisis of morbid mistrust to pass. To this end, it was maintained, the loyalty of the Party to its present leadership must be stressed as often and as emphatically as possible; that the thing to do was to burn incense before Stalin and extol his person on all occasions. The argument ran as follows: He has a weakness for such adulation and his vengefulness can be appeased only by huge doses of flattery, laid on with a trowel; there is nothing else to be done about it. Moreover, it was added, we must learn to forgive these trifles because of the big things Stalin has done for the Party in guiding it through the critical years of the First Five-Year Plan, and at the same time we must speak ever louder and with increasing emphasis of the tremendous changes now taking place, of the new "happy days" into which we were now entering, of the new Party policy, the basis of which was to cultivate in the masses feelings of human dignity, respect for human personality, and the development of "proletarian humanism." Alas, how naïve were all these hopes of ours! Looking back now, we find it hard to understand how we could have failed to note the symptoms which indicated that the trend was in quite the opposite direction: not toward reconciliation inside the Party, but toward intensification of the terror inside the Party to its logical conclusion, to the stage of *physical extermination of all those whose Party past might make them opponents of Stalin or aspirants to his power*. Today, I have not the slightest doubt that it was at that very period, between the murder of Kirov and the second Kamenev trial, that Stalin made his decision and mapped out his plan of "reforms," an essential component part of which was the trial of the sixteen and other trials yet to come. If, before the murder of Kirov, Stalin still had some hesitation as to which road to choose, he had now made up his mind.

The determining reason for Stalin's decision was his realization, arrived at on the basis of reports and information reaching him, that the mood of the majority of the old Party workers was really one of bitterness and hostility toward him.

The trials and investigations which followed the Kirov affair had demonstrated unmistakably that the Party had not reconciled itself to Stalin's personal dictatorship; that, in spite of all their solemn declarations, the old Bolsheviks rejected Stalin in the depths of their hearts, that this attitude of hostility, instead of diminishing, was growing, and that the majority of those who cringed before him, protesting devotion, would betray him at the first change of the political atmosphere.

This was the basic fact that emerged for Stalin from the documents compiled in the course of the investigation of Nikolaev's act. It must be conceded that Stalin was able to provide a reasonable basis for this deduction, and from it he fearlessly drew his ultimate conclusions. As Stalin perceived it, the reasons for the hostility toward him lay in the basic psychology of the old Bolsheviks. Having grown up under the conditions of revolutionary struggle against the old regime, we had all been trained in the psychology of oppositionists, of irreconcilable nonconformists. Involuntarily, our minds work in a direction critical of the existing order; we seek everywhere its weak sides. In short, we are all critics, destructionists— not builders. This was all to the good—in the past; but now, when we must occupy ourselves with constructive building, it is all hopelessly bad. It is impossible to build anything enduring with such human materials, composed of skeptics and critics. What must be considered now, first and foremost, is the necessity of enduring Soviet construction, particularly because Soviet Russia is facing tremendous perturbations, such as will arise inevitably with the coming of war. It was thus that Stalin reasoned.

The conclusion he drew from all this was certainly daring: If the old Bolsheviks, the group constituting today the ruling caste in the country, are unfit to perform this function, it is necessary to remove them from their posts, to create a new ruling caste. Kirov's plans presupposed reconciliation with the non-Party intelligentsia and enlistment of non-Party workers and peasants in the tasks of social and political life, as a means of widening the social basis of the Soviet regime and promoting its cooperation with the democratic elements of the population. Under Stalin's plan, these very same proposals acquired quite a different significance; they were to facilitate a complete revision of the personnel of the ruling caste by expelling from its midst all those infected with the spirit of criticism, and the substitution of a new ruling caste, governed by a new psychology aiming at positive construction.

It would take too much space to describe in detail the preparatory measures taken for the realization of this plan. Attention, of course, was directed principally to renovation of the Party apparatus, which, in many parts, was altered from top to bottom. There can be no doubt, also, that Stalin had determined to conclude these preparations before the new constitution was to go into effect. Our expectation had been that if there was any group that would receive some guarantees of "human and civic rights" from this constitution it would be the old Bolsheviks. In Stalin's scheme, however, the constitution played quite a different role: It was to help him eliminate us completely from any influence upon the fate of the country. Other elements that facilitated the task Stalin had set himself in this respect were supplied by circumstances more or less accidental.

Gorki's influence had greatly fallen after the second Kamenev trial, but his star had not set altogether: There was an outward reconciliation between him and Stalin, and he remained until his death the only person whom Stalin was compelled to take into consideration, to some extent at least. It is possible that had Gorki lived, the August trial might have had a different *denouement*. Be that as it may, it is certain that Gorki's death finally untied the hands of those in Stalin's immediate entourage who demanded haste in the contemplated crucifixion.

At the end of July, a small group of Komsomol students, charged with plotting the assassination of Stalin, were tried in Moscow. The trial, of course, was behind closed doors. Nearly all the defendants were raw youths. They had not committed any overt act, their conspiracy never having gone beyond mere discussion, which was quite serious, however, indicating that they had apparently intended to put their plans into effect. Such cases have, of late, become not infrequent in Russia: plenty of explosive material has accumulated in the country. In this particular case, the majority of the defendants did not deny their plans and were merely concerned with saving their personal friends who quite by accident had found themselves in the defendants' dock. The case was a simple one, and there could be no doubt about the verdict. After Nikolaev's act, all talk about terror meets only with one punishment—death. The judges were, therefore, all the more surprised when the prosecution demanded that the case be held in abeyance for further investigation.

Later, it became known that this demand was made on the initiative of highest authorities, who, in turn, acted on direct instructions from the secretariat of the Central Committee, the latter having decided to utilize this minor case for political purposes. The task of further investigation was entrusted to Agranov. This immediately determined its tone. From the accused students, threads were drawn to professors of political science and Party history. It is easy to find pages in any lectures on the history of the Russian revolutionary movement highly conducive nowadays to the cultivation of critical attitudes in respect to the government, and young hotheads always like to buttress their conclusions concerning the present by citing facts which they have been taught in school to regard as officially established. All Agranov had to do was to pick the professors who, in his opinion, were to be regarded as fellow conspirators. This was how the first batch of defendants in the trial of the sixteen was recruited.

It was even a simpler matter to draw threads from them to the old Bolsheviks from among former leaders of the Opposition. Parts of the material had been prepared beforehand: since the Nikolaev case Agranov had had charge of all cases involving Oppositionists, and he had manufactured a plentiful and ready supply of necessary "documents." The only question was what scope the higher Party authorities desired the case to be given. The preparatory work was conducted in greatest secrecy. There was no preliminary discussion in the Politburo. Molotov and Kalinin had gone on vacation, not knowing the surprise that was awaiting them. Since the Nikolaev case, prosecution of prominent members of the Party before the revolutionary tribunal in cases involving terrorist activity no longer requires preliminary consent by the Politburo. Vyshinsky was initiated into the case from the very beginning. Directing the whole affair was Yezhov.

The trial came as a complete surprise not only for the rank and file of Party workers, but also to members of the Central Committee and some members of the Politburo. Stalin had given his consent to everything and, when the trial was in full swing, left for a rest in the Caucasus: His departure was designed to make impossible the convocation of the Politburo to discuss the fate of the accused. Determination of this question was left entirely to officials: the presidium of the Central Executive Committee, where none dared to raise their voice against executions. There was some conflict with respect to the advisability of additional trials and the persons who were to be incriminated. Under pressure of some members of the Politburo, announcement was made rehabilitating Bukharin and Rykov. Characteristically enough, it was made even without an examination of the accused. Yezhov now regrets this concession, vowing that he will yet make good the "mistake."

While on his holiday, Stalin systematically dodged giving any replies to these questions, but has now taken the position that the cleaning-up must proceed to the end. He is not impressed by the argument that public opinion in Western Europe must be taken into consideration. To all such arguments he replies contemptuously: "Never mind, they'll swallow it." In his opinion, those who may resent the trial cannot exert any determining influence upon the policies of their countries, and "little articles" in newspapers do not disturb him in the least.

Whether additional trials will follow is not yet certain, but Agranov has received sweeping instructions to clean-up to the bitter end. Yagoda has been deposed because he showed some mild opposition to the staging of the trial, of which he learned only after all preparations had been completed, and urged that the case be discussed in the Politburo. Agranov thereupon accused him of protecting the old Party leaders, and he is now actually under home arrest. Yezhov, having taken over direction of the People's Commissariat for Home Affairs, has removed all high officials of the OGPU, leaving only Agranov. The new apparatus of the commissariat has been recruited, both in the center and local branches, from the ranks of Party secretaries. All these are persons who had previously worked with Yezhov and are his trusted men. Reports are that many of those arrested have died in prison: Interrogations are very brutal, and those interrogated have but one simple choice —to confess to everything Agranov demands or to perish. As yet, there have been no new executions, if we exclude the executions of foreigners charged with maintaining connections with the Gestapo, the Polish secret service, etc. But included in the lists of such foreigners are also native Russians. It is said that Sosnovsky has been dispatched in this manner. It is hardly necessary to mention the lawlessness with which immigrants who have become naturalized Soviet citizens are treated.

All of us old *Bolsheviks* who have any sort of prominent revolutionary past are now hiding in our lairs, trembling. For has it not been demonstrated theoretically that under present circumstances we are an undesirable element? It is sufficient for any one to have crossed the path of a person implicated in an investigation for his fate to be sealed. No one will dare defend us. At the same time, all sorts of "benefits" and "alleviations" are being heaped upon the general population. The purpose of this is deliberate: Let the memory of our crucifixion be inextricably bound in the minds of the people with the "improvements" they have received from Stalin.

TWO

Stalin and Kirov

The Murder of Kirov*

K HRUSHCHEV'S report to the secret session of the Twentieth Congress of the Soviet Communist Party has not as yet been made public, but detailed information about its contents has gradually been finding its way into the world press. In particular, we now know that at the center of the accusations made against Stalin personally is the charge that he was involved in the murder of Kirov. It is reported by reliable sources that Khrushchev informed the Congress that a new, formal investigation of this matter has been ordered by the Presidium of the Central Committee of the Party and that work on this investigation has already begun. The results no doubt will be of enormous interest, even though, of course, twenty-two years after the murder there is already a great deal that can no longer be established with the necessary accuracy. This is especially true because over these years there were so many

* This article appeared in the May, October, and December, 1956, issues of *Sotsialistichesky Vestnik*.

bloody purges during which the real organizers of Kirov's murder, headed by Stalin, systematically annihilated everyone who was an inconvenient witness. It is also known that Khrushchev mentioned other mysterious gaps in Stalin's biography: the death of his wife, Allilueva, whom he shot, and the death of Gorky, which was hastened by people who, at Stalin's order, administered treatment detrimental to Gorky's health.

These disclosures by Khrushchev made a tremendous impression on the Congress delegates. His report is now being read at meetings of all local Party organizations and the effect is always the same. An even greater impression is made by the publication of these facts abroad. Undoubtedly these disclosures are not the end of the matter. It is thus all the more important to understand the general nature of Stalin's secret activities which are now being revealed.

In 1929–30, Stalin defeated the "Rightists" of the Bukharin-Rykov-Tomsky group, but his victory was truly complete only in the question of establishing the dictatorship of the Party apparatus over the governmental soviet apparatus. Only on this question did Stalin have a clear majority in the Party behind him. As a rule, Stalin conducted his policy of "total collectivization" in the country-side, as well as his foreign policy (alliance with German militarists for a joint struggle against the "Anglo-Saxons"), by presenting the leading Party bodies with *faits accomplis*. This is why there was a continual foment of opposition within the formally Stalinist ruling bloc on the part of people who quite literally the day before had been fervent Stalinists; the case of the Syrtsov-Lominadze group (December, 1930) is especially characteristic in this respect.*

Of all these opposition groups, it was the Riutin group that played the most important role. Riutin was the son of a peasant

---

* Syrtsov, Lominadze, and Shatskin were accused by Stalin in 1930 of forming a group consisting of comparatively young Party members, who, as opponents of collectivization, gained a degree of influence in Party circles. This group insisted on the necessity of limiting the power of Stalin. They were all expelled from the Party and later, during the Yezhovshchina, died in prison. In 1930, Syrtsov occupied the post of Chairman of the Soviet of People's Commissars of the R.S.F.S.R.; Lominadze joined this group together with Heinz Neumann, who, in 1927, instigated the uprising in Canton; and Shatskin was one of the first organizers and leaders of the Komsomol in Russia.—B. N./1964.

from Irkutsk Province. He attended a local teachers' seminary, which, in the 1905 era, was a hotbed of Social Democratic propaganda. Riutin became a Social Democrat and taught primary school. In 1914, he was called into the army and became an officer. In 1917, he was elected Chairman of the Soviet of Soldiers' Deputies in Harbin; he aligned himself at this time with the internationalist faction of the Social Democrats. There, in November, 1917, Riutin headed an uprising which was both provoked and crushed by Chinese working for the management of the East China Railway. In the years following, Riutin was in hiding; at that time, he took part in the peasant guerrilla movement against Kolchak.* After the coming to power of the Bolsheviks, he joined the Communist Party and played a prominent role first in Siberia, then in Moscow, where, in 1927–28, he was a secretary of one of the most important districts, Bauman. At first he distinguished himself by his toughness in dealing with the "Trotskyites," but later he became one of the most active opponents of Stalin. In 1931–32, he drew up a draft program which aimed at bringing together Stalin's opponents. The most characteristic aspect of this program was not so much Riutin's pro-peasant sympathies (he was, of course, influenced by his peasant origin) as its harshness against Stalin personally. As reported by Bukharin [see p. 11], Riutin depicted the Soviet leader as being "the evil genius of the Russian Revolution, who, motivated by vindictiveness and lust for power, had brought the Revolution to the verge of ruin," and he argued that "unless Stalin was removed from Party domination, there could be no recovery in the Party or in the country."

Stalin declared that Riutin's program was a call for his, Stalin's, murder, and he demanded the execution not only of Riutin himself, but also of those functionaries involved in disseminating Riutin's

---

* In the fall of 1918, Admiral Alexander Kolchak, former commander of the Black Sea Fleet, was declared "Supreme Ruler" of Russia after a coup by White forces supported by British and Allied officers and conservative Russians. In the spring of 1919, while the Bolsheviks were pushing east against his forces, a Siberian peasant partisan movement harassed Kolchak's rear lines. He was thus prevented from joining forces with those of another White commander, Denikin. By 1919, Kolchak was completely defeated. For an excellent review of Kolchak's rise and fall, see George F. Kennan, *Russia and the West* (Boston: Little, Brown and Company, 1960).—Ed.

draft. The matter was investigated at the highest levels. At that time, an effort was still being made to abide by Lenin's wishes not to resort to executions to settle accounts within the Party. For this reason, the Presidium of the Control Commission declined to consider Stalin's demand as it stood, and referred the matter to the Politburo for a decision on the general principle of whether or not it was permissible to apply the death sentence in cases involving opposition groups within the Party. The question was considered first in the Politburo, then at a Plenum of the Central Committee (this was the so-called September Plenum of 1932, which met from September 28 to October 2).

Both in the Politburo and at the Plenum, discussion was very fierce. Stalin's chief opponent was Kirov, who, using old "Leninist" arguments, said that resorting to executions would be disastrous for the Party. Kirov, with varying degrees of firmness, was supported by Ordzhonikidze, Kuibyshev, Kossior, and Kalinin, as well as by Rudzutak, then Chairman of the Central Committee. (Kalinin was the only one among the group who survived the Great Purge.) Only Kaganovich was completely on Stalin's side; the others took an evasive position. Stalin also found little support at the Central Committee Plenum. The sympathies of an overwhelming majority were on the side of Kirov. The extraordinary popularity Kirov enjoyed in wide Party circles during the last two years of his life was due primarily to the role he had played in this matter.

The defeat suffered by Stalin was an extremely cruel blow to him, especially since it was his first major defeat at a Central Committee Plenum; he had never before brought important controversies to a vote unless he was sure of victory. This is how he had always acted, even in the Politburo, let alone in Central Committee Plenums. This time he had obviously miscalculated.

But the victors had no desire to bring matters to a head and start anything resembling an open struggle with Stalin. Riutin and his associates were, of course, expelled from the Party, sent to "isolators," and exiled. The Party press attacked the "Riutinites" with unprecedented harshness: "a wretched little counterrevolutionary" group, with an "out-and-out, blatant program of capitalist restoration . . . the desperate convulsions of the dying class enemy," and so on. On Stalin's demand, a decision about a new general purge

72

was reached soon afterward (December 10). Stalin, of course, was perfectly aware that all this did nothing at all to make up for the loss of prestige he had suffered through the rejection of his proposal; he secretly swore vengeance on his opponents and began to prepare a counterblow. The conspiracy organized by Stalin against the "collective leadership" that until then nominally existed at the top level of the dictatorship had its beginning in the Plenum of September, 1932. It was at this time that Stalin began to prepare the Great Purge.

The first victim was Stalin's wife, Allilueva, who was killed by him on the night of November 9, 1932. M. V. Vishniak's story of this murder, which was first published in *Novoye Russkoye Slovo* on December 21, 1949, is based on information from a completely reliable source. The story told by Elizabeth F. Lermolo in her recent book [*Face of a Victim,* New York: Harper and Brothers, 1955], as well as a number of other materials at our disposal, add substantially to our picture of this event, which is so important for an understanding of the general state of affairs at that time. But this would take us too far away from our account of the great political struggle then raging within the Soviet leadership; the story of the tragic death of young Allilueva is only incidental to the major conflict.

Just before his wife's death, Stalin, who had obviously decided to make himself dictator, began to seek the company of people who encouraged him in his dictatorial aspirations. The most prominent were certain figures in the intellectual community, particularly Alexei Tolstoy, who persuaded Stalin that he was one of the "chosen," that he should lead those around him and not submit to the majority. In conversations, Tolstoy frankly admitted that one of his purposes in writing *Peter the Great* was to influence Stalin along these lines. Stalin was similarly affected by conversations with Kaganovich's younger sister, R. M. Kaganovich.* These ideas were completely different from Allilueva's. Thus, from the point of view of Stalin's new development, her death just then could not have been more timely.

Formally, the discussion over the death penalty in the Riutin case

* Rosa M. Kaganovich became Stalin's third wife, after the death of Allilueva.—Ed.

in September, 1932, had arisen merely as a matter of intra-Party policy. But, in fact, at the root of it there was a profound difference of understanding of the general situation and of the tasks of the dictatorship at that point. This is apparent from the articles in which the Stalinists justified Riutin's expulsion from the Party. They maintained that an intensification, not a relaxation, of the "class struggle" was taking place within the country; therefore, they said, it is necessary to "increase class vigilance," and "relentlessly repulse attitudes of Philistine complacency," to "struggle against any manifestations whatever of conciliationism and rotten liberalism with respect to anti-Party views and aims" (*Bolshevik,* December 30, 1932, p. 11). These are no doubt the same arguments that Stalin and his adherents put forward in proving the necessity of shooting Riutin. We have no reason to believe that the opponents of the death penalty for Riutin had already in the fall of 1932 countered Stalin's ideas on the subject with one of their own. Only later—beginning in the summer of 1933—do we find in their writings traces of any such counterargument. There is no doubt, however, that the basic feature of Kirov's approach—his optimism about people and events—also played a role in the disputes of 1932.

At the Plenum of January, 1933, opposition to Stalin's policy was intensified and broadened. It was one of the stormiest plenums of that time; the country was going through the period of "organized famine" on which Stalin had deliberately launched the country in order to crush the resistance of the peasantry. The famine was particularly severe in regions that had previously been the most prosperous: the Ukraine and the northern Caucasus, the central Volga region and western Siberia. Delivery quotas exceeded the actual harvest. Grain was extorted by the most brutal measures— mass arrests, deportations, executions. The countryside was left entirely without grain and in early fall, terrible reports about the situation in the provinces began to arrive in Moscow. The exaction of grain from the countryside continued right up until the January Plenum, although it was common knowledge that there was a famine. The cities were filled with starving women and children, and every day corpses had to be carted off the streets.

As is bound to happen, there were other misfortunes as well:

the total disruption of agriculture (which was directly linked with the extortion of grain from the most prosperous regions) led to disorganization of bread supplies for the urban population, including industrial workers. And this set off a wave of unrest (in Leningrad, the Donbas, etc.) and also resulted in a general decline in productivity. Measures of a repressive nature did not help, since the diminished productivity was the result of malnutrition which at times bordered on starvation. As far as the food supply of white-collar workers was concerned, the situation was no better; at times it was even worse. As a result, there were signs of a breakdown of the government apparatus, and there was a growth of a "Kronstadt mood," (that is, the mood that caused the 1921 Kronstadt uprising).

It was only natural for the atmosphere of the Plenum convening at this time to be very strained, particularly when the discussion turned to the situation in the famine-stricken regions. I had an account from a very well-informed person about some dramatic moments at this Plenum. Thus, for example, during a speech by Kaganovich, who was on the whole the most garrulous speaker there, one of the members of the Central Committee who had returned from a famine area cried out from his seat: "But in our region they've started eating people!" To this Kaganovich retorted: "If we don't get hold of ourselves, you and I will be eaten. . . . Will that be better?"

This exchange hit the very core of the ambivalent mood of the Plenum delegates. Many of them had been shaken by the horrors of what was happening and spoke with indignation about Stalin's agricultural policy which had brought the country to such a pass. But at the same time, everyone realized that the fate of the regime was hanging by a thread, and any false step could lead to catastrophic ruin for all. None of them wanted such ruin. This forced them to close ranks, though they all were looking for a way out of the situation.

It was at this Plenum that Kirov's line and tactics, distinct from Stalin's, began to take shape.

Kirov's speeches at this Plenum were not published. Collections of his speeches published after his murder were selected and edited extremely tendentiously, and with the years this tendentiousness steadily increased. His real position can be judged only from those documents that were printed while he was still alive.

From these documents it is clear that in his speeches, Kirov did not align himself with the critics of the Central Committee's point of view. On the contrary, even in those instances where criticism was directed against resolutions that Kirov had at one time disagreed with, he did not now join the criticism. He obviously did this deliberately, striving all the while to show that he was remaining entirely within that intra-Party bloc which had played the leading role at the previous stage of the Revolution—the period of the First Five-Year Plan and complete collectivization—and that he made no distinction between his personal fate and the fate of the bloc as a whole. His motives were clear: at that time, the possibility of the regime's collapse began to occur to many people, and therefore the main cadres of "builders of the Five-Year Plan" had developed a distrustful and contemptuous attitude toward anybody suspected of "weak nerves."

Kirov did not suffer from weak nerves, and he firmly rejected the slightest suggestion that it was necessary to retreat. (In one of the speeches at that time, Zinoviev had referred to the "vague idea of retreat," which was then widespread.) Kirov insisted on the need for continuing the "socialist offensive." More vigorously than anyone else, with greater optimism and conviction, he spoke about the successes already achieved, about the victories already won, and never tired of pointing to the "full grandeur of the historical problems we have already solved." (Kirov's report at the Fifth Leningrad Regional Conference, January 17, 1934.)

Kirov urged that all attention be focused on working out a solution of existing problems, not on past disputes. At the Plenum of January, 1933, the main problem concerned the overcoming of the consequences of the famine and the organization of the spring sowing campaign, since a number of districts reported that the depopulated countryside would not be able to carry out the sowing. Stalin's proposal for organizing political sections attached to the MTS*—which was reported on at the Plenum by Kaganovich—

---

* Political sections under the MTS were decreed by the Central Committee Plenum on January 11, 1933. They were meant to strengthen the power of the MTS over the kolkhozes by giving the MTS political power.—B. N./1964.

was not opposed by Kirov, but it was he who raised the question of suspending extreme forms of mass repression against the peasantry, in particular an end to mass deportations to the north. Special commissions were sent to the most important agricultural districts to ascertain the state of affairs in the provinces, and with the authority to release prisoners. It is known to the writer that one such commission, which carried out an investigation in the central Volga region, was headed by N. Krylenko, who was then Public Prosecutor of the U.S.S.R. and a member of the Central Committee. His report, especially the section dealing with his visit to the Saratov prison, made a particularly strong impression in Moscow. In it he told how they had dug a special huge dungeon of several floors, in which thousands of arrested peasants lay side by side with corpses. And so the result of the work of these commissions was the "Instruction" of May 8, 1933. Over the signatures of Stalin and Molotov, this was distributed to "all Party and soviet workers and all organs of the OGPU, the courts, and the Prosecutor's offices." (The "Instruction" was first published by S. Y. Wolin in *Sotsialistichesky Vestnik* of February–March, 1955.)

These measures were only one of the consequences growing out of Kirov's plan of reforms. The basis of his ideas, as he himself said more than once, was Marx's old notion that with the change in the economic base, sooner or later a reorganization of the entire ideological superstructure must inevitably take place. The reason he dwelled on the colossal changes in the economic base of Soviet society was that in his view this obliged the Party to tackle the business of changing the "superstructure." It was only later—at the closed sessions of the Seventeenth Party Congress and at plenums of the Central Committee elected at that Congress—that he unfolded the basic features of his master plan. But he had given expression to his main ideas before this and these earlier statements fully bear out the summary of Kirov's views given in the *Letter of an Old Bolshevik*:

The period of destruction, which was necessary to extirpate the small proprietor elements in the villages, was now at an end; the economic position of the collectives was consolidated and made secure for the future. This constituted a firm basis for future development, and as the economic situation continued to improve, the broad masses of the population would become more and more reconciled to the government; the number of "internal foes" would diminish. It was now the task of the Party to rally those forces which would support it in the new phase of economic development and thus to broaden the foundation upon which Soviet power was based.*

Stalin, and in particular the young members of his entourage corrupted by power, were at this time particularly insistent on the inevitability of "sharpening the class struggle at the new stage" and demanded the stepping up and wider application of the policy of terror. (As I have shown above, it was with these arguments that they defended the need for ruthless reprisal against Riutin.) Quoting Marx, Kirov demonstrated the validity of relaxing the struggle and urged the Party to become reconciled with all who were willing to engage in a joint effort to improve the economic situation of the country.

Of course, in my present account the difference between the two points of view stands out in greater relief than it did at the time, even to the astutest observer of the Soviet scene. But nonetheless this difference existed. Stalin saw it, and in 1933 he had already begun to lay the groundwork for his struggle against Kirov.

Khrushchev's secret report at the Twentieth Party Congress makes it superfluous to collect legal evidence, so to speak, proving Stalin's involvement in the murder of Kirov. Although many points in the story of this murder still are obscure, even simply with regard to fact, the personal role of Stalin nonetheless emerges with sufficient clarity; Stalin's successors strongly hint that he may have been the organizer of this murder. It therefore becomes important to ascertain the reasons that caused Stalin to organize this crime. Why did the removal of Kirov, whom Stalin in 1924 called his "friend and beloved brother" (*Works,* VI, 422), become so vital a matter to Stalin in 1934 that he ran the huge risk connected with this murder?

The answer to this question is all the more important because the concealment of the real motives for Kirov's murder, as well as the motives for all the rest of the crimes of the Stalin era, is the most important purpose of Khrushchev's report. A study of this report shows that Khrushchev and others with him are trying to shift the

---

* For the full remarks, see *The Letter of an Old Bolshevik,* p. 33.—Ed.

responsibility for the crimes entirely onto Stalin, explaining his conduct by his personal qualities—his malevolent vindictiveness and the megalomania and paranoia from which he is said to have suffered. In the entire speech there is not even a hint of the political nature of the struggle which was being waged within the Communist Party at the beginning of the 1930's and which ended in the murder of Kirov and in the Yezhovshchina. It is not hard to understand what forces Stalin's successors to this omission: they are compelled to expose Stalin for a number of reasons, including the hatred of him in wide Party circles, but they cannot reveal the substance of the *political struggle* of that time, since basically they are now pursuing the same policy as Stalin did then.

What was the nature of this political struggle?

The first issue to reveal the existence of significant disagreements within the Stalin Politburo of 1930–33 was the question of the death penalty for Riutin and other Oppositionists. At that stage, questions nominally referring to *intra-Party relations* provided the focus of the struggle—the demand for removing Stalin from the post of General Secretary was central to these. Within the very next months, at the Plenum of the Central Committee in January, 1933, it turned out that there were also divergences on questions connected with the major domestic problem of the dictatorship: how to treat the peasantry. The terrible aftermath of the famine deliberately brought on by Stalin in 1932 in an attempt to break the resistance of the peasantry made the leading cadres of the Party (who until now had obediently followed Stalin) more receptive to the arguments of the advocates of a change of policy. The desire "to come to terms with the muzhik" became the prevailing sentiment—to come to terms, however, without abandoning the collectivization already carried out, but only by softening the methods.

The prestige of Stalin, who was responsible for the horrors of that terrible winter which took 5 to 6 million lives, suffered badly. All the same, the severest blow to him was not the catastrophic famine, but the collapse of the very foundations of his *foreign policy*.

The importance of this foreign policy—which comprises of course the strategy and tactics of world revolution—for the emergence of groupings within the Communist Party is often underestimated. Many people think that the primacy of internal policy over foreign policy was paramount for Stalin. At times this is postulated almost as a law providing the key to an understanding of the development of Soviet policy. I believe this to be one of the main misconceptions that prevents a correct understanding of what goes on behind the Iron Curtain. In reality, the opposite has been the case in all major conflicts: from the very first days of accession to power, Bolshevism has invariably subordinated its domestic policy to the needs of its foreign policy. The *degree* of this subordination has varied; its *forms* have changed; ideas on the correct roads to the "ultimate goal" have changed; even the interpretation of the ultimate aim itself has varied. But the subordination of the regime's internal policy to its external political aims has remained unchanged. None of the groups in power has as yet managed to break away from this relationship of internal to external policy, even though there have been attempts in this direction.

Stalin himself never tried to put domestic interests first. He knew how to conceal his real plans. He knew even better how to bide his time until conditions were favorable. He made many amendments and additions to both the general concept of world revolution and the old, "Leninist" idea on the methods involved. But in his own way he remained faithful to the aim of world revolution in its destructive aspect. He subordinated his entire internal policy to this aim.

This applies especially to the period under discussion, the period of the First Five-Year Plan. The decisive debate between Stalin and the opponents of this policy—the "Rightists" of the Bukharin-Rykov-Tomsky group—took place at the Central Committee Plenum of April, 1929. We know about the stand taken by Stalin there only from the concluding speech he made on April 22, the day before the close of the Plenum. His main speech was never published, and his concluding speech was published in its entirety only twenty years later, in his collected works; before that this speech appeared only in greatly abridged form. The speech leaves no doubt as to the meaning of Stalin's policy at that time. He began it with an analysis of "class changes" which had taken place in recent years both in the U.S.S.R. and in capitalist countries, emphasizing with particular force the growth in them of "elements of a new revolutionary upsurge." "The present slogans of our Party both in internal policy and in Comintern policy have grown out of these changes." Stalin illustrated there slogans with a story about fishermen on the Yenisei who during a storm headed their boat right into the waves shouting: "Hold the rudder tighter, boys, ride the waves. We'll make it!" Stalin compared his policy with that of these experienced fishermen and appealed to people to "ride the wave of the new revolutionary upsurge."

Stalin believed at that time that in 1928 the world had entered the period of "the second round of wars and revolutions," which would decide the fate of humanity, and he wished to throw everything into the scales for the success of these wars and revolutions. His internal policy—the policy of total collectivization—represented hasty preparation of the Soviet home front for the coming "final conflict."

This policy of "riding the wave" was pursued by Stalin with exceptional vigor and cynicism in the Comintern. Germany became the main arena of its application. There were no elements of revolutionary upsurge there. In the trade-unions and factory-committee elections in 1927–29, the Communists invariably lost votes; in the Ruhr, a Communist stronghold, 1,065 Communists were elected to factory committees in 1925, and only 242 in 1929. But economic crisis fostered the growth of the Hitler movement, which in 1928 had just begun to receive generous support from overlords of German heavy industry like Fritz Thyssen. They needed Hitler because they were disturbed by the growth of the workers' influence, the broadening of social legislation, and the high level of wages. They used Hitler as a battering ram against the workers' organizations and social democracy.

For the same reason, Stalin also needed Hitler. Since 1924–25, Stalin had been carrying on the "Bolshevization" of sections of the Comintern, creating a secret-service *apparat* consisting of professional revolutionaries appointed and paid by Moscow. This made Stalin the actual boss of the Comintern, although officially it was headed by Bukharin on behalf of the Soviet Party. Behind the scenes, a struggle had been going on between Stalin and Bukharin

since 1927, or perhaps even 1926. The insurrection in Canton*
had been organized by Stalin against Bukharin's opposition. A
sharp clash occurred in the summer of 1928 at the meeting of the
Soviet faction of the Sixth Congress of the Comintern, at which
Stalin won a number of victories over Bukharin; for one thing, he
succeeded in having amendments inserted in Bukharin's draft program labeling the Social Democrats the main enemy of the Communists. (O. H. Kuusinen gave the most detailed account of these
disputes in the *Communist International* for 1930.) In the fall of
1928, a struggle developed in the Comintern on the question of
tactics in Germany. This struggle was cut short by the Politburo,
which by a majority of four to three removed Bukharin from his
Comintern post. When a major political battle unfolded between
Stalin and the "Rightists" in the Politburo and later in the Central
Committee, Stalin sent a special mission headed by Manuilsky and
Heinz Neumann to Berlin; they were supposed to prove that there
was rising in Germany a revolutionary wave, which Stalin was calling on people to "ride." It was this mission which, on the evening
of May 1, 1929, provoked a series of armed attacks on the Berlin
police; *Pravda* thereupon declared these to be the beginning of the
proletarian revolution.

This was, indeed, the beginning—not, however, of the proletarian revolution but of a new, Stalinist phase in the life of the
Comintern. It was not based only on adventurist *putschism*. It was
something much worse. For a long time, there had been technical
military collaboration between the Kremlin and German militarists.
Secret factories built with German money had, since Lenin's time,
been manufacturing airplanes, hand grenades, machine guns, and
poison gases for the German Army. German military schools for
pilots, tank men, chemical-warfare specialists, etc., were built on
Soviet territory. In 1926, this collaboration was dealt a heavy blow:
the German Social Democrats publicized a delivery of grenades

* The Canton uprising, which was organized by a group of special emis-
saries of Stalin acting without the consent of the official organs of the
Chinese Communist Party, took place on December 11, 1927. It ended in
failure four days later, as the earlier uprisings in Swatow and Hunan had
failed. The failure of the Canton uprising brought about a decline of Russian influence on the Communist movement in China.—Ed.

from the U.S.S.R. At about the same time, the voices of those opposing the theoretical ideas on which this collaboration was based began to be heard in the ranks of Soviet Communists. The Communists at that time regarded Germany as a country reduced to the status of a "semicolonial" power and equated nationalist movements in Germany with the "national-liberation" movements of oppressed peoples. In the Locarno period, Bukharin issued a special letter saying that Germany had now become a full-fledged capitalist country and that therefore a change of attitude toward it was necessary. But this view did not prevail; it evidently ran into opposition within the Party itself.

Judging from articles appearing in German publications on the history of the army, statements such as Bukharin's in practice led to fewer changes in the secret collaboration between the U.S.S.R. and Germany than might have been expected. But the political atmosphere of these relations undoubtedly changed: the "friendly ties" had somewhat loosened by 1927-28.

On the other hand, after 1929, with the beginning of the Stalinist offensive on the Comintern level, the collaboration took on a new lease on life. The full facts about these relations have not as yet come to light, but it is this period that marks the beginning of cooperation between the "political generals" of the German Reichswehr and the Hitlerites, and, simultaneously, the closest political collaboration between these same generals and Stalin. In a memorandum which he submitted to the international tribunal in Nuremberg in 1946, A. Rechberg* gave an account of his conversation with General von Schleicher† in 1930, in which von Schleicher in-

---

* Arnold Rechberg was one of the wealthiest members of a small group of German industrialists that opposed the policy of military retaliation against France and England, although it held an extremely right-wing position on social and political questions. The group's ideas on relations with the Soviet government were set out by Rechberg in an interesting memorandum, which was presented at the war crimes trial in Nuremberg. This memorandum appeared in Russian, with an introductory article by me, in *Narodnaya Pravda* (Paris), October, 1949. Arrested by the American military forces, Rechberg suddenly died under mysterious circumstances. A big box containing his notes has disappeared.—B. N./1964

† Kurt von Schleicher, the right-hand man to the Minister of Defense, was in charge of a Ministry Bureau for political and press affairs of the army

formed him that the advice to collaborate with Hitler was given him by Stalin, who pointed out that Hitler was a highly talented agitator and could be very useful. The purpose of this collaboration is known: the German republic had to be destroyed as the prelude to a war of revenge in the West. True it was known that Hitler favored war in the East, a new crusade against Russia, rather than war in the West; but von Schleicher was certain that he could keep a tight hand on "this housepainter," and Stalin believed him.

In the name of this program, the joint effort of the Communists and the Hitlerites began under the direction of Stalin and von Schleicher. Outwardly, the Communists were the extreme, irreconcilable opponents of Hitler and attacked the Social Democrats for their allegedly too-tolerant attitude toward the Nazis. The Communists themselves behaved very provocatively toward the latter, with constant clashes and skirmishes, but the brunt of their scathing propaganda invariably was directed against the Social Democrats rather than the Nazis. Although for different reasons and under different slogans, both the Communists and the Nazis were engaged in the same work: they were destroying German democracy and clearing the way for Fascism.

It must not be thought that all German Communists were blind to this. Many of them began to have doubts. When, for example, the question arose of supporting the Nazi plebiscite against the Prussian government of the Social Democrat Otto Braun, the Communist Party Central Committee at first declared itself opposed. In order to obtain the desired Central Committee resolution, the intervention of a special emissary of Stalin was necessary—the very same Heinz Neumann. Neumann gave assurances on behalf of the Soviet leader that Hitler would not be allowed to assume power and that Stalin had received special guarantees to this effect. (I

---

and navy. At the end of the 1920's and the beginning of the 1930's, he became the spokesman for the policy of uniting the Reichswehr and the Soviet government for a joint struggle against the West. Believing the German Social Democratic Party to be the chief opponent of this policy, von Schleicher became the covert organizer of attempts to defeat the Social Democrats and to create a strong, authoritarian government; he hoped that, supported by the Reichswehr, such a government would be capable of conducting a *revanchist* policy.—B. N./1964.

have in my possession an account of this meeting given me by one of the participants.) A theory was developed about Hitler, which held that he was playing the role of "icebreaker of the revolution," clearing the way for the Communists. No one knows, of course, exactly what Stalin was thinking, but it was not only the German Communists who failed to understand the meaning of his treacherous game.

Stalin kept a tight hand on the rudder, without regard for anything else. The plunge his boat took was thus all the more severe when, in January, 1933, Hitler came to power—without von Schleicher, against von Schleicher, in a struggle against all the political generals of the Reichswehr who so thoughtlessly had given Stalin guarantees.

For a long time Stalin did not want to believe that this accession of Hitler was serious or that it would last very long. He did not believe it even after Hitler, in the summer of 1933, ordered putting an end to the military collaboration with the Red Army. In none of Stalin's addresses in 1933 was there a single political attack on Nazi ideology. Even in his speech at the Seventeenth Party Congress (January 26, 1934), Stalin did not attack Hitlerism, but only tried to convince its leaders of the madness of their plans for a crusade against the East.

Stalin's speech was constructed very cleverly—very skillfully "dosed out," in Bukharin's words. Compared to his speech of 1930, there are new notes: less talk about the "revolutionary situation," more emphasis on the desire for peace. But there was not a single word in it, not a single gesture, to indicate that he had relinquished his idea of a joint struggle with the German generals against the West, that tomorrow, if the situation changed, he would not return to the same old positions. As the future showed, this is indeed what happened.

Nominally, Hitlerism was a dominating concern of the Seventeenth Congress. But not everyone viewed the question the way Stalin did, and even fewer took issue with him, since the whole assembly felt that in the then prevailing critical situation the Party ranks had to be closed as tightly as possible. It was in this spirit that during the months prior to the Congress many Oppositionists were released from exile and labor camps. Moreover, the most prominent Oppositionists—the leaders of the "Rightists" as well as Zinoviev and Kamenev—were invited to speak at the Congress, thereby emphasizing this necessity for unity. It was evidently for this reason that even those who, like Kirov, had spoken about Nazism in a substantially different manner on the eve of the Congress now chose not to touch upon the question at all. Those who did speak—there were very few—stayed within the framework laid down by Stalin, only coarsening and vulgarizing his presentation, as, for example, Manuilsky.

Only one of the speakers on this subject differed with Stalin's point of view. This was Bukharin. He, too, tied in his speech with Stalin's. His starting point was Hitler's military plans. He did not, however, dwell on establishing the existence of these war plans, but linked them with the very essence of the ideology of Nazism—with the apologia for barbarism which permeated the writings of Nazi philosophers and publicists, with their acute hostility toward culture ("When I hear the word 'culture,'" Bukharin quoted the words of a Nazi, "I reach for my revolver."), and with their harping on the theme that man is a "predatory animal." Having shown up this bestial aspect of Nazism with great forcefulness, Bukharin said that the coming "colossal historical battles" with this enemy would be a struggle for "technical progress, science, culture, for people's happiness," a "fight for the future of humanity."

This short speech provided what was missing in Stalin's lengthy one, and what was missing at the Congress in general: a complete program under whose banner the struggle against Nazism could be waged. The enormous impression it made is not reflected in the official proceedings of the Congress, but it may be judged from the fact that immediately after the Congress, Bukharin was appointed editor of *Izvestia,* which he made the central Soviet paper in the ideological fight against Nazism. This appointment could not have been made unless an overwhelming majority on the Central Committee and in the Politburo supported it, although it was known that Bukharin was in disfavor with Stalin after their extremely sharp clashes in 1928–29, at which time Bukharin called Stalin a Genghis Khan. Stalin, as we know, was not one to forget personal insults. The relationship probably was not improved, either, by Bukharin's speech at the Seventeenth Congress, despite its many highly flattering references to Stalin. The delegates could not fail to interpret Bukharin's speech, so sharply anti-Nazi, as a condemnation of Stalin's Comintern policy which had made possible Hitler's victory. And it was such a condemnation.

The delegates to the Congress were well aware of this. These topics were widely discussed at the many closed meetings of the delegates to the Seventeenth Congress. These meetings were not nearly so unanimous as were the open sessions and, consequently, the choice of Bukharin as editor of *Izvestia,* which gave him the leading role in the cultural and political struggle against Nazism, was a vote of censure against Stalin. Thus, to the struggle against Stalin's intra-Party practices and his domestic policy was added the struggle against his external policy.

One event, which partly by chance coincided with the Seventeenth Congress, focused the attention of the delegates on Stalin's foreign-policy maneuvers. This was the attempted Fascist coup in Paris on February 6–7, 1934, and the role played by the French Communists.

As we know, those were weeks of acute political crisis in France; Fascist-Monarchist groups, with ties to the Nazis and egged on by them, were attacking the Republic. In full accordance with Stalin's directives, the French Communists played a game of provocation, as though repeating the game of the German Communists in 1930–33. While mouthing extreme Left slogans, the French Party was in fact helping the Fascists destroy the Republic. There was a frenzied campaign to discredit the Republic; there was no Fascist slander too vile to be taken up by the Communists, especially if it was directed against Socialists and leaders of non-Communist workers' organizations in general. But the Communists were not content with echoing the words of others; they also made their own contribution to this campaign. With Stalin conducting, the French Communists were playing the same tunes which their German friends had played a year previously in preparing the way for Hitler.

True, the events in Paris did not have a Berlin-type ending. On the night of February 7, right-wing extremist groups tried to storm the Chamber of Deputies and seize power. Lacking popular support, they suffered shameful defeat. The criminal nature of the game played by the Communists is illustrated by the following fact:

the day after the rout of the Fascists, the Communists called a protest meeting at which they demanded the trial of the "Fascist butchers" who had used force in defending the Chamber against the Fascists.

This was too much even for many French working-class Communists, as well as for most of the delegates to the Seventeenth Congress. (It was at this time that the revolt of the Communists in Saint-Denis began, led by Doriot,* who until then had been the most faithful of the faithful.) It was clear that Stalin's policy was both criminal from the viewpoint of the working-class movement and dangerous from the viewpoint of the Soviet Union. A Fascist victory in Paris, even if it would not have made Hitler the master of Western Europe, would in any case have secured his rear for his *Drang nach Osten*. One had to be blind not to see it.

Moscow heard of the events in France shortly before the end of the Congress. (Debate on the new Party rules, despite their enormous importance for the Party future, was cut short.) Most of February 8 and virtually the entire next day were spent on a discussion of the situation at meetings of various delegations. In the whole history of the CPSU there had never been such a long interruption in the work of a Congress before the elections of the governing bodies. It is clear from this what importance was attached to their composition. The details are not known, but the fact that new directives were flown from Moscow to Paris instructing the French Communists to change their policy radically can only be seen as an indication of the mood which had made itself felt at the delegates' meetings. (On February 11, the French comrades officially announced they were joining the movement to safeguard the Republic, the initiative for which had originated with the trade unions and Socialists.)

There is no doubt that it was then that the general feeling arose

* Jacques Doriot, who had gone from his position as head of the International Young Communist League to build a Party stronghold in the Paris suburb of Saint-Denis, came out in opposition to the tactics prescribed for the French Party by Moscow in 1934. The Moscow tactics led some French Communist groups to support the Fascist attack on the National Assembly. Doriot, however, favored a united front with the Socialists. He was expelled by the French CP for his opposition to the general line in April, 1934, and later by the Comintern as well.—Ed.

in favor of the new policy the regime put into practice in 1934. The basic feature of this new strategy was the attempt to revise Soviet *foreign policy.* If, as was shown above, Stalin, in the years 1929–33, worked toward an alliance with the German militarists against the "capitalist democracies" of the West, then, after the Seventeenth Congress, he attempted to substitute a policy of joint action with the West European democracies against militant Nazism. It was this decision—we do not know in what form it was adopted by the Seventeenth Congress or by which particular Party body—that determined the policy of the CPSU in that period. Later, Stalin managed to use this anti-Nazism as a cover for an attempt to restore the alliance between the U.S.S.R. and German militarism. But this came at the next stage of development of the dictatorship, after the Great Purge which Stalin conducted largely for the purpose of liquidating the opponents of such an alliance. In 1934, and even in 1935, a part of the ruling group sincerely attempted to implement the new policy of fighting against Hitler. As a rule, the fate of any one person in the years of the Great Purge is a true indication of his sincerity as regards this policy: with few exceptions, all of its *sincere* supporters were liquidated.

The changes in various spheres of Soviet internal policy—and there were many—derived from this attempt to revise radically the principles of the past foreign policy. The main goal of the sponsors of these changes was the creation of a solid home front for a prolonged and difficult struggle against Nazism.

The foreign correspondents then in Moscow (for example, Walter Duranty, who knew and understood much more than he thought advisable to publish) labeled the new policy the "policy of reconciliation," and they were completely right in linking it with the name of Kirov. It was the logical outgrowth of Kirov's optimistic appraisal of the general situation. He argued that the basic difficulties of the dictatorship had already been overcome, that there was an objective possibility of reducing the terror, and that the irreconcilable enemies of the new regime were so few that they could be ignored. Therefore, Kirov argued, it was necessary to discard the policy of general suspicion and universal terror and replace it with one based on trust and persuasion. In many respects this policy resembled the "policy of trust" which Sviatopolk-Mirsky attempted to pursue in the autumn of 1904.* It should be said that measures to this effect rapidly followed one another after the Seventeenth Congress. This is not the place to discuss them in detail, but in looking at them now from the vantage point of history, one can see that they were part of a grand design.

Countless Communist Oppositionists incarcerated during the years of the First Five-Year Plan returned from prison and exile. Simultaneously, numerous cases of so-called wreckers were reviewed; the regime tried to bring back as many as possible of its old, lost cadres.

The OGPU was replaced by the NKVD, and the change was more than nominal; suffice it to say that the regulations of 1934 deprived the NKVD of the right to pass death sentences, of which there had been so many.

Of great importance were the attempts at reconciliation with the intelligentsia; the most important stage in this process was the Writers' Congress held in August, 1934. The central figures of this Congress were Bukharin and Gorky, who jointly came forward as advocates of "proletarian humanism," which they contrasted to the antihumanism of fascism.

At the same time, much was being done to give effect to the switch in Soviet foreign policy. In September, 1934, after appropriate preparation, the U.S.S.R. entered the League of Nations. In previous years the Soviets had called the League the main imperialist weapon of the "capitalist democracies."

These measures, however significant in themselves, were, according to the plans of the sponsors of this new policy, only a preface to the great program of reforms they had mapped out. After the Seventeenth Congress, the reforms became the major preoccupation of the Politburo and of the special conferences convened under the Central Committee and the Council of People's Commissars to work out separate aspects of the program. The major issue was the

---

* Prince P. D. Sviatopolk-Mirsky succeeded the reactionary Minister of Interior von Plehve in 1904, when the latter was assassinated by a revolutionary terrorist. He attempted to pursue an enlightened policy designed to meet the complaints of the moderate liberals. However, revolutionary feeling was too strong and his support from the Czar too weak for his measures to have much effect. He was replaced in January, 1905.—Ed.

revision of the Constitution of 1924 to eliminate the provisions by which workers' representatives were assured an artificial majority on all Soviet bodies, to the detriment of the peasants. The new Constitution was conceived as one based on universal and equal suffrage; it was to make impossible any talk of the unequal position of the peasant in the U.S.S.R.

Kirov played the leading role in all this. His most active supporters in the Politburo were Ordzhonikidze and Kuibyshev. These three also formed the leadership of the new majority, which had in fact emerged after the Seventeenth Congress both in the Central Committee and in the Politburo.

Organizationally, the new majority had not taken very firm shape and had not been at all consolidated. This was because of the genuine wish of its representatives, particularly Kirov himself, to put the regime's new policy into effect with as few repercussions as possible in the apparatus of either the government or, particularly, of the Party. This was the logical consequence of the group's general attitude toward the Party, which they regarded as the basis of the whole Soviet system. We must not forget that the horrors of collectivization, famine, and terrible economic distress were still fresh in their minds. The regime could only get over the recent difficulties by playing on the fear of Party workers of what would inevitably happen if the whole system collapsed and the enraged peasants took merciless vengeance on the towns. Even when addressing closed meetings, Kirov never spoke in this vein; he always remained optimistic about establishing friendly relations with the peasantry. Yet there is no doubt that he was not entirely free of these fears and that the special urgency of his constant appeals for preservation of Party unity at all costs and for considerate treatment of its members grew out of these feelings.

Kirov called upon all Party members for the closest unity, based on the voluntary subordination of the minority to the majority, since only with such unity could the Party exercise hegemony in the country. These views of Kirov are the key to certain features of the Seventeenth Congress and the period that followed it, particularly to the new majority's attitude toward Stalin, an attitude that otherwise would be inexplicable.

At the Congress, Stalin's policy suffered a severe defeat and there was an abrupt change in course. Yet to the outside world the Congress looked like a sheer glorification of Stalin—and not only to the outside world; even in the closed sessions there was no criticism which might have undermined Stalin's role as leader. This was only logical: if it was considered necessary to raise morale by calling the Congress the "Congress of Victors," then Stalin, as the official leader of the Party, had to be extolled.

But in fact, Stalin's position after the Congress was greatly shaken. A close reading of the official documents published at the time provides clear evidence of this. If one compares the list of members of the permanent Central Committee bodies elected by the Plenum, as officially reported, with the similar lists published after previous Congresses, one cannot help being struck by one peculiar feature of the 1934 list: It does not contain the usual phrase about the "confirmation" by the Plenum of Stalin's appointment as General Secretary of the Central Committee. This formula had always appeared in such official reports of the Central Committee, beginning with the Thirteenth Congress; this time it was missing. Of course, this was no accident; nothing is ever accidental in official CPSU documents. It meant that *after the Seventeenth Congress, Stalin ceased to be General Secretary of the Central Committee,* that he had lost all those special privileges which went with the position and which set him apart from the other members of the Central Committee Secretariat.* Previously these special rights had made him boss, in the full sense of the word, of the Secretariat and of its whole apparatus. Now he became the first of the four secretaries of the Central Committee, all of whom formally had equal rights. This was a real revolution from above in the Central Committee apparatus.

Another major event of this session was the inclusion of Kirov among the secretaries of the Central Committee. The significance

---

* This analysis of the Seventeenth Party Congress as a moment when Stalin's influence weakened was based on Bukharin's account. It agrees with that of other authors writing on these events. It is all the more important to note that now even Soviet historians are beginning to interpret the Seventeenth Congress in this way. L. S. Shaumian, the son of the well-known S. Shaumian, in an article in *Pravda,* February 7, 1964, states that certain delegates to the Seventeenth Party Congress had considered removing Stalin from his post. Learning of these plans, Stalin moved to consolidate his position, and thus began the Yezhovshchina.—Ed.

of this decision was obvious: the new majority was gaining a foothold in the apparatus of the central bodies of the Party. Kirov had a reputation in the Party as an experienced and gifted organizer, a good disciplinarian with a knack for choosing the right people. Although the Plenum's decision to keep Kirov in his post of First Secretary of the Leningrad Regional Committee meant that he would have to devote some of his time and energy to Leningrad matters, it also enhanced Kirov's authority in the Central Committee apparatus: he had Leningrad behind him.

The two other secretaries were not of great importance at that moment. One was Zhdanov, who, being a newcomer to the job, could not play a major role; the other was Kaganovich, whom many considered Stalin's evil genius, but who at that moment was not quite so close to Stalin—evidently because he was looked upon suspiciously by the "younger" members of Stalin's personal secretariat, especially Poskrebyshev and Yezhov. Although these two were both creatures of Kaganovich, they did not completely trust him. They may have had good grounds for this; there are certain indications that in the climate prevailing in Moscow in 1934, Kaganovich had begun to waver in his "ultra-Stalinism" and had begun to wonder whether it would not perhaps be advisable for him to go over to the camp of those supporting the new course.

Be that as it may, at the top of the Party apparatus the great struggle between the two political lines turned into a duel beween Stalin and Kirov. The duel was an uneven one, because the adversaries fought it on different levels and with different weapons. Kirov treated it as a political struggle, to be conducted in terms of common loyalty to the Central Committee and acceptance of the line adopted at its Plenum, the highest Party authority. Stalin treated it as a *personal* struggle and saw every defeat as a personal affront.

After his defeat in October, 1932, in the Politburo and in the Central Committee on the question of the death sentence for Riutin, Stalin by no means resigned himself to the situation but began, in the innermost recesses of his personal secretariat, to prepare his revenge. This secretariat had formerly also had a section that gathered materials on the activities of the OGPU. After the Riutin affair, this section was expanded and a special body, which became known as the Special Secret Political Department of State Security, was formed. It is not known exactly when this special department was created; its existence was the greatest of secrets and there was never any mention of it in print.* But there is no doubt that it already existed in embryonic form in the summer of 1933.

The chief organizer of the department was, of course, A. N. Poskrebyshev, for many years head of Stalin's personal secretariat and the person who enjoyed his confidence.† Originally, the heads of this department, as far as can be established, were: (1) M. F. Shkiriatov, one of the original directors of the Central Control Commission and, later, after the Seventeenth Congress, Deputy Chairman of the Party Control Commission of the Central Committee. Shkiriatov was one of Stalin's closest assistants in matters of this sort; (2) N. I. Yezhov, in 1933 head of the Records and Assignments Department of the Central Committee, which was later reorganized into a "Department of Cadres"; (3) Y. D. Agranov, then a member of the collegium of the OGPU, and later one of its deputy chairmen. Later there were changes in the personnel of this commission. New people were added, for example, Malenkov and Serov, who later became notorious as a general in the MVD. But in 1933–34, the only active members of the department were the ones mentioned above. It was headed by Poskrebyshev, and of course it was masterminded behind the scenes by Stalin himself. It was officially charged with supervising the OGPU, whose heads, Menzhinsky and Yagoda, were not trusted by Stalin.‡

It was not difficult to organize this surveillance. With the aid of

---

* It is mentioned in the books of some foreign correspondents who were living in Russia at that time, but the information I am now publishing is derived from interrogations of refugees from the U.S.S.R., among whom were some who in years past had some connection with this department. Unfortunately, none of them has yet published his recollections about those times.—B. N.

† For more about the role of Poskrebyshev, see pp. 105 ff.—Ed.

‡ A. Orlov, in his book *The Secret History of Stalin's Crimes* (New York: Random House, 1953), depicts Yagoda as a man who "in the course of fifteen years became Stalin's *alter ego.*" This is not at all in accord with the facts. It is known from documents (for example, the record of a secret talk between Bukharin and Kamenev in June, 1928) that Yagoda, as well as Menzhinsky and Trilisser, was on the side of the "Rightists" against Stalin. It is also known that in 1929, Yagoda signed the joint memorandum from the leaders of the OGPU to the Politburo warning against forced collectivization.—B. N.

the Central Committee Department of Cadres and the Orgburo, the Secret Department planted its people in all the local offices of the OGPU—usually as deputies to the chiefs of these departments, since according to established practice the appointment of the latter was in the hands of the collegium of the OGPU. This network of the Secret Department of Stalin's personal secretariat later, during the Yezhovshchina, provided the core of the NKVD apparatus, while the regular cadres were almost completely eliminated. It was with the help of this secret apparatus that Stalin prepared his blow against Kirov.

As we now know, Nikolaev, Kirov's assassin, a dupe of *agents provocateurs* from Stalin's personal secretariat, was unsuccessful in his first attempt to assassinate Kirov. He was arrested by Kirov's bodyguard and a loaded revolver was discovered in his briefcase. But he was released and was able, approximately ten to twelve days after his first attempt, to go back to Smolny and kill Kirov.

Kirov was assassinated on December 1, 1934. The first attempt therefore must have taken place around November 20. From November 25 to 28, a Central Committee Plenum was meeting in Moscow. This was one of the most important plenums in the entire history of the CPSU. On its agenda was the question of the great plan of reforms which had been worked out on the initiative of Kirov. The official report on its results mentioned only the decision to abolish the food-rationing system in the cities (then the most important demand of urban workers) and the abolition of the political departments of the Machine-Tractor Stations; these political departments were tentacles of the police apparatus reaching into the very depths of the countryside. It is also known, however, that this same Plenum adopted resolutions that later formed the basis for the agricultural statute, which became known as the "Bill of Rights of the Collective Farmer." This statute, had it actually been put into effect, would really have brought about substantial improvements in the situation of the collective farmer. Finally, as we know from later statements, though not from the report published at the time, this Plenum also discussed the question of the new constitution and other political reforms planned by Kirov. Moreover, these were approved in principle by the Plenum, but it was decided to make no public announcement until after the next Plenum, when they were to be discussed in greater detail.

In other words, *the Plenum accepted the whole of Kirov's grand plan,* but decided to publish only those parts dealing with *economic* reforms that would considerably improve the situation of the workers and peasants. But for some reason or other, it postponed the publication of the *political reforms* that had been approved in principle.

In the light of this, the dates of Nikolaev's first, unsuccessful attempt, and his second, successful one, when his bullet killed Kirov, acquire new significance.

The first attempt took place practically on the eve of Kirov's departure for the Plenum. Before the session, Kirov, a member of the Politburo and one of the secretaries of the Central Committee, naturally had a great deal of important work in Moscow; therefore, he had to leave several days before it began. It was the intention of the brain behind the assassination, Stalin, that Nikolaev's bullet wreck the Plenum and thus prevent the adoption of Kirov's plan for reforms. This first attempt at assassination failed by accident, for reasons beyond the control of the *provocateurs.* Kirov was able to attend the session, and there, in a political controversy, Stalin suffered defeat.

It is necessary to add that one more resolution of an organizational nature was adopted at this Plenum. At both previous plenums, in February and June, the question had been raised of moving Kirov to Moscow and having him take over important aspects of the everyday work of the Central Committee Secretariat. These proposals met with the ill-disguised opposition of Stalin. Even Kirov himself received them coolly, pointing to pressure of work in Leningrad. There are grounds for believing that for him the question of moving to Moscow was bound up with the question of his grand plan of reforms. At the November Plenum, the question of Kirov's move was raised again. This time Kirov did not object, and the Plenum adopted a resolution to that effect, setting a very early date for his transfer. Kirov was to return to Moscow within a week and immediately take over a substantial part of the work of the Central Committee Secretariat, above all the work connected with putting his reforms into practice.

This prospective transfer filled the central Party apparatus with many misgivings; for the first time after nearly thirteen years of the one-man dictatorship of General Secretary Stalin, another "strong man" was going to make his appearance in the Central Committee building. The situation was all the more perilous in that the new Party statutes adopted by the Seventeenth Congress had also substantially changed the position of Stalin's notorious personal secretariat. Until the Seventeenth Congress, the statutes did not provide for the staffing of this personal secretariat—it was under the exclusive authority of Stalin himself. No one else had any say in the control of it. The statutes of the Seventeenth Congress regularized the position within the Party apparatus of this now vastly swollen personal secretariat and officially incorporated it into the machinery of the Central Committee as its "Special Sector." But the same resolution of the Congress also gave a legitimate pretext for an inquiry into the affairs of this Special Sector if the alignment of forces in the Central Committee were favorable to such a move. What this foreboded for the members of the Special Sector only they themselves knew. Is it any wonder, then, that Nikolaev repeated his attempt? Stalin's personal secretariat, which had now been converted into the Special Sector of the Central Committee's General Secretariat, had every reason to eliminate Kirov.

The Plenum ended on November 28. Kirov cannot possibly have left Moscow the next day. After the Plenum there was bound to be a meeting of the Politburo and the Secretariat and, perhaps, of the Orgburo, of which Kirov was also a member. Most likely, he got back to Leningrad on the night of the thirtieth. And the next day, Nikolaev made his way through the now so familiar corridors of Smolny, carrying in his briefcase the same revolver that had recently been taken from him by Kirov's bodyguard, only to be returned to him later by Zaporozhets, the Deputy Chief of the Leningrad branch of the NKVD, who had been named to this post by Yezhov, then head of the Central Committee Department of Cadres.

The duel between Stalin and Kirov was over. The struggle for Kirov's grand plan still continued, and there were still some tense moments, but Stalin's victory was already assured. Kirov's place in the Secretariat was filled by Yezhov.

More on Stalin and Kirov*

K IROV'S assassination is one of the most important landmarks in the history of the U.S.S.R.

The murder was actually committed by the unfortunate young Communist Nikolaev, whose personal motives are of only secondary interest; there is no doubt whatever that he was merely a pawn in a big game whose meaning he himself did not understand. What we are mainly concerned with are the forces which were directing Nikolaev from behind the scenes.

Where should we look for these forces? Now, after Khrushchev's famous secret speech about the crimes of Stalin, it is clear that the inspirers and real organizers of the murder must be sought in Stalin's immediate entourage, in his personal secretariat, among people who acted with his knowledge and at his instructions.

* This article appeared in *Novoye Russkoye Slovo,* December 6, 1959.

Speaking of this murder, Khrushchev said on February 25, 1956:

> To this day the circumstances surrounding Kirov's murder hide many things which are inexplicable and mysterious and demand a most careful examination. There are reasons for the suspicion that the killer of Kirov, Nikolaev, was assisted by someone from among the people whose duty it was to protect the person of Kirov.*

Khrushchev, of course, understood the full meaning of his words, and he had every reason for saying them. If the leader of the ruling Party and head of the dictatorship says this, it means that he is obliged to carry out an investigation and uncover the truth about the crime, to find the guilty parties and name them. But almost four years have passed since these words were spoken. Of course, after a quarter of a century such an investigation is a highly complicated and difficult matter, especially as the investigators of the assassination were intent on destroying all traces that might have helped to get at the truth. But Khrushchev, after all, is the virtual dictator of the U.S.S.R., and he has enough power in his hands to overcome many of these difficulties. He is not doing it. True, the most recent official *History of the CPSU* greatly tones down the wording of Stalin's *Short Course (Istoriia Vsesoiuznoi Kommunisticheskoi Partii [Bolshevikov]: Kratkii Kurs* [Moscow, Gosudarstvennoe Izdatelstvo Politicheskoi Literatury, 1938]), which placed the responsibility for the murder on every opposition group in the Party, without exception. On the whole, however, the latest *History* also upholds this false version, repeating the phrase about Nikolaev's links to "the Zinoviev anti-Party group" and ignoring the "mysterious" and "suspicious" aspects of the case referred to by Khrushchev. All other Soviet authors who have written about Kirov's murder are also silent about these aspects, thereby giving tacit support to the false Stalinist version.

Investigation of the case, I repeat, indeed presents enormous difficulties, but it is still possible. There are a number of clues that point to the real organizers of the murder, and these could be followed up even today, the most important being the one to which

---

* For the English text of this speech, all references are to *The New Leader* Supplement, "The Crimes of the Stalin Era," 1962. This passage appears on p. S 22.—Ed.

Khrushchev referred in his report, namely, the circumstances surrounding the death of the Chekist Borisov, who was assigned to protect Kirov and who was, apparently, the only witness to the murder. The story of his death needs to be told.

Borisov, who for a number of years had been Kirov's bodyguard and general factotum, was, by all accounts, personally devoted to Kirov. By virtue of his position he was bound to know much that would have been important for clearing up the circumstances of the murder. His interrogation was essential to the investigation, but his testimony does not appear in the materials of the investigation. Before he could be questioned, he was killed in an automobile "accident" whose circumstances Khrushchev himself calls "unusually suspicious." This is putting it mildly. In fact, the circumstances of Borisov's death are not suspicious—they are completely obvious and clearly point to the circles to which the organizers of Kirov's murder belonged.

Immediately after being told of Kirov's murder, Stalin left Moscow by special train for Leningrad. He was accompanied by a Politburo commission (Voroshilov, Molotov, and Zhdanov), by a member of the NKVD collegium (Agranov), a group of people from his personal secretariat, and a gang of his bodyguards. They arrived in Leningrad before dawn on December 2, and the first thing Stalin did was to take the whole staff of the Leningrad branch of the NKVD off the case. Stalin put Agranov in charge of the Leningrad NKVD, and entrusted him with the investigation of the Kirov affair. No one else examined the matter.

Agranov was greatly trusted by Stalin. This was not only because over the years he had gained a reputation as a feared and brutal investigator,* but also because in the power struggle at the

---

* Yakov Agranov was the chief investigator in a number of outstanding cases, including the Kronstadt uprising, when thousands of sailors and others were shot, the so-called Tagantsev conspiracy in the summer of 1921, when, among many others, one of the greatest poets of the time, N. Gumilev, was shot, the peasant uprising in Tambov, etc. He was distinguished for his brutal and unscrupulous methods in conducting investigations. Later, Agranov became founder and chief of a special department in the GPU watching over writers—the so-called Litcontrol—a member of the GPU executive, etc. He was arrested and shot in 1939, after the liquidation of Yezhov and his replacement by Beria.—B. N./1964.

top of the dictatorship he had always been devoted to Stalin and had become a trusted Chekist in Stalin's personal secretariat.

By putting Agranov in charge of the investigation of Kirov's murder, Stalin in effect was taking personal charge of the investigation, and he was therefore responsible for everything that was done during this investigation.

Early in the morning of December 2, Agranov summoned Borisov for interrogation. He was called for in a car by Agranov's men, that is, members of Stalin's own bodyguard, and it was this car that had the "accident" in which Borisov was killed. These were the circumstances of the so-called accident that Khrushchev called "suspicious." In fact, everybody else in the car was unhurt. Only Borisov was killed. Such accidents are most unlikely. There can be no doubt that the whole thing was staged in order to get rid of an awkward witness. Moreover, those responsible for the bogus accident were so sure they would get away with it that they did not even consider it necessary to take precautions.

By whom was it staged? We do not know the names of the actual murderers since they were never identified in the press. But their position in the apparatus is clear: They were people from Stalin's secretariat acting on the orders of Poskrebyshev, Yezhov, or Malenkov. These people were not called to account and did not suffer any punishment; otherwise, Khrushchev would have mentioned it in his speech. Stalin, too, knew about their deed. He personally interrogated all the most important witnesses. Borisov's death must have come to his attention. If the stagers of the murder did not suffer punishment, it means that Stalin himself was behind the murder.

The business of Borisov's death in itself is sufficient proof of Stalin's direct involvement in the murder of Kirov. And that is why the circumstances surrounding this affair remain uninvestigated. In his speech to the Hungarian Party Congress in December, 1959, Khrushchev explained in effect that because his secret speech had created such complications within the apparatus of the regime, it had proved necessary to put off the investigation. But delay is needed only by those who wish to preserve and strengthen the dictatorship. Those who wish to liberate the country are interested in the exact opposite—in getting at the truth about the bloody crimes of Stalin.

Why was Kirov's murder necessary to Stalin? This is part of the broader question of why Stalin needed the Yezhov purges of 1936–38. Why did he find it necessary to liquidate more than 60 per cent of the delegates to the Seventeenth Congress, which had elected the Central Committee? Why was it necessary to liquidate more than half a million Communists who held responsible posts in the regime, and no fewer than 10 million non-Communists?

Unless we regard Stalin as a madman—and this he was not—there can be only one explanation: at the top level of the CPSU, a muted but nonetheless intense struggle was in progress between the adherents of two different policies. On the one hand, there was Stalin's policy, which became clearer as the years went by. It was a policy of stepping up terror in the country as a whole, but particularly the application of terror to the Party itself—a policy of exterminating all dissidents. It was at the same time a policy of foreign ventures based on a firm understanding with Nazi Germany. Opposed to it was Kirov's "policy of conciliation," which never became public knowledge in its entirety. However, there is no doubt that it comprised profoundly anti-Nazi attitudes, an attempt to come to an understanding with the peasants, a desire to conduct Party propaganda in the spirit of "proletarian humanism," and above all insistence on an immediate abatement of the reign of terror within the Party.

It was this last demand which gave Kirov the support of the majority of the delegates to the Seventeenth Congress. His policy toward the Party is in many ways reminiscent of Khrushchev's present policy. This makes an understanding of Kirov's policy all the more important. The past—the struggle between Kirov and Stalin—extends into the present. Of course, it must be emphasized as strongly as possible that Khrushchev's policy cannot be regarded as a direct continuation of Kirov's, even on the plane of internal Party relations. It is by no means mere chance that the new edition of Kirov's selected articles and speeches published under Khrushchev omits all but one of Kirov's speeches of 1933–34, which deal with the very period in which Kirov's new ideas found open expression. On this plane, Khrushchev still has no intention of telling the truth about Kirov. Nevertheless, there is no doubt he is trying to learn from him.

THREE

Stalin's Death
and the Aftermath

The Poskrebyshev Purge*

Events of enormous importance to Russia and the whole world are taking place in the Kremlin. It is not just that the doctors arrested earlier this year [1953] have been released and the charges against them declared false. It is not even that S. D. Ignatiev, the Minister of State Security, and his deputy, Riumin, have been removed from their posts and called to account. However important they may be, these facts are overshadowed by the nature of the charges brought against Ignatiev and Riumin by the Soviet Government, which in its official statement accuses them of abuse of power, inadmissible methods of investigation, "barefaced lies," and violation of the "rights of Soviet citizens guaranteed them by the Constitution."

One must know Soviet conditions in order to appreciate the full significance of these words. For decades, the Soviet regime has

* This article appeared in the April 17, 18, and 19, 1953, issues of *Novoye Russkoye Slovo*.

105

told its citizens that the MGB-MVD never makes mistakes, and that therefore there could be no protest against its actions, which had resulted in the arrest, deportation, and death of millions. Now the government itself has openly stated that the MGB has made mistakes. This makes it permissible for everybody to have doubts and to demand an investigation.

Another aspect is even more important: Not only has the government made legitimate the right of Soviet citizens to question certain actions, but it has in effect turned to these citizens for moral and political support in the fight against government officials who, on achieving high office, violated the constitutional rights of citizens. This means that the struggle at the top is no longer confined to the leadership itself, but that there are now certain social groups in the country with which the protagonists in this struggle consider it important to maintain good relations.

If this were not so, we should not have had this announcement from Beria, which sounds more like a proclamation than a sober government communiqué. With his thirty-odd years of police work, Beria knows better than anyone else just how dangerous to the regime his report is. He could have gotten rid of an opponent without even making the fact public, as he has done many times in the past. There is only one possible explanation why the Ignatiev-Riumin case was publicized in this provocative tone: because an intense struggle is taking place behind the Kremlin walls and one of the contending groups—Beria's—thinks it necessary to show that part of the Soviet public which can read between the lines of official statements what is at stake in this struggle.

There can be no doubt whatsoever that Beria, who is now the head of the Ministry of Internal Affairs (MVD) and of the whole police apparatus of the country, is out for the blood of Ignatiev, who until Stalin's death headed the Ministry of State Security (MGB) now absorbed into the MVD. From the tone of Beria's announcement it is clear that a personal factor is involved in this struggle. But it is also clear that the issue is so important and the conflict so acute that it cannot be reduced merely to a matter of personalities. Moreover, Ignatiev himself is such a minor figure compared with Beria that he cannot possibly have opposed Beria all by himself. There must be somebody behind him, and the first step in trying to solve this latest Kremlin riddle is to find out who it is.

In the American press, Ignatiev is now being portrayed as one of Malenkov's men, and consequently the developments in the Kremlin are being explained as a struggle between Beria and Malenkov. This interpretation strikes me as fallacious. Under no circumstances should Ignatiev be portrayed as a Malenkovite. Our information about Ignatiev is extremely limited, but we do know that he began to make his career when Malenkov was in decline.

As a comparatively young man, not yet fifty, Ignatiev was secretary of the Regional Party Committee (*obkom*) of the Bashkir Autonomous Republic during the war. He held this post until February, 1946, when he was elected to the Supreme Soviet of the U.S.S.R. as the deputy from Ufa. He immediately began to play a role in the Supreme Soviet: At the opening session, it was he who presented the motion concerning the agenda, and he was elected to the Credentials Committee, of which Patolichev, who a few days previously had been elected to the Orgburo of the Party Central Committee, was chairman. Because of the struggle then going on in the Central Committee, there was intensified recruitment of supporters from among provincial officials and attempts to get such recruits into the Central Committee apparatus. Ignatiev was one of those provincial officials who remained in Moscow to work in the Central Committee.

Knowing what we do about the posts Ignatiev has held, it is possible to state unequivocally that he was not aligned with the supporters of Malenkov. At the same time, he did not hold posts that would put him among the Zhdanovites. On October 9, 1946, he was mentioned in *Pravda* as Deputy Chief of a Central Committee directorate. No indication was given as to which directorate. But since at that time the Central Committee had only two directorates according to the Party statutes—Personnel and Propaganda—and since the top officials of the latter are known, it is to be assumed that Ignatiev was made Deputy Chief of Personnel.

The Personnel Directorate had been the brainchild of Malenkov, but in July, 1946, when he was removed from his post as secretary of the Central Committee, the Directorate was also taken from him; his deputy in the Directorate, N. N. Shatalin, who has now been brought back into the Central Committee Secretariat by Malenkov, was dismissed. Patolichev, a member of the Central Committee Secretariat since July, 1946, became head of the Directorate. He knew Ignatiev from the Credentials Committee and he now made him his deputy in the Personnel Directorate.

That is how Ignatiev came to hold his prominent post in the Secretariat. Soon he received further promotion: He was made a member of the government's Council for Kolkhoz Affairs, the chairman of which was A. A. Andreev, a Politburo member and one of the most implacable opponents of Malenkov. Patolichev was one of the Council's deputy chairmen. Ignatiev's work on this council undoubtedly was connected with personnel, for one of its tasks was the setting up of new cadres of kolkhoz executives. Ignatiev was also concerned with personnel in the years following, when he was transferred to Belorussia, then Daghestan, and later Uzbekistan. In 1950, while in Uzbekistan, he was elected to the All-Union Soviet.

These facts are, of course, meager, and they shed little light on Ignatiev's personality, but they are sufficient to rule out Ignatiev's being a Malenkovite. One can also state with equal certainty that Ignatiev was not a Zhdanovite either. All of Zhdanov's prominent supporters had been liquidated, or at least removed from positions of leadership, in 1949–50.

If Ignatiev was neither a Malenkovite nor a Zhdanovite, what was he? Was he a member of any group at all? These questions can be answered only after a brief digression into past history.

From the very first moment that he became General Secretary, Stalin set about building the special apparatus of his personal secretariat, the functions of which gradually grew, as did its importance. Without knowing the history of this secretariat and its activities one cannot understand the secret of Stalin's success. At times the secretariat employed several hundred people. Ultimately, it acquired unlimited resources and colossal power, including access to the most secret materials of all government and Party agencies, including the NKVD-MVD. This secretariat was the eyes, ears, and hands of Stalin. His chief assistant in constructing this apparatus was a certain Tovstukha, a very interesting figure whose biography will continue to intrigue the historian of the period.

But it was A. N. Poskrebyshev who soon became the most devoted and trusted member of the secretariat and remained in it until the very last day of Stalin's life. A Communist since 1917, he began working in the secretariat in 1922 or 1923, when already past the age of thirty. (He was born in 1891.) Poskrebyshev was a man with a magnificent memory, a very talented organizer, and exceptionally self-possessed. He was totally self-effacing and put himself entirely at Stalin's service. On orders of Stalin he would carry out the most distasteful, dirtiest, and bloodiest deeds. He became Stalin's *alter ego*. If Stalin ever trusted anyone, it was Poskreybyshev, to whom he even gave a rubber stamp with his signature to affix to documents of a certain kind.

It is not possible here to go into detail about Poskrebyshev's activities, but it should be mentioned that he was responsible for setting up the Special Secret Political Section of State Security, which was created as early as 1934 as part of Stalin's personal secretariat. This Special Sector, which also included Yezhov, Shkiriatov, and, somewhat later, Malenkov, made the behind-the-scenes preparations for, and then carried out, the bloody purge of 1936–38.* Malenkov compiled the first lists of victims; Poskrebyshev maintained liaison with Stalin and personally supervised the removal of top figures whom Stalin, for one reason or another, did not want arrested openly. For instance, he quietly got rid of Ordzhonikidze. It was for this work that Stalin, at the beginning of 1939, gave him his first Order of Lenin.†

He was awarded his second Order after the war, when he began to play an even more important role. From 1946 onward, he started to make public appearances, was elected Chairman of the Supreme Soviet's Committee on Draft Legislation, and his name began to appear in the press. This, of course, happened with the blessing of Stalin, who by this time had virtually transferred to Poskrebyshev his supervisory powers over the Secretariat of the Central Committee.

As the conflict between Zhdanov and Malenkov deepened,

* See pp. 93 ff. for details on this Special Department.—Ed.
† For an account of this affair, see *Na Rubezhe* (Paris), Nos. 3 and 4, 1952.—B. N.

Poskrebyshev's duties were bound to become more and more complex. It is known from Yugoslav sources that Stalin, supported by Molotov, at first tried to prevent this conflict from becoming more acute and to confine it within the narrowest possible limits. It is very likely that it was because of this that the death penalty was abolished in the spring of 1947, at a time when Zhdanov's influence was at its height. It was only natural that Poskrebyshev should try, once the Zhdanovites had been crushed, to unite all those forces capable of resisting the Malenkovites; the latter were not formally combined in a caucus, but they were very strong, assertive, and well led. In this, as in all his other dealings, Poskrebyshev was merely the obedient executor of Stalin's orders.

Backed by Stalin's authority and in fact acting on his directives, Poskrebyshev was the only person during the postwar years with whose support Party functionaries like Ignatiev, who belonged neither to the Zhdanov nor the Malenkov factions, could survive. Poskrebyshev was the only one able to appoint a candidate like Ignatiev as Minister of State Security and allow him to pursue a policy that was, apart from everything else, directed against the mighty and influential Beria.

Thus, the conflict whose final acts are now unfolding in the Kremlin around the case of Ignatiev is merely one aspect of the great conflict between Poskrebyshev as Stalin's agent on the one hand, and Beria and some other top leaders on the other hand. The outlines of this conflict become much clearer if we take another look at the events in the few months preceding Stalin's death.

It is not known exactly when the appointment of Ignatiev as Minister of State Security took place, but there now can scarcely be any doubt that it was done to make Poskrebyshev complete master of the MGB and enable him to prepare a new purge similar to the one of 1936–38.

This preparation for a purge was first brought to light by the official announcement of the arrest of the nine doctors accused of poisoning Zhdanov and Shcherbakov and of attempting to poison Marshals Vasilevsky, Konev, and others. This announcement, published by *Pravda* and *Izvestia* on January 13, 1953, called them "vile spies and murderers in the guise of professors." The main accusation against the arrested doctors was "trying to undermine the health of leading Soviet military figures, to put them out of commission, and thereby weaken the country's defenses." They had done this on the instructions of "foreign intelligence services."

In the tone of this official announcement, the attentive reader will detect echoes of Stalin's infamous speech of March 3, 1937, in which he gave the signal for extending the purge. Here we have the same kind of talk about complacency and lack of vigilance that help the enemy; the same phrases against the "opportunistic theory" of the "dying down of the class struggle," a theory which plays into the hands of "hidden enemies supported by the imperialist world." The article urged that all such enemies "be squashed like disgusting vermin," and that, for this purpose, "an end be put to lack of vigilance in our ranks." The similarity between these two documents—the announcement in *Pravda* on January 13, 1953, and Stalin's speech of March 3, 1937—is so great that now, in the light of subsequent events, there can be no doubt about the meaning of the arrest of the nine doctors: It was in preparation for a new Yezhov-style purge, to be conducted by the same Poskrebyshev who, under Stalin's direct guidance, had also conducted the purge of 1936–38.

A lead article in *Pravda* of January 18, 1953, actually ended with a direct reference to Stalin's speech of March, 1937. Anybody who knew how to interpret the use of quotations in *Pravda* editorials could no longer have the slightest doubt that a new purge was being prepared.

The Soviet newspapers of the ensuing weeks confirmed this interpretation of events. Every day they reported instances of "lack of vigilance" on the part of Soviet institutions, and by studying these reports, one could get a good idea of which targets would come under Poskrebyshev's fire.

First in line, of course, was the Ministry of Public Health, particularly the Special Medical Administration of the Kremlin; its chiefs, the first to be arrested, were charged with being agents of the American intelligence service, especially one of its "branches" —"the international Jewish bourgeois-nationalist organization 'Joint.' "* The Americans, and particularly the Joint, were cast in

---

* The doctors allegedly established contact with the American intelligence service through the Joint Distribution Committee, a U. S. Jewish philanthropic organization. A British organization also was supposed to have been involved.—Ed.

major roles and this accounted for the anti-Semitic bias of the campaign.

The attack was not, however, limited to the Ministry of Public Health. Cautiously, but clearly in a concerted manner, the Soviet press gradually got around to the economic ministries: trade and cooperative organizations, transport machine building, the oil industry, the Ministry of Supply, the Ministry of Nonferrous Metals, etc. It should not be forgotten that the campaign was only beginning and that the press carried only a small part of what was being "prepared" in the offices of the security organization, to say nothing of what was being planned by Poskrebyshev in the behind-the-scenes headquarters of the purge: Stalin's secretariat. Nevertheless, it was quite plain that the primary targets were the economic ministries, and in particular Tevosyan and Malyshev, who, as Stalin's deputies on the Council of Ministers, controlled the work of a number of these ministries.

It is noteworthy that these attacks did not implicate either the armed forces or the Party. It is now impossible to say how far the purge would have gone; but there is no doubt that during this, its first stage, it was directed by the Party *apparat,* under the guidance of Stalin's personal organization and with the assistance of the MGB, against the "managerial" group of Communists. The influence of the latter had grown considerably in recent years, and in the elections to the Party bodies at the Nineteenth Congress, they gained a number of key positions.

On the other hand, the large-scale purge of the Ministry of Public Health makes it clear that a savage blow was being dealt as well at the so-called non-Party Soviet intelligentsia, which the regime had courted during the war and whose relative importance in Soviet society had continued to grow in spite of its victimization during the recent Zhdanov and Malenkov purges.*

To weaken these two important groups of Soviet society and, consequently, to increase the relative importance of the Party ideologists and organizers—this was the *social* objective of the Poskrebyshev purge. The Army, in the broad sense of the word, was

* This refers to the notorious purges of writers, philosophers, musicians, etc., carried out by Zhdanov in the postwar years. After Zhdanov's death in 1948, the hounding of intellectuals was intensified by Malenkov.—Ed.

not touched by the purgers; the nature of the charges against the doctors shows that they wanted to have the Army on their side and even curried favor with it.

The purge did not last very long. At the beginning of February it had already begun to ease off, and by the middle of the month it had petered out. The words "lack of vigilance," which had been the keynote of the purge, completely disappeared from the pages of *Pravda*. In re-examining the newspapers of that time, one gains the distinct impression that behind the scenes there was a struggle going on between those who wished to step up the campaign and those who, on the contrary, wished to let it die down.

Who were the protagonists in this struggle? On one side, undoubtedly, stood Stalin and Poskrebyshev, with the apparatus of the MGB. In the light of Beria's present statements it becomes clear that he played an important role in organizing resistance to the backers of the purge. How are we to explain this unusual behavior on the part of Beria? After all, we know him well enough not to entertain any illusions about him. He is one of the most ruthless and unscrupulous of the Soviet leaders—in effect a public executioner. People who know Beria depict him as a man devoid of any human feelings, a machine functioning as organizer of the police apparatus. If *such* a man opposed Stalin's plans for a new purge, he must have had good *personal* reasons for doing so. He must have felt personally threatened by this purge. If we consider only the known facts, then we can see that he had every reason for this fear.

The January 13 announcement of the arrest of the doctors contained criticism of the state-security organization for "failing to uncover" in good time this "terrorist organization." Beria knew better than anyone what such a reproach meant at such a time, particularly as Beria could quite easily have been charged with being a direct accomplice of the "terrorist organization" of Jewish doctors acting on the instructions of the Joint. We know from the memoirs of Lucian Blit, a close friend and aide of the well-known Jewish Socialist G. M. Erlich, who was shot by Beria in 1941, that Mikhoels, head of the Jewish State Theater in Moscow, was made chairman of the "Jewish Anti-Fascist Committee" in 1942 on Beria's suggestion, and it was on Beria's recommendation that he was permitted to visit New York in this capacity.* According to the indictment published on January 13, it was in New York that Mikhoels established his ties with the Joint, which allegedly provided the Jewish doctors with the means for their terroristic and poisoning activities. One can easily imagine what webs the agents of Ignatiev and Poskrebyshev could have woven out of this. If there had been a public trial of the "doctor-poisoners," Beria might well have figured in it as a defendant. And Beria knew that at such a trial he would "confess," just as Yagoda, and not so long before Slansky and others, had also confessed. And since Beria knew all this much better than most others, he had no desire to let events take this particular course.

There were also other signs that must have seemed ominous to Beria. He could hardly have been pleased with the purge that had been carried out in Georgia the summer before. It destroyed the whole Party apparatus, which had consisted almost entirely of Beria's henchmen as well as his personal friends.

But almost worst of all was the state of affairs in the Atomic State Trust No. 1, of which Beria was head and for which he was responsible. It was being said that the work of this trust was proceeding much less successfully than that of other trusts. It is rumored that this was the main reason for Stalin's dissatisfaction with Beria, since the failure of the atomic-bomb production program curbed Stalin's aggressive and risky foreign policy.

Beria's campaign against Ignatiev is therefore a logical consequence of everything that has happened in recent months, of all those developments which turned Beria into a determined opponent of the purge launched by Stalin, Poskrebyshev, and Ignatiev. Against such adversaries, however, Beria could not act alone. Who was allied with him?

We may not know for some time exactly what the alignments were at the summit of the Soviet regime. It is important, however,

* Mikhoels visited New York at the height of World War II to enlist material support from American Jews for the Soviet war effort. Mikhoels remained head of the "Jewish Anti-Fascist Committee" until it was liquidated in 1948. Shortly afterward, he was killed in an automobile accident which is now officially admitted to have been arranged by the Soviet secret police.—Ed.

to establish the main fact, namely that *Malenkov must have been an ally of Beria.*

The Western press, particularly the American press, believes that Malenkov was Beria's adversary. The line-up in the Kremlin is therefore frequently described in terms of this supposed conflict between Malenkov and Beria. There is no evidence for this theory. The main argument in favor of it—the depiction of Ignatiev as a Malenkovite—is, as I have shown above, completely incorrect. Ignatiev was one of Poskrebyshev's men. (Let us note here that Poskrebyshev is somehow connected with the Bashkir Republic; he came up from the Belebey District of the Bashkir Republic to the Supreme Soviet, and this supports the assumption that he was born there; Ignatiev for a number of years was secretary of the Bashkir Republic *obkom.*)

On the other hand, study of Soviet newspapers in recent months reveals a certain reserve toward Malenkov. *Pravda's* lead articles are particularly important in this respect. As is well known, *Pravda* editorials are authoritative; among other things, they are broadcast in their entirety over the radio, etc. The number of references to a person in these articles is an accurate index of his standing within the leadership. For example, in the first weeks after the Nineteenth Congress, references to Malenkov in these articles were almost obligatory. In November and December, however, the frequency of references had dropped by about 50 per cent. Moreover, a certain pattern in these references to him is discernible: he was not quoted in matters concerning foreign policy; only Stalin was quoted in this connection. On the other hand, articles on domestic policy, Party and particularly economic matters, almost always included some reference to Malenkov. The situation changed this January, soon after the announcement of the arrest of the doctors, that is, after the beginning of open preparations for a purge. From that time on, Malenkov was mentioned no more than once a week. After February 15, his name disappeared altogether from *Pravda* editorials. He was still mentioned in other articles and news items, but infrequently. As to lead articles, his name was obviously taboo.

This could not, of course, be accidental. In Moscow such factors never are. If references to Malenkov, who was then First Secretary of the Central Committee, disappeared from *Pravda* editorials, it

115

meant that his influence was on the wane, that Stalin was displeased with him for some reason, since only Stalin could have ordered *Pravda* to omit references to Malenkov. And this can only have been an indication of how Malenkov's stock stood on the "black market" manipulated by Poskrebyshev behind the scenes, where the purge was being prepared.

The story of Malenkov's relations with Poskrebyshev is a special page in the history of the Kremlin underworld, and it will be very difficult for future historians to decipher it. It is all the more difficult for a contemporary. There is no doubt that Poskrebyshev greatly assisted Malenkov in the first stages of his career. Louis Fischer even holds that it was Poskrebyshev who brought Malenkov into Stalin's personal secretariat. In subsequent years they worked together in carrying out the dirtiest and bloodiest jobs for the Kremlin's "Genghis Khan with a telegraph" (to borrow Leo Tolstoy's phrase). But this certainly does not mean that they could not have quarreled and become enemies.

What is more, if the above analysis is correct and if the purge prepared by Stalin and Poskrebyshev was to strike at the managerial class and the Soviet "technocrats," Malenkov had to part company with Poskrebyshev. For, in playing his big political game, Malenkov was banking on this particular group of Soviet society. Though himself a Party *apparatchik* to the marrow of his bones, he began to oppose the dictatorship over the Party by the *apparat,* and he advocated granting a large share of influence to Communists outside it, i.e., to the managers, the military, and so on.

It is almost certain that there were also some personal motives pushing Malenkov in this direction. We do not know yet what they were, but we know enough to warrant the conclusion that Malenkov turned against Poskrebyshev and allied himself with Beria.

Thus, during the critical days at the end of February, when the course of the purge planned by Stalin, Poskrebyshev, and Ignatiev was being decided, the alignment of forces was as follows: Stalin and Poskrebyshev were readying a new Yezhov-type purge with the support of the Ministry of State Security headed by Ignatiev and the backing of substantial groups within the leadership of the Party *apparat*. Opposed to them was a bloc headed by Beria and Malenkov, or rather, Malenkov and Beria, for Malenkov was a much more significant figure than Beria, despite the latter's police and political talents.

We do not know what exactly happened on the night that Stalin suffered a stroke. But we can say with certainty that this stroke (if it was a stroke) was not the *cause* of the subsequent changes but a *consequence* of the struggle that led up to them. If there had been nothing more to Stalin's death than meets the eye, then we should now constantly see Poskrebyshev's name as a faithful secretary and retainer of Stalin. He was flourishing until literally the very eve of Stalin's stroke. On February 22, he was elected to the Moscow Soviet, and six days later his name was included in the list of its newly elected members (*Vecherniaia Moskva,* February 28). In the seven weeks that have elapsed since then, there has not been a single mention of Poskrebyshev.* This omission shows that there is something odd in Stalin's death. Whether he really did suffer a stroke after some particularly acrimonious argument, or whether this stroke was brought on by a well-aimed bullet from a pistol is not known. The only thing that matters for us now is that he died because of a major political defeat.

This fact must be established beyond a doubt, for a great deal depends on it not only in our diagnosis of the past, but also in our forecast for the future. If Stalin had died a normal death, there would be a very good chance that his successors might maintain the unity of the ruling Party for a long time—a necessary condition for the preservation of the dictatorship in its present form. If, however, Stalin did not die a normal death but was *helped* (this vague formulation most accurately corresponds to what we know at present about this welcome event), then there is little chance of the ruling Party preserving its unity, and the Kremlin is entering a period of fierce and bloody struggle which may be very far-reaching.

In these circumstances, the undertones of Beria's official an-

---

* It is interesting to note that not long ago the Western press carried reports that Poskrebyshev was living and writing his memoirs. It seems the writer Galina Serebryakova spoke of it during the celebrated meetings of government representatives with writers and artists which took place in Moscow in December, 1962. These rumors have not been echoed in the Soviet press.—B. N./1964.

117

nouncement about the release of the doctors acquire special significance. By this announcement, Beria, Malenkov, and those of their colleagues involved in the events leading up to Stalin's death are addressing themselves to those groups of Soviet society who understood that the arrests of the doctors were a mere preparation for a new purge and who therefore had particular reason for alarm. It is to these people in particular that Malenkov and Beria appeal when they talk about safeguarding the "rights of Soviet citizens as guaranteed in the Soviet Constitution," by implying that it was this that forced them to remove the criminals in charge of the state apparatus, despite their awareness of the risk for the whole system that this entailed.

Herein lies the hidden meaning of the seemingly obscure words in Beria's oration at Stalin's funeral on March 9. "The workers, collective-farm peasantry, and the intelligentsia of our country," Beria said, "may carry on their work calmly and confidently, in the knowledge that the Soviet Government will constantly safeguard the rights guaranteed them in the Stalin Constitution."

Beria is not, of course, concerned with the rights of the population at large. But Malenkov and Beria really did want to guarantee certain minimum rights for the Soviet ruling elite. The fact that it was Beria who, in 1938–39, was given the task of winding up the purge no doubt argues somewhat in his favor.

From the point of view of the new rulers of the country, things are made more difficult by the fact that they had to get rid of the old leader at a particularly difficult moment in the international situation. Stalin was playing a mad game, not only at home but also abroad. His foreign policy was particularly reckless, and it was this criminal recklessness in foreign policy that constantly increased the folly of his domestic policy. By the time of his death, Stalin had brought things to such a pitch that his gamble on the unwillingness of his opponents to risk a war was ceasing to be effective, and he might have had to take upon himself the responsibility for the outbreak of war. What will Stalin's successors do?

While Stalin was alive, they were by no means in favor of making Soviet foreign policy less aggressive. If they differed from Stalin, it was in the sober realism of their approach to the problem of war. They saw the next war as a total war, in which equipment and manpower would play the deciding role. It was they who, more consistently than the rest of their colleagues, rid themselves of the revolutionary romanticism of the early Bolshevik period, though they also attached tremendous importance to the Cold War as a preparation for hot war, and they were past masters in the conduct of it.

Now that they are in power, they have not changed their nature. They are just as much for foreign aggression as they were under Stalin. If anything has changed, it is their potential: *dat Deus immiti cornua curta bovi*. The death of Stalin and the struggle now being waged behind the walls of the Kremlin are an unexpectedly lucky gift of fate. But only the wise use of this gift will give the Western democracies a chance to save the world from the horrors of a new, atomic war.

Russia Purges the Purgers*

INSTEAD of being given a show trial in keeping with established Moscow ritual, which might, as *The New York Times* said, have developed as "the most sensational trial in Soviet history," Beria was tried behind closed doors without any of the usual "confessions." The world, of course, is sorely disappointed. But the "liquidation" of Beria, even without a sensational trial, is a tremendously important event. Only half a year ago he was the second most powerful and influential person in the Soviet Union. Many even felt at that time that he would be the first to crush everyone else; after all, he was First Deputy Chairman of the Council of Ministers, a member of the Presidium of the CPSU Central Committee, a Marshal of the Soviet Union, etc., and above all, he was the Minister of Internal Affairs. As such, Beria was the undisputed head of the powerful secret police of the greatest police state in the

* This article appeared in *Novoye Russkoye Slovo*, December 27, 1953.

world, in command of dozens of special divisions of the best-drilled and -disciplined armed forces in the U.S.S.R. Who, we might ask, could possibly stand in his way after the death of Stalin?

The possibility that Beria would be dealt with so quickly and so mercilessly seemed unlikely. Why, then, was he eliminated? For major political reasons? For reasons connected with the deep split within the ruling clique of the Kremlin? Or was it merely a matter of dog eat dog, as the Russian *émigré* press so frequently contends?

It is not easy to answer these questions, and not only because our information is extremely scanty and by no means always reliable. What is important, however, is the fact that the situation in the Kremlin is still far from stable. The death of Stalin, who held so many threads in his hand, gave rise to many involved realignments, particularly because his death took place at a moment when such realignments had already begun. This process is by no means over yet, but the Beria case marks an important stage in the stabilization of the post-Stalin alignment of forces in the Kremlin.

The first question is: On whom did Beria rely for support? Who are the associates who shared his fate? The most important among them was Vsevolod Merkulov, who in 1945 was awarded the title of General of the Army and in recent years has been Minister of State Control, but who in reality is one of the oldest and most experienced Chekists. Born in Baku at the end of the nineteenth century, he graduated from the Baku Polytechnic Institute, the same school where Beria studied in 1918–20. Merkulov's work in the Cheka-GPU-NKVD began in the very first years of the Bolshevik's arrival in Transcaucasia (1920–21), and it was then that he formed his lasting association with Beria.

It was in the Transcaucasian period also that Beria began his close collaboration with three other persons who have been eliminated with him: Sergei Goglidze, Bogdan Kobulov, and Vladimir Dekanozov. All were the same age as he and all began to work at about the same time he did in the Cheka-GPU-NKVD, where they all rose to high positions. Goglidze became People's Commissar for Internal Affairs of Georgia, Kobulov his deputy, and Dekanozov chief of this Commissariat's foreign section. Beria's transfer in 1931–32 to the post of Secretary of the Transcaucasian Committee of the Communist Party further strengthened his ties with these men, since this made him boss of all Party matters for Transcaucasia and also head of the NKVD there.

The following incident serves to demonstrate the closeness between these men and Beria: In the autumn of 1938, Yezhov ordered Goglidze to arrest Beria. Not only did Goglidze fail to carry out this order, but he even told Beria of it, thereby making himself guilty of the worst possible offense an NKVD functionary could commit. Goglidze's warning saved Beria and enabled him to go to Moscow to see Stalin. Beria then was able to play a great part in overthrowing Yezhov and putting an end to the Great Purge, which, as far as Stalin was concerned, had by then served its purpose anyway.

Beria, named to Yezhov's post by Stalin, was allowed to bring with him from Transcaucasia some reliable and experienced associates; these naturally included Goglidze, Kobulov, Dekanozov, and Merkulov, who became Beria's closest collaborators in the NKVD from 1938 until his arrest. This was a group of really stanch Beria supporters, bound up with him in life and death. Each of them played his own part, frequently a very important one.

Goglidze became Beria's trusted agent for particularly delicate matters. His first assignment was to the Leningrad region. This area was particularly important in 1939, when the seizure of the Baltic states and the war against Finland were being planned, since the preparations for this aggression were largely concentrated in the hands of the Leningrad NKVD. Soon after, in 1940 or at the very end of 1939, Goglidze was transferred to the Soviet Far East, a region that was becoming more and more important for Soviet foreign policy. From then on, the control of Soviet agents in Korea, Japan, China, and the Pacific countries in general was in Goglidze's hands. One only has to recall the events taking place in this part of the world during the last twelve to thirteen years to understand the enormous scope of Goglidze's work. It should be realized that the undercover work of Soviet agents is by no means confined to gathering secret information about other countries; it also includes the confusion of public opinion in these countries, the subversion of groups that oppose Soviet policy, and the support of groups whose influence furthers Soviet policy. Recently much has been written in the United States about Richard Sorge, the top Soviet agent in Japan on the eve of the war, who played a major role in Japan's decision not to enter the war against the U.S.S.R.* on the side of her Germany ally. Sorge's immediate superior was Goglidze, who was in daily contact with him in Tokyo. Yet Sorge was only one of Goglidze's many agents in the Far East.

Of course, Goglidze also had enormous responsibility in the sphere of domestic policy. He had jurisdiction over a territory probably as big as the whole of the U.S.A.; in particular, he had over-all charge of all gold-mining in the Kolyma area,† of the work of the Dalstroy group of camps, as well as that of many other concentration camps east of Lake Baikal. It is even more important that, as has now become known, he was in direct charge of all work on atomic and hydrogen bombs.

This is by no means a complete list of the activities of Goglidze and of the organization which he headed, but it is enough to give some idea of the importance of this man who has now been executed together with Beria. As a comic sidelight on the nature of Soviet reality it should be added that Goglidze was also a member of the Supreme Soviet in the Council of Nationalities for the Jewish Autonomous Region in Birobidzhan on the Amur.‡

---

* Richard Sorge was a grandson of Friedrich Sorge, a friend of Karl Marx and an active participant in the revolution of 1848–49 in Germany who emigrated to America. Before and during World War II, Richard Sorge worked as a German journalist in Japan and acted as a Soviet agent. A personal friend of the German Ambassador in Tokyo, Sorge was privy to secret developments at the highest levels of the Japanese government.

The "Sorge case" has now been written about, and although a number of points in the case still remain obscure, there is no doubt that Sorge supported those military circles in Japan which pushed Japan into war against the United States with the aim of preventing its advance against the Soviet Far East. Knowledge of Japan's plans for attack on Pearl Harbor enabled the Russians, as a recent *Pravda* article (September 3, 1964) acknowledges, to stop the German advance on their west flank in 1941.—B. N./1964.

† The Kolyma area was a forced-labor center. For a study of this and other forced-labor areas, see D. Dallin and B. Nicolaevsky, *Forced Labor in Soviet Russia* (New Haven, Conn.: Yale University Press, 1947).—Ed.

‡ The Jewish Autonomous Province was created on May 7, 1934. Publicized in the early days as a "Jewish nation on Soviet soil," it never had more than a minority of Jewish residents. In 1937, the entire leadership of the region was destroyed in the Great Purge; the migration of Jews to the

123

Dekanozov, who had been head of the foreign section of the NKVD in Georgia, also rose rapidly as Beria's protégé. His specialty was diplomacy. As early as March–April, 1939, he was appointed to the Ministry of Foreign Affairs, where he headed the consular, financial, and personnel sections. He thus became Beria's representative there and, as such, prepared the way for Litvinov's removal. There are a number of indications that Beria was an active supporter of a *rapprochement* with Nazi Germany. After Molotov's appointment to the Foreign Ministry, Dekanozov became even more important; he played a major role in preparing the Hitler-Stalin Pact. Beria's ministry in general was instrumental in bringing about this pact. Dekanozov's appointment as Soviet Ambassador to Berlin was therefore simply the logical outcome of Dekanozov's personal role and of the activities of Beria's department in general. These leaders were thus all the more shocked by Hitler's treachery in June, 1941. It is significant that during the war years, Dekanozov invariably figured in all attempts to establish secret contacts with Berlin. He did so, of course, with the knowledge and blessing of Beria.

In recent years Dekanozov did not play a prominent role and apparently even fell into disfavor, since at the Nineteenth Congress he was not elected to the Central Committee. Beria, however, did not forget him; after Stalin's death, when Beria purged the apparatus in Georgia, he secured the appointment of Dekanozov as Minister of Internal Affairs there. It was from this post that Dekanozov was sent to prison.

The other two men brought by Beria from Tiflis to Moscow—Merkulov and Kobulov—were given jobs in the central NKVD apparatus, and from that moment on, they played crucial roles in the entire so-called operative work of the NKVD—that is, the

---

area continued to decline until after the war, when there was a revival of interest in the Jewish Autonomous Province on the part of Soviet Jews. At this time, the regime shifted its policy and undertook a series of actions against Jewish schools, newspapers, and other organizations. The region is rarely ever mentioned now. For a detailed account of the history of the Province in particular and the situation of Jews in the Soviet Union in general, see Solomon Schwartz, *The Jews in the Soviet Union* (Syracuse, N. Y.: Syracuse University Press, 1951).—Ed.

work of exposing and combating opponents of the dictatorship at home and abroad. Since Beria, after his appointment as Minister of Internal Affairs, was immediately co-opted into the Politburo and thus found himself concerned with questions of grand policy, the day-to-day work of the NKVD fell entirely on Merkulov, who was hence Beria's closest assistant. From this moment, Merkulov was in effect head of the Main Administration of State Security (the name under which the old GPU continued to exist and function within the Ministry of Internal Affairs). Therefore, it was only natural that in early 1941, when State Security was first set up as a separate ministry (NKGB), Merkulov became its head. During the early years of the war, the NKGB was again merged with the NKVD, but in 1943, the planned separation took place. This division between State Security and Internal Affairs lasted until Stalin's death.* Merkulov was again head of State Security for a short time until 1946, when he was replaced by Abakumov. Merkulov then spent four years abroad as chief of the Soviet Reparations Commission in the occupied areas—an extremely important post at the time, though not, of course, comparable to that of Minister of State Security—until he was appointed Minister of State Control. He held this post at the time of his arrest.

The reasons for Merkulov's removal as Minister of State Security are not known, but it coincided with the period when Zhdanov's influence was at its height. The appointment of his successor, Abakumov, was confirmed by the Supreme Soviet on October 18, 1946, simultaneously with the confirmation of Malenkov's appointment as Deputy Chairman of the Council of Ministers. There is no doubt that Merkulov's removal was somehow related to the struggle that was then going on. Merkulov was not a Malenkovite, and on the whole it is difficult to assume that he took sides in the quarrels

---

* It was announced in February, 1941, that the NKVD would be divided into a People's Commissariat of State Security (NKGB) and a People's Commissariat of Internal Affairs (NKVD). But the war intervened, and the division did not take place until April, 1943. In 1946, the commissariats were renamed ministries, and in March, 1953, after Stalin's death, the MGB and MVD were once again merged in a new Ministry of Internal Affairs. (See Merle Fainsod, *How Russia Is Ruled* [rev. ed.; Cambridge, Mass.: Harvard University Press, 1963], p. 452.)—Ed.

of that time. Most likely, he was penalized because he was carrying out the policies of Beria, who was then close to Malenkov.

Kobulov was Merkulov's assistant and permanently held his post up to his arrest. In recent years, judging from a number of indications, he headed MGB activities abroad, particularly in occupied areas. It was he who directed the MGB work in East Germany and gave orders to Zaisser, head of the East German secret police, who was deposed after the June Berlin uprising.*

The remaining two members of the group who were eliminated along with Beria, namely Vlodzimirsky and Meshik, were also major MGB functionaries, though of somewhat lesser stature. Regarding Lev Yemelyianovich Vlodzimirsky, we know that in July, 1945, when military titles were conferred on officials of the central MGB apparatus, he received the rank of lieutenant general, while Merkulov was made a general of the army, and Goglidze, Kobulov and the present Minister of Internal Affairs, Kruglov, were made colonel generals. It is clear from this that even then Vlodzimirsky's position in the MGB already must have been an important one, probably department head.

We have absolutely no information on the past of Pavel Meshik. The first mention of him in the press dates back to May–June of this year [1953], when, during the purge of the Khrushchevite leadership of the Ukrainian Party (removal of Melnikov, etc.),

---

* Wilhelm Zaisser, a German Communist, was an officer in the German Army during World War I, who took an active part in the organization of Communist uprisings in Germany between 1919–23. After the crushing of the Hamburg uprising, Zaisser went to Moscow, where he attended a special military school under the general staff of the Red Army; this school prepared selected Communists for work with Soviet military intelligence. Zaisser went to work in this area. He was one of the Soviet agents in China. Then he went to Moscow and played an important role in the Spanish Civil War. In World War II, he worked directly under Beria. He was also instrumental in setting up the German National Committee in Moscow.

After the defeat of Hitler, Zaisser returned to Germany, where he became Minister of National Defense in the Soviet zone, directly subordinate to Beria. Following Stalin's death, when Beria and Malenkov were preparing for some kind of settlement on East Germany, Zaisser played a major role in East Germany in formulating such a policy, which Ulbricht has since called the policy of capitulation before the West. Zaisser was ousted not long after the fall of Beria.—B. N./1964.

Meshik suddenly appeared in the post of Ukrainian Minister of Internal Affairs, with the obvious assignment of putting a halt to the forced Russification of the Ukraine, especially the recently annexed Western part.

Thus, together with Beria, six of the most prominent MGB functionaries were liquidated, including no fewer than four of his old colleagues in Transcaucasia. All of them held top posts in the MGB, chiefly in the Ministry's central administration. To illustrate this group's importance to the Ministry, I shall recount one interesting circumstance.

In recent years, the composition of the Central Committee of the CPSU has been such as to give representation to the most prominent groups of Party officials working in various branches of the regime. Moreover, the proportion between the various groups is determined by the idea which the leaders have of the relative importance of the group concerned at the time when the lists are drawn up.

Thus out of the 125 members and 111 alternates of the latest Central Committee, elected last October at the Nineteenth Congress, the MGB-MVD supplied only 3 full members (including Beria himself) and 7 alternates, including Merkulov, who was not nominally in the MGB at the time of the election but who was by his very nature a part of this MGB-MVD group. This is a very small number, comprising only 2.4 per cent of the full members and 6.3 per cent of the alternates. And even so, half of them were not MGB officials. The names of the MVD top officials at the time of the Congress are known, since not long before, *Izvestia* had published an obituary of the Deputy Minister of Internal Affairs, V. V. Chernyshev, signed by all the leading officials of the Ministry. From these signatures we know that even such old MGB operatives as Serov and Riasnoy had joined the MVD. This is no doubt explained primarily by the great amount of work that the MVD had had to handle in connection with the "Great Stalin Construction Projects" —projects carried out by slave labor under the direction of the MVD.

Of the active MGB officials, only one, apart from Beria himself, was elected a member of the Central Committee. This was S. D. Ignatiev, then Minister of State Security. Goglidze, Kobulov, and

Merkulov were elected alternates. Ignatiev, author of the doctors' plot, disappeared from the scene last April; it is very likely that he was liquidated by Beria at that time.* The three alternates have disappeared together with Beria. Thus, the "MGB faction" in the Central Committee of the CPSU has now been completely wiped out, while the "MVD faction" remains untouched. The blow fell only on those members of this venerable establishment who had been concerned with "operative" work and apparently wanted to apply their methods in order to influence government policy.

To understand this event it is, of course, essential to know the political background, the nature of the political conflicts, which led to the smashing of the MGB. And it really was a case of the wiping out of a whole department, for the physical annihilation of its representatives on the Central Committee inevitably brought in its wake not only the mass annihilation of other, lesser officials of the department, but also a considerable reduction in the weight of the security police in the apparatus of the dictatorship. Our major conclusion from the Beria case is that there must have been a demotion of the role of the "operative" political police in the Soviet state.

Never in the entire history of the Soviet regime has the role of the MGB been as huge as it was under Beria during the war and afterward. This was due, above all, to Beria's personal standing. Ever since the beginning of the regime, the leaders of the Party saw great danger in any excessive growth of the police apparatus. They approached the question, of course, from the viewpoint of Party interests; those of the masses even in the early days were of little concern to them. Hence the tradition of never including the head of the political police in the supreme Party body. Let us recall that even Dzerzhinsky, despite his tremendous authority in

* It would seem that in the days of Beria's decline, Ignatiev was in an extremely difficult position, and there is every reason to think that his trial was being prepared by Beria. Soon after Beria's fall, it was found that the information on which Ignatiev's trial was based was fabricated. Khrushchev then took Ignatiev under his wing and gave him an important post in the Party apparatus, albeit in the provinces—first in Ufa, then in Kazan. Recently, however, the name of Ignatiev has disappeared entirely from the lists of leading Party functionaries, and it is not certain what has happened to him.—B. N./1964.

the Party, was never a member of the Politburo, let alone his successors. The rule was first broken in the case of Yezhov, but this was an exceptional measure necessitated by the exceptional nature of the tasks placed on the weak shoulders of this secondary figure in the Great Purge.

Under Beria the situation changed radically. For fifteen years he not only combined direction of all the Soviet police forces (the scope of whose activities had vastly increased since Dzerzhinsky's days) with membership in the Politburo, but he also became one of the most influential members of this supreme political body. Whether he actually harbored plans to seize power, as the official announcement asserts, no one can tell. But everything we know about internal developments in the U.S.S.R. gives a sure indication that objectively, whether anybody had consciously willed it or not, this was a real possibility in the context of the Soviet situation. In this sense, the official announcement is absolutely right.

Unlike the cases of 1936–38, the Beria case *is* the result of a ruthless struggle for power. Furthermore, it is a stage in a continuing struggle, and it is for this reason that the regime could not afford to have a public trial.

The Meaning of the
Beria Affair*

BERIA and six of his "accomplices" (this is the official term) have been shot. The last of the "indignant" public meetings condemning them has been held. Beria's name has disappeared from the pages of the Soviet press. The government of Malenkov and his colleagues is making every effort to ensure that what has happened will be forgotten as quickly and as completely as possible. From their point of view they are quite right, of course, yet despite all the attempts of the regime to gloss over the real reasons of the split in its ranks, the Beria affair has not only shed light on relations within the ruling Kremlin clique, but it has also given us a glimpse of the mood of the Soviet people. In both these respects, the situation proves to be much more tense than it had seemed to outside observers looking at it from afar. Beria has been shot, but the underlying causes of the Beria affair continue to exist.

* This article appeared in *Novoye Russkoye Slovo,* December, 1953.

What is the real significance of what is happening in the U.S.S.R.? In answering this question, we must remember that the internal development and the present power struggle take place on two different levels, which correspond to the basic social and political structure of the country. One level is that of relations within the ruling Party, chiefly at the top—i.e., among those groups that determine and direct policy. The second level is that of the relations between the ruling Party as a whole and the population at large.

There is no way in which the people of the Soviet Union can formulate, let alone express, their moods and wishes. The regime deliberately tries to atomize them, allowing no independent organizations and barring any legal means of influencing the country's policies. The masses are simply a passive object of policy, of any experiment which the regime considers fit to carry out in the country. They can only defend their interests by resorting to extra-legal means. By means of brutal repression, the regime drives any such attempts, even the most timid ones, deep underground. Yet it is powerless to prevent entirely the emergence of popular opinion, and the rejection of existing conditions finds ready expression—sometimes in the most unexpected forms.

These popular moods are carefully recorded and studied by the authorities. They sometimes exert an indirect influence on policy, but only as an external, alien, and even hostile force which must be reckoned with if the harmful consequences of possible dissension are to be avoided.

The fountainhead of all policy is the ruling Communist Party, or rather its leadership. This leadership, in formulating its policy, always takes account of what it regards as desirable from the point of view of its final aims, and what is possible in the light of the existing situation. The mood of the masses is just a component of the objectively existing situation and nothing more.

Disagreements on what is desirable and what is possible at any given moment are the determining factor in the emergence of rival groups in the Party leadership. Even in Lenin's days, Party factions had been forbidden—and this applied to the leaders as well. But it has always been difficult for the leaders to prevent the rise of factions, for in the process of working together, members of the

Soviet elite develop ideas and arrive at conclusions concerning the desirable and the possible which necessarily lead to the creation of more or less stable groupings. While Stalin was alive, this process continued at a slower pace, because Stalin virtually monopolized the right to decide important questions. He had reduced the other members of the Politburo to expert consultants; they did the groundwork on problems and then, having discussed them among themselves, passed them on to Stalin for a decision. But Stalin could only slow down this process of group formation; he could not eliminate it altogether. For the emergence of cliques among the top leadership is a reflection of the emergence of different social groups within the ruling classes.

In the distant past, when the regime was still in its infancy, a discussion was conducted in the Communist press about the danger of the "inner degeneration" in the Party, because, in carrying out the New Economic Policy, it had to take into account the interests of classes and groupings of Soviet society other than those of the proletariat, which was then still regarded as the only vital social force. A writer who treated the question seriously, the young Communist Ossovsky,* tried to show that the Party was faced with

---

* Y. Ossovsky was a rank-and-file Party member, known only for the fact that in 1926 he published two interesting articles against the Cheka in *Bolshevik*: "On the Path to the Development of the Soviet Economy," in Nos. 7–8, and "The Party on Its Way to the Fourteenth Congress," in No. 14. As is evident from the author's notes to the second of these articles, it was written almost a year before it was published and was rather widely circulated in Party circles in manuscript form. Its basic thesis was that of the danger, if not inevitability, of the internal degeneration of the Communist Party. "Only fools can think," wrote Ossovsky, quoting Lenin, "that parties, even revolutionary parties, are proof against degeneration if objective conditions lead in this direction. The basis of this danger lies in the necessity for the party, if it stands at the head of a government of a country the majority of the population of which is not proletarian but peasant, to conduct a policy corresponding to the interests of both groups." The difficulty which arises from this objective situation can, in the opinion of Ossovsky, be overcome only by "real, unqualified building of inner-party democracy."

Ossovsky's position drew sharp attacks from various sides. His article was declared "the platform of opposition liquidationism" in an article by Sleptsov (*Bolshevik*, No. 14, 1926), as a result of which Ossovsky was persecuted, and eventually arrested. I learned from people who met him in Vorkuta that he later died there.—B. N./1964.

the same choice as in the old Russian ballad the horseman at the crossroads: If you go to the right you will lose your horse, if you go to the left you will die. In a society that has more than one class, Ossovsky argued, a political party cannot be both united and unique. If it is to be the only party, then it will cease to be united, because its ranks will inevitably be penetrated by representatives of different classes and groups and it will become a forum for the struggle among them. If, on the other hand, it wants to be really united, then it should realize that it is in its own interests to allow the existence of other parties for the benefit of people who wish to voice the interests of other classes.

About three decades have passed since then. Ossovsky himself has died in Vorkuta, and Stalin solved the dilemma by conducting the Great Purge—i.e., by annihilating anyone who even tried to raise the question. Present-day Soviet society is very different from the society of Ossovsky's day, but the question he posed still stands, even though today, after thirty years, the actual form in which it is put differs radically.

The social groupings now forming in the Party and its governing apparatus are conditioned by the nature of the functions of the different components of the apparatus. Today, this apparatus is enormous and complex, extending its feelers into each and every aspect of Soviet life. What is more, in recent years there has been a rapidly growing specialization among the members of the apparatus, according to the particular field for which they are responsible. It used to be thought that a responsible Communist could direct any type of activity, although in fact, not having the necessary knowledge, he could not really control anything and was completely at the mercy of the specialists whose advice he followed. This type is now a thing of the past. Now all executive positions are staffed by Communist specialists, a fact which in the last fifteen years has made for greater stability of the governing groups. The rapid turnover of personnel (the game of leapfrog, as they say in the Soviet Union) is now true only of Party leaders and ideologists. Wherever special knowledge is called for, we find relative, sometimes even absolute, stability among the executive personnel.

These Communist executive-specialists are a comparatively well-knit group and very frequently know exactly what they want. They know what is needed for the successful functioning of their particular departments. It is possible for them to defend their views in the highest bodies of the apparatus, since their most prominent representatives usually are members of the Supreme Soviet, the Central Committee, and the Council of Ministers; and sometimes they are members both of the inner, political, caucus of the Council of Ministers and even of the Party Presidium.

This situation had crystalized while Stalin was still alive; his death merely made it possible for the conflict of interest among the various groups to emerge into the open. The Beria affair can only be understood if it is seen as an aspect of this conflict among the Kremlin leaders.

The facts published in connection with the Beria affair leave little room for doubt that in the months following Stalin's death, Beria proposed policy changes which can best be defined as "liberal," in the Soviet sense of this term.

At first sight, this scarcely tallies with what we know about Beria's personality and past. If anyone cannot be suspected of the sin of "rotten liberalism" it is Beria, so it would seem. He was not so much a human being as a kind of robot, completely devoid of any generosity and humanity, capable of calculating with mathematical precision the consequences of highly complex police-political operations. It was Beria who raised the Soviet terror machine to its present height, if one can call it that, converting it from a weapon of terror and violence against individuals into a sociological instrument able to bend Soviet society to the will of the dictatorship.

But however incredible it may seem, the fact that Beria proposed a plan of liberal reforms is beyond doubt. He actually favored a let-up in the campaign to amalgamate the collective farms;* he wanted to halt the campaign of Russification in the non-Russian areas of the Soviet Union, and he was in favor of concessions to the Western democracies. This is known not only from the Soviet Government's indictment of Beria, it is confirmed by reliable information coming from other sources.

* Amalgamation of the kolkhozes was inaugurated by Khrushchev in early 1950 in order to tighten the regime's control over the collective farms and raise their productivity. The campaign gathered momentum during 1951 and 1952.—Ed.

Beria Affair

The reports about the secret relations Beria entered into with representatives of the British government in the spring of last year [1953], if they are corroborated—and they were published in the American press by Joseph Alsop, one of the best-informed journalists*—may throw new light on some aspects of the Beria case. But this will only confirm the general picture. The fact of Beria's conversion into a champion of liberal reform within the country and of relaxation of Soviet aggression abroad must now be considered a certainty.

What accounts for Beria's change? It is entirely possible that he had some personal reasons: rumors of a Russian nationalist mood in Kremlin circles against the "Georgian overlords" from the NKVD were coming out of the Soviet Union already during the war years. After Stalin's death, these feelings must have grown stronger. Under these circumstances, Beria, a Georgian, must have felt somewhat uncomfortable, and it was only natural that he, wishing to change his popular image, should plan to head up a liberal program. But even if he had such personal motives, they are only of secondary importance. Factors of an entirely different order played the decisive role.

Clearly, for the Soviet dictatorship the secret of staying in power lies in the skill with which it toes the dividing line between the desirable and the possible. Stalin was famed for his skill in not overstepping this line, and it is no mere chance that Bukharin used to call him the *genialny dozirovshchik*.† Stalin knew when it was necessary to stop and take a breather in the offensive on the domestic or foreign front. It was this feeling for the limit of the pos-

* On May 11, 1953, Churchill delivered a major speech in the House of Commons on the changes in the U.S.S.R. He said that the West needed to wait for a "healthy internal evolution." Churchill spoke of the desirability of a personal meeting of the heads of state of Great Britain, the United States, and the U.S.S.R. An article by Joseph Alsop, which appeared soon after in the *New York Herald Tribune,* reported attempts of Soviet agents to make contacts with London and Washington. This has never been clarified, but it is very likely that some such approach was made by Beria. —B. N./1964.

† This was the term Bukharin used in his conversations with me in March–April, 1936, and refers to Stalin's mastery of administering the right political dose at the right time.—B. N./1964.

sible that at one time enabled Stalin to be the arbitrator in the disputes within the Politburo.

But in the postwar years, especially in the very last years of his life, he lost this gift. Recently a French bulletin, *B.E.I.P.I.*,* published some interesting material claiming that almost throughout his entire reign, Stalin was out of his mind. Be that as it may, there is no doubt that toward the end of his life Stalin lost his touch, that he ceased to have a feel for the limits of the possible. Victory, not only military but more especially political victory, so turned his head that he seems to have lapsed into a state of near insanity. He made the war-torn country shoulder the burden of ever-more grandiose construction projects, without regard for what these projects meant for the working masses of the country. It is public knowledge that on this issue Stalin did not tolerate any objections, that he became frenzied if any were raised. He clearly felt his end approaching and strove to erect monuments to himself. His successors had to pay for them. Of these, Beria was the person who, by virtue of his position, best knew the real situation in the country—both with respect to objective possibilities and with respect to the subjective moods which had been coming to a head among the people. That is why he was the one who insisted most on the need to relax dictatorial rule within the country. That is why he was more insistent than the others about the need for concessions in the sphere of foreign policy as well. More clearly than the others, he saw the possible consequences of an aggressive foreign policy if it were to meet with resistance.

That is the explanation for Beria's unexpected "liberal zigzag." Of course he had not changed. He had not suddenly become a "democrat." It was because he remained what he had always been that he saw more clearly than the others that the dictatorship had reached an impasse out of which it could be led only by a radical change of course.

Malenkov's government did not embark upon such a shift. No doubt it was informed of Beria's plans and approved them; at any

* The *Bulletin de l'association d'études et d'information politique internationale* was put out in Paris from 1949 on with the close participation of Boris Souvarine, L. Lauret, Branko Lazitch, and others. Now this periodical appears under the name of *Est et Ouest*. It published articles by Souvarine maintaining that Stalin was mad and paranoiac.—B. N./1964.

rate, it looked upon them tolerantly. What Beria did do in the months before his arrest he could not have done without the consent of Malenkov. But the support of Malenkov's government was far from complete. The facts at our disposal leave virtually no room for doubt that the decisive dispute and rupture occurred in the realm of foreign policy, in the matter of concessions to the West which Beria considered necessary. There is almost no doubt that these concessions were to be very substantial and go as far as withdrawal from East Germany; they were to go almost as far as agreement on questions connected with the Far East, Korea, Indochina, etc. This, at any rate, seems to be indicated by the chronology of events. It was, however, the very scale of the concessions contemplated by Beria which stretched the patience of his colleagues to the breaking point and which led to his arrest.

Instead of an agreement with the West based on substantial concessions, the Soviet Union reverted to past policies, to the double game which "dialectically" combines negotiations and even concessions in one sector of the vast political front with intensification of aggression in other sectors. Thus, for example, this policy can easily combine concessions in East Germany with the shipment of arms to rebels in Indochina.

The failure of Beria's attempt has undoubtedly delayed the process of change in the policy of the dictatorship which had been dictated by the death of Stalin. Beria was liquidated by people who, more than he, were attached to the old "Stalinist" formulas, especially in foreign-policy matters. This liquidation could have extremely dangerous consequences both for the peoples of the U.S.S.R. and for the rest of the world. However, it would be wrong to see only this side of the Beria affair. There is another and extremely important side as well.

In the dispute under discussion, Beria was a supporter of the reformist tendencies among the leaders, and he sought to modify the dictatorship. But the force on which he relied, the police apparatus of the MVD, was the one most hostile to the people, the most antipopular force in the entire apparatus. And it was Beria who had created this force in all its magnitude, making it hated not only by the people but by other sections of the apparatus. From this point of view, the Beria affair represents not simply the annihilation of a group of leaders of the Soviet political police; it also represents a severe blow to the MVD as a part of the apparatus. The fact is not only that the entire leadership of the operative organs of the MVD, in charge of its work for a full decade and a half, has been physically destroyed, nor even that, in accordance with Soviet practice, numerous *apparatchiks* will share their fate. Even more important, the Soviet Government will now have to limit the rights and powers of the MVD. As an indication of this prospective change, the article by the new Prosecutor General of the U.S.S.R., R. Rudenko, which talks about strict supervision of the MVD, is noteworthy. Even more important are the foreign press reports about depriving the MVD of its administrative role in major projects carried out with the help of slave labor. It is still not clear to whom the administration of these jobs is being transferred, but apparently they have been permanently taken out of MVD control.

The matter does not stop here. Reports have been circulating about the abolition of the Economic Board of the MVD, that is, of the branch which supervised the economic organs working with the aid of "free" labor. During the last fifteen years, this MVD board expanded widely and interfered in the internal affairs of economic enterprises, causing great resentment on the part of industrial managers. At this writing, it is not clear whether the abolition of the Economic Board means that the MVD has been deprived of the right to interfere in the work of economic enterprises. But there is no doubt that this development is in the offing.

This is a very important trend, very much in keeping with new developments in general in the U.S.S.R. Under Beria, the MVD played a highly important role in all spheres of Soviet life; without Beria, with Kruglov at the head, the MVD cannot hope to play anything like its former role. Who is moving in to fill the void? Which group within the apparatus is laying claim to power and has a chance of acquiring it?

The foreign press sees the Soviet Army as such a group and makes much of the role of the marshals, especially Zhukov, and their growing influence. The question of the army's role is a large and important one, but it does not arise at present. Today the army still has no influence and does not play a decisive role. It has no representatives in any of the crucial centers of power—neither in the Presidium nor in the Council of Ministers nor in the Council's Presidium, for Bulganin was never a representative of the army and in no measure reflects its attitudes.

The real victor coming up to take the place of the former leaders of the MVD is the new type of Soviet economic administrator. It was the economic administrator alone who, after the liquidation of Beria, got a foothold in the apparatus, and a very firm one at that. In the light of this, the recent appointment of five new deputies to Malenkov in his post as Chairman of the Council of Ministers is especially important.

In March of last year, after the death of Stalin, Malenkov found himself with five deputies—Molotov, Beria, Kaganovich, Bulganin, and Mikoyan, all former members of the Politburo. After the removal of Beria, and at the end of the year, Malenkov added Saburov, Malyshev, Pervukhin, Kosygin, and Tevosyan as deputies. All of them, of course, are old and tried Communists with a long period of service in the Party. But they are also engineers and experienced in industry. In March, 1953, all of Malenkov's deputies were old members of the Politburo, and only two—Kaganovich and Mikoyan—had practical knowledge of the problems of economic organization; as a group they were *Party* leaders whom the Party had assigned to the economic sector. Today, five of Malenkov's nine deputies are engineers by education, of whom four actually came up from the factory bench. If we take into account that this group is also strongly represented in the dictatorship's second command post—the Presidium of the CPSU Central Committee—with two members, Saburov and Pervukhin, out of a total of nine, then we shall see that the development at the top level during the ten months following the death of Stalin can be summed up as a process of systematic and rapid advancement of a new type of Soviet economic administrator.

This process is exceptionally important to the general fortunes of the Soviet regime, and the fact that Malenkov is the one who is pushing this development strengthens its importance, for the events of recent months should have convinced even the skeptics that Malenkov is a highly dangerous and talented adversary. There are many reasons for thinking that the U.S.S.R. is approaching a new period, one in which the managers of the economy will play the major role.

The Beria case has nothing in common either in substance or in form with the show trials of the Great Purge. Those trials were based on deliberate lies, whereas the Beria affair is based on truth. In 1953, Malenkov and his henchmen filled the prisoners' dock with some of the most prominent members of the Soviet terror apparatus, men who actually did aspire to seize power—and moreover, to seize power not merely for its own sake, but to put into effect a definite program different from the one now being carried out by Malenkov and his colleagues.

The main features of Beria's program can be gleaned from official and semiofficial statements published by the Soviet authorities. There have been three of these: (1) the articles published in *Pravda* and *Izvestia* on July 10, that is, after Beria's arrest; (2) the statement from the Prosecutor's Office published in Soviet newspapers on December 17; and (3) the statement on the trial and conviction, published on December 23.

It should not, of course, be assumed that everything in these statements is true; it would be even less accurate to think that the whole truth about the case has been told. But the situation was such that the government could not help giving some information about the actual conduct of the trial; too many people knew about the struggle which preceded the liquidation of Beria's group, and it was impossible to keep completely silent about the truth or to tell only lies. This would have compromised the regime too much in the eyes of its defenders.

Consequently, in the main—especially where the political substance of the charges is concerned—these official announcements had to have some measure of truth. For this reason, these documents are extremely valuable for an understanding of the Beria case and for the mechanics of the power struggle in the Kremlin. One merely has to know how to read the statements.

Central to all the accusations leveled against Beria is the charge of his subversive activities in agriculture. The statement of the Prosecutor's Office says that Beria set out to "undermine the collective-farm system and create food difficulties in the country," and "in every possible way sabotaged and interfered with the carrying out of vital Party and Government measures for the improvement of the kolkhozes and sovkhozes, and the welfare of the Soviet people."

This charge sounds all the more grave in view of the details of the agricultural crisis made public just after Beria's arrest. The Malenkov regime is unquestionably trying to shift responsibility for this crisis onto Beria and his codefendants. How much truth is there in these accusations?

The basic pattern of the agricultural crisis is the collective-farm system's total failure to satisfy the interests and wishes of the peasantry, which has not become reconciled to the collective farms and is trying by every means to throw off the fetters of this system. But the present scale and acuteness of the crisis were brought on by the new campaign against the countryside. This was begun by the Soviet government in 1950 under the slogan "amalgamation of the kolkhozes," and it is still continuing.

For the last quarter of a century, all of Soviet policy with respect to the collectives has been an extraordinary game: forced into the kolkhozes and unable to abolish them, the peasants try to adapt to the forms of the collective-farm system which exist at any given stage. By hook or by crook, they find loopholes in the system which enable them to exist and somehow—not as well, of course, as before—to do their work. At that point the government steps in and begins a new phase in the campaign against the peasants. The ultimate aim of this campaign was quite clearly outlined in Stalin's last "scientific work," *Economic Problems of Socialism in the U.S.S.R.,* where he speaks of the contradiction between the state form of property, which exists in Soviet industry, and group property, as it exists in the kolkhozes. The aim of the Soviet policy concerning the peasants is to eliminate this contradiction, to convert the collective farmer into a hired worker for the state.

The amalgamation of the kolkhozes, as projected in the original plan of 1950, was to be the decisive step in this direction. Connected with the forced resettlement of peasants from small villages and settlements to large centers, to "agricultural cities" (*agrogorods*), the amalgamation of the kolkhozes was intended as a general shake-up of the entire Soviet countryside—a new agrarian revolution no less sweeping than the radical break accomplished in the countryside in the period of "complete collectivization" in 1929–32. The amalgamation plan was not completely carried out in 1950–51: at the beginning of March, 1951, the initiators of this plan, among them notably Khrushchev, suffered a severe setback. The dictatorship gave up its plans for agricultural cities, and much less was heard about amalgamation itself. But the amalgamation policy continues to this day. This may be said with complete certainty on the basis of data reported by the most authoritative spokesmen for the regime. At the Nineteenth Congress of the CPSU, Malenkov reported that the total number of kolkhozes had been reduced from 254,000 on January 1, 1950, to 97,000 by October, 1952; and at the September Plenum of the Central Committee, Khrushchev spoke of 94,000 kolkhozes. Thus, in the last ten months, the number of kolkhozes has been reduced by another 3,000—that is, during that period, another 5,000–6,000 kolkhozes, or no less than 5 per cent of their present total number, were amalgamated.

The present agricultural crisis is doubtlessly caused by this amalgamation, and in the final analysis the essence of the power struggle on this particular issue is a dispute over whether to continue or to modify the policy. In this dispute, Beria advocated the modification or abandonment of the amalgamation. This can be asserted on the basis of the following facts:

We know that in March and April, 1951, Bagirov, then Secretary of the Central Committee of the Azerbaidzhan Communist Party, and Arutiunov, Secretary of the Central Committee of the Armenian Party, came out openly against Khrushchev's "excesses" in the matter of amalgamation. Their statements were published in the local press—in the Erevan *Kommunist* and the *Bakinsky Rabochy*. But both of these men were definitely Beria people, particularly Arutiunov, a pupil of Beria, who worked under his direct guidance as Secretary of the Tiflis Municipal Committee of the CPSU. From this post he was promoted by Beria in 1947 to Secretary of the Armenian Communist Party, which was then undergoing a general purge. Therefore, it can be assumed that even then their statements against amalgamation had the direct, behind-the-scenes support of Beria. It now becomes clear that the opposition to Khrushchev at that time was headed by Beria. He was the one who struck at Khrushchev in March, 1951. Arutiunov, Bagirov, and the others who spoke out with them were so bold *because* they had the support of Beria. Now they are all paying for it: immediately after Beria's fall, Bagirov lost his post and now it is Arutiunov's turn. Past attitudes toward amalgamation of the kolkhozes are playing an important role in all the other purges now sweeping the country.

As yet, we do not have precise information on the program Beria advocated in the recent disputes with Khrushchev. But the fundamental lines of both sides, it seems to me, are not difficult to determine. Beria was in favor of relaxing the offensive against the countryside. His opponents were in favor of continuing this offensive, of continuing to consolidate the kolkhozes and "eliminating the contradiction" between collective-farm property in the countryside and state property in industry.

However, it should be noted that now that Beria has been eliminated, the present rulers of the Kremlin are also making great efforts to convince the peasant of the need to work, and for this purpose they are taking various measures to increase his stake in the economy. These measures in no way affect the collective-farm system itself and will not prevent its further development. The measures which Beria proposed evidently must have been of a different nature.

The question of amalgamation was undoubtedly central to the power struggle that led to Beria's downfall. But it was not the only critical issue around which the struggle was waged. The reports on the Beria case show that the nationalities question was also at issue. According to the announcement by the Prosecutor's Office: "Beria and his accomplices undertook criminal measures aimed at reviving the remnants of bourgeois-nationalist elements in the Union republics, at sowing enmity and dissension among the peoples of the U.S.S.R., and, in particular, undermining the friendship of all the peoples of the U.S.S.R. with the Great Russian people."

With minor variations, this charge is repeated in all the relevant documents and articles. The reference to the "insidious methods" to which Beria resorted in this matter is particularly interesting. A study of the political relations in the Kremlin in recent months leaves no doubt that this second charge also has a basis in fact.

It is generally conceded that in the last phase of Stalin's life, his policy on the nationalities question was highly chauvinistic and played on traditional Russian national feeling. In effect this meant that the Czarist policy toward the non-Russian nations of the country was resuscitated by the Bolsheviks in a camouflaged form as a means of consolidating the state. The years 1948–52 were marked by purges, many of which were carried out in a spirit of Russian nationalism against non-Russian intellectuals, etc., who had, however cautiously, tried to preserve some vestiges of a separate national identity for the various ethnic groups of the U.S.S.R.

The first months after Stalin's death were marked by a tendency to abandon or, at any rate, moderate this trend in the nationalities policy. In all the non-Russian republics, leading officials of the Party and government who had championed Stalin's nationalities policy were replaced. This new nationalities policy of the post-Stalin period culminated in the June Plenum of the Central Committee of the Ukrainian Communist Party, at which the Central Committee policy was declared to be unsatisfactory. The Secretary of the Central Committee, Melnikov, was accused of allowing "a distortion of the Leninist-Stalinist policy of our Party, which was manifested in the faulty practice of filling leading Party and Soviet positions in the western regions of the Ukraine primarily with workers from other regions of the Ukrainian Soviet Socialist Republic, and also in changing the language of instruction in western Ukrainian institutions of higher education to Russian" (*Pravda,* June 13).

Similar resolutions were adopted by the Central Committee of the Communist parties of Latvia, Lithuania, Estonia, and other Union republics throughout most of the U.S.S.R.

No matter how great Beria's power may have been, he could not have conducted such a broad campaign by himself. He had to have either the support or at least the acquiescence of both the Central Committee Secretariat of the CPSU, headed by Khrushchev, and of Malenkov, as head of the government. But Beria's leading role in this change of policy on the nationalities question was obvious. Apart from other evidence, this is indicated by the fact that the article in the June issue of *Kommunist* substantiating this new line was written by such a prominent supporter of Beria as P. N. Fedoseev.*

But internal issues were always secondary in Stalin's major plans. Domestic policy was geared entirely to his schemes for destroying "capitalist encirclement." This is particularly true of the last years of his life.

As a disciple of Lenin and henchman of Stalin, Beria understood the need of gearing domestic policy to foreign policy, and he was undoubtedly planning a retreat on foreign policy as well. The official statements on the Beria case bear out this view.

When these statements deal with Beria's "crimes" in the realm of foreign policy, the language becomes obscure. Newspaper reports of nationwide denunciatory meetings describe Beria as a man who "sold himself to international imperialism," whereas the official statements are more cautious on this point. The statement of the Prosecutor's Office confines itself to pointing out that Beria "based his criminal calculations on support for the conspiracy by reactionary imperialist forces abroad" and, for this purpose, "maintained and developed his ties with foreign intelligence services." But not one of these services is ever named in the statement, unless we include the charge that in 1919–20, Beria was connected with the Azerbaidzhan and Georgian intelligence services, which allegedly worked for the British.†

This was expressed more bluntly in articles published on July 10 in *Pravda* and *Izvestia*. There it was stated that Beria was "an agent of international imperialism," on whose orders he developed plans "to replace the policy worked out by the Party over many

* The support of Beria by Professor Fedoseev, presently chairman of the Academy of Sciences of the U.S.S.R., is evident from his stand on the question of amalgamation of the kolkhozes. Fedoseev, like Beria, was an opponent of the policy, which Khrushchev had initiated. Fedoseev maintained his opposition even in the face of attacks by Suslov. He held to this position until recent years, when Khrushchev began to advocate a more conciliatory policy toward the kolkhozes.—B. N./1964.

† Beria's contacts with "foreign intelligence services" have often been mentioned in the Soviet press. These allegations continue to appear, although not the slighest shred of evidence has ever been offered.—B. N./ 1964.

years with a policy of capitulation which in the last analysis would have led to the restoration of capitalism."

Let us hope that the future will bring new information that will enable us to analyze Beria's foreign-policy ideas more precisely and, consequently, learn how this question is being handled in the Kremlin. But even without additional information, we have grounds for saying that Beria's plans included an agreement with the West based on concessions by the U.S.S.R., at least in regard to the Soviet zones of Germany and Austria. The Iron Curtain over these countries is not so tightly drawn, and we are sufficiently well-informed about the struggle which was taking place among the leaders of the German Communists. Zaisser, head of the East German Department of State Security, was undoubtedly Beria's man, and on direct orders from Beria he launched the "new course" policy, which included not only concessions on the economic front, but also an agreement with the clergy, major concessions to the bourgeois parties, and so on. The West German press labeled these plans the "German NEP," but in reality they were considerably more than that. They were plans for releasing in East Germany (to use the expression current in the Soviet Union during the NEP) "the brakes on the transition from dictatorship to democracy."

This, of course, by no means completes the list of Beria's "crimes." But anyone who has carefully read the relevant documents will agree that these three charges are the essential points of the indictment against Beria and his companions. As I have shown, knowledge of the events of recent years makes it possible to determine the meaning of the generalities of the indictment and to supply specifics. Malenkov's government accuses Beria and the others of having committed the following acts, which from Malenkov's point of view are very grave crimes: (1) favoring the relaxation or even the stopping of the offensive against the countryside carried on under the slogan of amalgamation of the kolkhozes; (2) favoring the easing of the persecution of minority nationalities; and (3) desiring the moderation of the U.S.S.R.'s aggressive foreign policy and the relaxation of the dictatorship of the Communist parties maintained in the occupied countries with the support of Soviet armies.

For good measure, one other item must be added: we know

from the statement of the Prosecutor's Office that Beria's "accomplice" Vlodzimirsky, who has now been shot, was chief of the special investigation department of the Ministry of Internal Affairs. This, however, is the same post held in the last months before Stalin's death by Riumin, the man who conducted the investigation of the doctors' plot and whose methods were so sharply criticized by Malenkov's government in the announcement of the doctors' release.

It is impossible to overemphasize the importance of this point. If Riumin was in charge of investigating the doctors, then Vlodzimirsky undoubtedly investigated Riumin's methods. Riumin was called an "adventurer" by the government, but as yet we do not know what became of him.* However, the investigator who exposed Riumin has been liquidated. We now know this beyond any doubt.

One should not think that this circumstance is purely coincidental. On the contrary, it also explains the charge brought against Beria in the *Pravda* and *Izvestia* articles of July 10, 1953, but which was not to be found in the statement of the Prosecutor's Office. This fourth charge against Beria and his associates read: "Having been charged with carrying out the instructions of the Party Central Committee and the Soviet government with a view to strengthening Soviet justice and clearing up certain illegal and arbitrary actions, Beria deliberately impeded the implementation of these instructions and, in a number of cases, tried to distort them."

Thus, the winding up of the doctors' affair, or, at any rate, the manner in which it was done, was a "distortion" by Beria and his followers of the instructions of the Party and Government.

These are the principal "crimes" for which Malenkov's regime sent Beria and his followers to their death.

* Riumin was executed in the summer of 1954 for actions taken against Communist economic managers.—Ed.

The Execution of Riumin*

THE July 23, 1954, announcement of the execution of Riumin, former Deputy Minister of State Security in the last months of Stalin's life, has caused considerable stir abroad. The reaction is mainly one of puzzlement. The Riumin affair is connected in most people's minds with the "doctors' plot," which attracted the attention of the entire world. Riumin's execution at this time does not fit into the usual interpretations of Soviet events on this side of the Iron Curtain. The Western press agrees that Riumin was made a scapegoat, but it has not explained why this particular scapegoat had to be shot; Ignatiev, Riumin's chief and Minister of State Security at the time of the doctors' plot, has already been rehabilitated, while Beria, who was mainly responsible for exposing the whole thing as a frame-up, has been liquidated.

The Riumin affair is of great significance because it shows the

* This article appeared in *Sotsialistichesky Vestnik,* August–September, 1954.

inadequacy of the oversimplified explanations of the events connected with the death of Stalin and the execution of Beria. The basic flaw in all these explanations is that they all regard the Riumin affair as merely a sequel to the doctors' plot. Actually, the situation is much more complicated. To begin to understand Riumin's execution we must first and foremost establish that he was *not* shot either because he directed the investigation of the Jewish doctors' case or because he was one of the organizers of this affair. We are forced to this conclusion by an analysis of the official announcement of Riumin's execution.

Strange as it may seem, none of the commentators writing about the Riumin affair has taken the trouble to decipher the juridical formulation of the charge for which he was sentenced to death. They all repeated the phrase about "a crime covered by Article 58, Paragraph 7, of the Criminal Code of the R.S.F.S.R.," but no one bothered to look up and figure out the actual meaning of the paragraph in question. The full text of this paragraph reads:

> 58.7 Undermining state industry, transport, trade, money circulation or credit system, as well as cooperatives, for counterrevolutionary purposes by utilizing state institutions or enterprises or obstruction of their normal activity, as well as using state institutions and enterprises or obstructing their activity in the interests of former proprietors or interested capitalist organizations, entails the measures of social defense [penalties] indicated in Article 58, Paragraph 2, of the present Code.

Article 58, Paragraph 7, is so irrelevant to Riumin's activity in connection with the arrest of the Jewish doctors that one might almost think that there was some mistake and that the wrong article of the Criminal Code was cited. But the reference to Article 58, Paragraph 7, is contained in all reports on Riumin. Proofreading in Soviet publications is very competent, particularly in the text of official communiqués. Therefore, any doubts on this score can be dismissed. Riumin was undoubtedly convicted and executed under this paragraph and no other.

But it cannot possibly be applied to Riumin's role in the doctors' plot, despite all the well-known "ingenuity" of Soviet prosecutors. Nor indeed was this necessary. There are two other paragraphs in the same article of the Criminal Code, which would have been completely appropriate, for example, Paragraph 10, concerning the "exploitation of religious or racial prejudices of the masses." Since Riumin was convicted under Article 58, Paragraph 7, this was done because the principal deed of which he was accused involved "undermining" the national economy or "obstructing the normal activity" of state industry, trade, cooperatives, etc.

This conclusion is not at all contradicted by the fact that in the same official announcement reference is made to Riumin's activity in connection with the arrest of "prominent medical figures." On the contrary, the nature of the reference merely confirms our basic conclusion. The text of the announcement states that Riumin, "acting as a secret enemy of the Soviet state, for opportunistic and adventuristic purposes, undertook the falsification of evidence on the basis of which provocations were fabricated and unwarranted arrests made of Soviet citizens, including prominent medical figures" (*Pravda,* July 23, 1954). In other words, Riumin was accused of attempting to stage not only the doctors' plot, but a whole series of other frame-ups as well.

In themselves, the actions of investigative organs in "employing methods of investigation prohibited by Soviet law," mentioned in the announcement of Riumin's execution, do not constitute a major offense, punishable only by five years' "loss of freedom" at the most (Article 115). Some such charge was no doubt considered in court; in the detailed indictment, Article 115 was mentioned, and it was under this article that Riumin was accused of actions connected with the illegal arrests of the medical figures. But this charge was so insignificant, the penalty to which Riumin was liable under it was so small compared with the sentence as a whole, that it was not thought necessary even to mention it in the official announcement.

Just as the official announcement of the Riumin affair mentions the arrest of "prominent medical figures" only in passing, in a subordinate clause, so Riumin's judges must have treated the whole matter of the attempt to stage the doctors' plot as a secondary matter. The trial concentrated on the other frame-ups mounted by Riumin—namely those which made it possible to describe his actions as undermining the normal activity of the Soviet economy. It was for these other misdeeds that Riumin was sentenced to death and executed.

Just what were these cases? The Soviet press neither mentioned them directly nor even alluded to them. Nevertheless, it is possible to answer this question if we turn to the events of the months immediately preceding Stalin's death.

The official announcement of the discovery of a doctors' plot to remove prominent Soviet leaders by poisoning was published in Moscow on January 13, 1953. It was the signal for the opening of an all-out campaign against foreign and domestic enemies threatening the Soviet regime. The main enemy was said to be the United States, which was allegedly behind the plotters, but the press devoted particular attention to the exposure of persons in positions of responsibility who "lacked vigilance" and allowed "enemy agents" to make their way into various Soviet institutions and carry on their subversive work.

The "poisoners" were needed in order to create the proper atmosphere for a new purge. The Party leaders of economic organizations, industry, transport, trade, and cooperatives were the main targets. A close study of the Soviet press and a comparison of the denunciatory articles appearing in various Soviet papers permit an even more precise definition of the first targets of this campaign. As I have stated, the first blow was directed at the economic ministries and, in particular, at Tevosyan and Malyshev, whose posts in the Council of Ministers at the time gave them control of the work of these ministries.

This far from exhausts the conclusions that can and should be drawn from the announcement of Riumin's execution. The execution also throws further light on the enigma of the Beria case.

Riumin was arrested on Beria's orders, and *Pravda,* commenting on the announcement of this arrest in an editorial on April 6, 1953, described Riumin's activities as an attempt to "incite in Soviet society, which is welded together by a moral and political unity and by the ideas of proletarian internationalism, feelings of national hatred that are profoundly alien to socialist ideology." *Pravda* was, of course, not giving its own version of Riumin's activities. It was simply voicing the views of Beria, who then ruled the police apparatus. It was Beria who put the emphasis in the Riumin case

151

on the business of inciting nationalist feelings and made Riumin's attempt to frame the Jewish doctors the central point of the indictment.

It is possible that even then not everyone within the Soviet leadership agreed with this version of the indictment. After Beria's arrest their disagreement was reflected in the press. An editorial about the Beria case appearing in *Pravda* and *Izvestia* on July 10 contained the following passage: "Having been instructed by the Party Central Committee and the Soviet government to strengthen Soviet legality and clear up certain illegal and arbitrary actions, Beria deliberately impeded the implementation of these instructions and, in a number of cases, tried to thwart them."

Today there is no doubt that the editorial of July 10, 1953, was a summary of those sections which were intended for publication of the long indictment brought by Malenkov against Beria at the Plenum of the Central Committee held between June 24 (the date of Beria's arrest) and July 10 (when the announcement of Beria's arrest was made public). It was here that Malenkov asserted that the version of the charges against Riumin as given in *Pravda* on April 6 was a "distortion" of the sense of the direct instructions of the Central Committee and the Soviet Government. On the other hand, the new formulation of the charges on which Riumin was executed is in complete accord with the "direct instructions" of the present, Malenkov-controlled majority of the Central Committee and the Government. It was indeed dictated by this majority.

In other words, the difference between these two formulations —the one in *Pravda* on April 6, 1953, and the one in the announcement of July 23, 1953—reflects the differences between Beria and Malenkov over the Riumin case.

The importance of this difference should not, of course, be exaggerated. There were also very substantial disagreements between Beria and Malenkov over certain other extremely important questions of Soviet policy. Nevertheless, so many different interests revolved around the Riumin affair that it played a very appreciable role.

At bottom, it was the difference in their attitude toward the whole complex of factors in Stalin's policy which, in January, 1953, led Stalin to attempt to carry out a new mass purge. This attempt was defeated by a bloc of two main forces—those behind Malenkov and those behind Beria. Whether, in order to accomplish this, they had to resort to some sort of "active" intervention to help Stalin die or whether Stalin died a natural death we do not know for the time being. Theoretically, of course, it is completely possible that Stalin died a natural death, but in this age of skepticism so timely a death of the man blocking the way of two such ambitious men as Beria and Malenkov automatically gives rise to all kinds of doubts. In any event, after the execution of Riumin, who was only a tool of Stalin, it can be regarded as certain that Malenkov was opposed to a new purge.

But although Beria and Malenkov were allied in their opposition to a new purge, it now seems clear that they differed considerably in their attitude toward those features of Stalin's policy which underlay his decision to carry it out. This policy had two elements—at any rate as far as the opening act of the purge was concerned. The first was anti-Semitic and anti-American, dictated above all by considerations of foreign policy; its tone was set by the announcement on January 13, 1953, of the doctors' plot. The second was that of a campaign against the economic administrators, which was dictated by considerations of domestic policy and which was a reflection of the struggle inside the Party between the Party apparatus as such and the economic apparatus. The chief opponent of the first element was Beria, and hence the emphasis on it in Beria's indictment of Riumin. Malenkov was an opponent of the purge because of the second element—the campaign against the economic administrators—and it was for this that he now had Riumin executed.

As was bound to happen, Beria and Malenkov, allies in their opposition to Stalin's new purge, quarreled the very day after their joint victory. Among the reasons for their falling-out was the question of which features of Stalin's policy were to be eliminated.

The *Pravda* editorial of April 6, 1953, indicates that Beria opposed the anti-Semitic and anti-American theme of the second purge, that is, its foreign-policy aspects. Having eliminated the issue of the doctors from the indictment of Riumin, Malenkov showed that he was not going to oppose the anti-Semitic theme

153

which Stalin had exploited during the last years of his life, much less the anti-American theme.

The mere fact that recent anti-Semitic comments in various Soviet publications have not found much support among Party propagandists does not mean that the exploitation of anti-Semitic feeling has been abandoned altogether, but rather that such remarks have hitherto been used to sound out public opinion. The dictatorship has not committed itself to abandoning this theme in the future. If it had accepted Beria's version of the indictment and mentioned the issue of the doctors in the announcement of Riumin's execution, if this announcement had spoken of inciting "feelings of national hatred," this would have indicated an intention of combating anti-Semitism. But the regime dropped these points from its charges against Riumin, thereby showing that it prefers not to bind itself on that issue.

As regards the anti-American theme, things are even worse. During the new purge this was firmly bound up with the anti-Semitic theme. Therefore, condemning the anti-Semitic aspect of Riumin's activity, as Beria did, would necessarily have led to discrediting the anti-American theme too. Now we know that the regime has not the slightest intention of abandoning its virulent anti-American campaign. On the contrary, it wages it with ever-greater vigor. The anti-American theme disappeared from the pages of the Soviet press only for a short time—during the months when Beria headed the unified MVD. Soviet anti-American propaganda is perhaps not as crude as it was in the last days of Stalin, but it is no less virulent.

Thus, from this point of view, the announcement of Riumin's execution confirms the hypothesis that Malenkov was opposed to a new purge because of its domestic significance, because its real organizers in Stalin's secretariat had decided to make it into a brutal purge of the economic apparatus, and they had already begun to strike against prominent representatives of this group in Malenkov's intimate entourage. The foreign-policy themes of the purge were not at all unacceptable to Malenkov in principle; he did not reject them and does not wish to reject them today. He was and continues to be very anti-American.

But the campaign against Beria was only one aspect of the great struggle waged by Malenkov over the Riumin case. The fact that

Riumin was not tried until fifteen months after his arrest shows that he must have had his defenders. They must have been very influential defenders at that, since Malenkov overcame their opposition only with great difficulty.

Who were they? It is less a question of individuals than of the groups for which they were spokesmen. The question of their identity overlaps with the question of who planned Stalin's new purge in early 1953 and of who still supports this policy at the present time.

Our information about Riumin himself is unfortunately extremely meager. His name is to be found neither in the lists of prominent members of the MVD-MGB nor of the Party apparatus. Two conclusions have to be drawn from this: first, that he was a comparatively young man, and second, that his work was performed in the most secret recesses of the apparatus, that is, most likely in Stalin's personal secretariat.

This conclusion is also supported by two references to Riumin's past in non-Soviet sources. The first of these is a statement by Erich Wollenberg. Wollenberg is a former prominent German Communist military officer who led a Communist uprising after World War I. He then emigrated to the U.S.S.R., where he held high posts in the Soviet Army. About 1934, he fled the Soviet Union. The April 15, 1953, issue of the bulletin *Die aktuelle Reportage,* published in Frankfurt am Main, carried an article by Wollenberg according to which Riumin had played a behind-the-scenes role in the organization of the show trials of the Great Purge (1936–38). The second reference, even more interesting, is by Yu. Chernomorsky, the Berlin correspondent of *Ukrainskiye vesti* (Ulm, Germany, August 1, 1954), who, in writing about the significance of Riumin's execution, says that Riumin, before being appointed to the post of Deputy Minister of State Security in 1952, headed the state security section in Stalin's personal secretariat.

It has not yet been possible to check whether these reports are correct. But there can be no doubt about the basic facts: Riumin could rise from obscurity to the responsible post of Deputy Minister of State Security only via Stalin's inner sanctum.

If this is true—in particular, if Riumin was really chief of the state security section of Stalin's secretariat and, therefore, a confidant of Poskrebyshev—then it is entirely possible that Riumin, not Ignatiev—who, as Minister of State Security, was Riumin's official chief—was the actual organizer of the new purge. In that case, Ignatiev might have served merely as a cover while Riumin directed the purge operations under the general behind-the-scenes supervision of Poskrebyshev and, of course, Stalin himself. If these are the facts, then Riumin, who has now been sent before the firing squad, was not a scapegoat made to pay for someone else's crimes; he was a major criminal, second in importance only to Poskrebyshev in the preparation of the new purge. This would make both the struggle to save him and Malenkov's determination to liquidate him all the more understandable.

Two additional factors are important to an understanding of the Riumin case: first, the fact that his trial lasted six days, from July 2 to 7; second, the fact that it came immediately after the special Plenum of the Central Committee which met in June, 1954.

There is no doubt whatsoever that these events were related and that Riumin's case had been investigated and decided upon by the Central Committee Plenum before his trial by a military tribunal. If Beria, with all the power he held at that time, was able to arrest Riumin only after receiving direct instructions from the Central Committee and the government, then such direct instructions were all the more necessary to bring Riumin to trial.

A real struggle over the Riumin case was fought at the June Plenum, and it was there that his execution was decided upon. There is no doubt that at this Plenum it was Malenkov who favored execution and that he had the support of all those whom Riumin, a year and a half earlier, was preparing to purge—that is, the economic administrators who constitute the second-largest group in the present Central Committee. It seems clear also that Riumin's defenders at this Plenum must have been made up almost exclusively of Party *apparatchiks* to whom Poskrebyshev looked for support in organizing the new purge. The purge of economic representatives was to have enhanced the role of the Party apparatus; this was what Poskrebyshev sought. But since the Party bureaucracy constitutes a vast majority in the Central Committee, the decision to bring Riumin to trial could have been passed only if a considerable number of Party bureaucrats also supported it. The memory of the

Great Purge is still all too vivid, so that the proponents of a new purge could not find much support even in these circles.

The fact that Riumin's trial lasted six days is especially interesting in view of the Plenum's prior decision. No report of the trial appeared in the newspapers, nor, of course, will there be any. But there is no doubt that the details given at the Riumin trial will become widely known in top Party and government circles. It is quite likely that many members of the bureaucracy attended the trial, and that it dragged on so long because many of Riumin's victims—people who had been subjected to "unwarranted arrest" —were called as witnesses. The intention of the trial is quite clear: Malenkov does not want to reveal to the general public the truth about the new purge, from which the Party and the government were saved only because Stalin died at an opportune moment. But he wants the Party and government elite to know the truth and make note of who supported the purge and who was against it.

There is no doubt that the trial of Riumin was a show trial for the benefit of the ruling circles, so that they would more clearly understand the danger from which they had been saved. The trial was a triumph for Malenkov.

In the very subtle game Malenkov has played, he has disposed of both sides: those who wanted to moderate the ultra-aggressive foreign-policy course adopted by Stalin during the period of preparations for the purge, and those who had carried on a campaign against the economic administrators. Malenkov was and continues to be an opponent of the domestic policy of the organizers of the new purge. But he has in no way abandoned the foreign-policy objectives which underlay Stalin's decision to embark on it.

The Execution of
Abakumov et al.*

IT looks very much as if the fight over Stalin's succession is entering a new and highly significant phase. On December 24, 1954, Moscow newspapers reported the execution of Viktor S. Abakumov, who was Minister of State Security from 1946 to 1951, and three of his closest associates. Two others were sentenced to long prison terms. The entire investigation department of the Ministry of State Security in that period has been wiped out. Sentence was passed by the Military Collegium of the Supreme Court, which met in Leningrad on December 14–19, 1951, under the chairmanship of General E. E. Zeidin. Abakumov and his associates were found guilty of having formed "a criminal, subversive group" which acted on instructions from Beria "to the detriment of the Party and the government." The main charge was their part in the "Leningrad case," which was marked by the false accusation of prominent

* This article appeared in *Novoye Russkoye Slovo*, January 2, 1955.

Party and government figures who, as the official announcement emphasizes, have now been completely rehabilitated and had their civil rights restored.

The Soviet announcement, of course, contains many obscure points and leaves many things unsaid. In particular, there are no references to the mysterious Leningrad case, which has never been reported in the Soviet press. Nevertheless, the meager information in the announcement and various other materials help in understanding the meaning of this latest trial.

Abakumov was the last of the "old Chekists" who had worked in the disreputable organizations concerned with state security since the very beginning and who had been closely associated with the first Cheka head, Dzerzhinsky. Serov, Kruglov, and the other chiefs of the MVD rose to prominence later, at the end of the 1920's and the beginning of the 1930's.

Abakumov, born in the Don region, took part in the Revolution as a youth of twenty. He did not complete secondary schooling and had no trade. He did not participate in the revolutionary movement before 1917, but he joined the Bolsheviks in the very first months of the Revolution and almost immediately after the October coup he went to work for the Cheka. During the Civil War he worked in Moscow, where, in 1919–20, he held the post of deputy chairman of the Cheka. In 1920, at the height of the partisan movement in the Ukraine, Abakumov headed the operations section of the rear staff of the Southwest Front; at that time, the staff was headed by Dzerzhinsky himself, and it was he who chose Abakumov for this post. After the Soviet-Polish War and the rout of Wrangel,* at the end of 1920, Abakumov was appointed deputy chief and later chief of the Special Section of the Ukrainian Cheka

---

* General Baron Peter Wrangel had assumed command in the Crimea early in 1920, gathering the remnants of the White troops into a volunteer army and restoring discipline among them. With this force, he won some minor victories which gained him French recognition as the government of south Russia. In the summer of 1920, Wrangel launched an offensive to the north. He got as far as the Northern Taurida region. But at this point, the armistice between the Poles and the Bolsheviks in Moscow was signed, and the Bolsheviks were free to turn their full armed strength against Wrangel's White Army. Frunze carried out this campaign, pushing Wrangel back and ultimately forcing his evacuation to Constantinople.—Ed.

—i.e., he was made head of the Cheka section of the Red Army in the Ukraine. In 1922, when special attention was being devoted to suppressing the peasant uprising in the Tambov Province, Abakumov was transferred to that area and made head of the Special Section of the Tambov Military District, which had been set up under the command of Tukhachevsky. Later, Abakumov became OGPU head in the Urals and Western Siberia. In 1927, he shifted to a job in the economic sector and was made head of the Donets Basin coal combine; there he played an important role in staging the Shakhty trial of 1928, when there was a brutal purge of "bourgeois specialists-technicians."* During the following years, he worked either as economic administrator or as secretary of a Party organization.

When Beria replaced Yezhov as head of the NKVD in the fall of 1938, the Central Committee, at Beria's insistence, mobilized all of the "old Chekists" who, for some reason or other, had left police work. Abakumov was among those mobilized. Apparently Abakumov had not known Beria personally before. The almost total lack of experienced personnel helped Abakumov to rise rapidly in the central department for "special sections" of the army, an area in which he was considered a specialist. By 1940, he had become one of Beria's deputies, and after the war started, when the Special Sections were made into a separate department

---

* The Shakhty trial of 1928 was directed against technicians of bourgeois origin who were accused of having connections with former mine owners. These proprietors had fled the country—some to Germany, others to France or England—and the accusation said that they had bribed the engineers to reduce coal production so as not to work out the mines. Among the accused were several Germans. The prosecution claimed that they had been instrumental in bribing the engineers.

At the trial, many of the accused denied the charge. Among them there were engineers who had belonged to independent democratic organizations. They were sentenced to death, as were a number of the Germans. The German Government demanded their release, threatening economic and other reprisals. The Soviets yielded and the Germans were expelled from the Soviet Union. Only the Russian engineers, who continued to deny any connection with the former mine owners, were executed.

The trial was conducted on the initiative and according to the plan of Stalin, and it signified the transition to a policy of repression against the old, independent specialists.—B. N./1964.

Abakumov's Execution

(SMERSH)* with special powers not only for the front and front-line areas, but also for work in the enemy's rear, Abakumov became head of this department directly under the authority of the supreme command, that is, of Stalin personally. Abakumov remained in this post until the end of the war. In the fall of 1946, when SMERSH was disbanded, he was appointed Minister of State Security and remained in this post until the end of 1951 or the beginning of 1952; on November 7, 1951, he made his last appearance in this capacity on the Red Square reviewing stand.

Now Abakumov and his associates are accused of having fabricated false charges against Party workers, government officials, and members of the intelligentsia. Not a single name has been mentioned, but reference is made to the so-called Leningrad case as a frame-up in which many people in these categories were arrested and indicted for crimes against the state.

Heretofore, the Soviet press had not mentioned the Leningrad case, but there is no doubt that the matter is connected with the liquidation of Zhdanov's supporters in 1949. Information about this purge first appeared in the Russian-language *Bulletin of the League for the Struggle for the Freedom of the People* (New York, April 10, 1949) and in *The New Leader* of April 23, 1949, in a letter from Berlin made public by the present writer.† Based on statements from recent Soviet refugees, the letter said that after Voznesensky's removal from the Politburo and as head of the State Planning Commission, M. Rodionov's removal as Chairman of the Council of Ministers for the R.S.F.S.R., and A. Kuznet-

---

* The title is a contraction of the Russian *Smert Shpionam,* "Death to spies." The organization developed during the war; it was designed to combat disaffection and conduct counterespionage in Russia itself and in occupied areas, as well as to fight anti-Bolshevism generally.—Ed.

† The reference to Berlin as the place from which this information was received was intended to protect the real source. In fact, the information came from an *emigré* living in one of the Baltic seaports, who received it from a Soviet sailor from Leningrad. The sailor told him that there had been a great number of arrests in the city. The nature of the charges against those arrested is still not known, but it is now apparent that they were fabricated. The main point about the affair was that it led to the total elimination of the Party and Soviet officials appointed by Zhdanov during his fifteen years as Stalin's deputy in Leningrad.—B. N./1964.

sov's as Secretary of the Central Committee, mass arrests were carried out in Leningrad of such men as Popkov, Kapustin, and Tikhonov, Secretaries of the Leningrad regional and municipal committees of the Party. As was then reported, the following charges were leveled against all those arrested:

> On the one hand [they were accused] of moral corruption: they were charged with indulging in drunken orgies, luxurious living, dressing their wives in costly clothes, driving expensive cars, and so forth. To obtain money for all that, they allegedly accepted bribes; Popkov, for example, was accused of selling food cards. On the other hand, it was said about them that they carried out their own economic policies, undermining those of the government. [*The New Leader,* April 23, 1949.]

This was possible only because they enjoyed the special protection of Popkov, Kapustin, and Tikhonov. The charge of carrying on their own economic policy was directed mainly against Voznesensky. Kuznetsov, who was then the head of the Personnel Directorate of the Party's Central Committee, was accused of "covering-up" and profiting from the misappropriations.

> All the above-named persons [the letter stated] have thus far only been dismissed from their posts and removed from work, but they face the threat of arrest and more severe punishment. There are generally many arrests and punishments. It is rumored that Afanasiev, head of the maritime commercial fleet, who was allegedly caught maintaining secret connections with England, was arrested and possibly shot. [*Ibid.*]

Later this information was confirmed in the foreign press; it was first made public by C. S. Sulzberger in *The New York Times* of June 19 and 23, 1949. At that time, two major actions were undoubtedly carried out against the Zhdanovites—one in Moscow, against Voznesensky, Kuznetsov, Rodionov, *et al.,* and the other in Leningrad, against Popkov, *et al.* There is little doubt that a number of persons were executed as a result of these proceedings, or at any rate as a result of the Moscow case, and that the institution of the death penalty for "traitors and subversive saboteurs" by a decree of January 12, 1950, was connected with these cases involving Zhdanovites. We still do not know just who was shot and who went to labor camp or prison at that time. But the words in the official announcement of Abakumov's execution about the complete rehabilitation of the victims and the restoration of their civil rights can of course only refer to those who survived.

The Leningrad case is the focal point of the official announcement, but it reveals only one side of the Abakumov affair: its *domestic* aspect. However, a careful reading of the announcement shows that there was another side to the Abakumov affair, a *foreign-policy* aspect, which the Soviet government is at great pains to conceal. It will be necessary to come back to this point, for it is of enormous importance.

The opening of the Leningrad case implies the rehabilitation of the Zhdanovites. But the purge of the Zhdanovites was not the work of Abakumov alone, or even of Beria alone. The decision to carry it out could have been made only by the highest bodies: the Presidium of the Council of Ministers and the Politburo. The main fight against Zhdanov and his followers was carried on by the Beria and Malenkov bloc, with the latter most likely playing the larger role. This bloc could only have had its way, however, if it had the support of the majority of the Politburo and, above all, of Stalin.

However, the composition of the Politburo at that time was almost the same as that of the present Presidium of the Central Committee. The majority of this Presidium, primarily its head, Malenkov, is responsible for the purges of 1949–50. This is the conclusion to be drawn here, and undoubtedly it is now being drawn by Soviet citizens as they listen to the stories of rehabilitated Zhdanovites. The execution of Abakumov and his colleagues is meant to placate them. But will it?

There is no doubt that the decision to rehabilitate the Zhdanovites was made in the Central Committee's Presidium, and it seems very much as if it was made after a fierce fight. Malenkov has recently exerted great efforts to minimize the ever-deepening rift between himself and Khrushchev.

The execution of Abakumov and the rehabilitation of the Zhdanovites will not, at any rate, help to mitigate the struggle which is going on behind the scenes between Malenkov and Khrushchev.

163

But this struggle is not the only important thing. An analysis of the background of the Riumin affair has shown a striking concern on the part of the Party and government to dissociate themselves from the methods used by the police organs of the dictatorship. The leaders have endeavored to shift responsibility for such methods onto Beria and his associates. This could hardly have been easy, even immediately after the death of Stalin; now it has become even more difficult. The circumstances which have come to light in connection with the rehabilitation of the Zhdanovites and the conviction of Abakumov will not make the position of the leaders any easier. Certain things said in the Soviet press, however cautiously, show that a highly critical attitude toward the methods of the police organs is taking hold among broad sections of the "Soviet public." It seems very much as if dissatisfaction is penetrating the highest strata of Soviet society, for such cases as the Leningrad affair show how precarious is the fate of each member of this society, regardless of how high his rank.

The Abakumov Case*

THE CASES of first Beria, then Riumin, and finally Abakumov are important landmarks in the post-Stalin period of Soviet rule. They throw light on the most obscure aspects of the recent Soviet past which are of particular relevance for an understanding of the present.

Just what was the reason for the execution of Abakumov, head of SMERSH during the war and then, from the autumn of 1946 to the end of 1951, Minister of State Security? Two elements must be distinguished in this case: first, the charges which were brought against him and of which he was found guilty; and second, those aspects of the charges which were stressed in the Soviet press. These two elements are by no means identical, but both are of great importance, and only if both are taken into account can the full meaning of the case be understood.

* This article appeared in *Sotsialistichesky Vestnik,* January, 1955.

We know about the actual charges against Abakumov only from the paragraphs of the Criminal Code cited in the official statement about the case. He was found guilty of actions covered by Paragraphs 1b, 7, 8, and 11 of Article 58 of the Criminal Code. These paragraphs deal with:

(Paragraph 1b) "high treason, i.e., acts committed by citizens of the U.S.S.R. to the detriment of the military might of the U.S.S.R., its national sovereignty, or the inviolability of its territory, to wit: espionage, betrayal of a military or state secret, desertion to an enemy," etc., if committed by military personnel;

(Paragraph 7) "undermining state industry," etc., "for counterrevolutionary purposes by utilizing state institutions or enterprises";

(Paragraph 8) "the perpetration of terroristic acts against representatives of the Soviet regime or functionaries of workers' and peasants' organizations," etc.;

(Paragraph 11) "organized activity aimed at preparing," etc., acts covered in the previous paragraphs.

It will be easier for us to understand the specific meaning of these juridical formulations if we recall which of these paragraphs were cited in the official statements about the Beria case, as well as the Riumin case. Charges against Riumin were based on only one paragraph, i.e., Paragraph 7. The charges against Beria were made under Paragraphs 1b, 8, 11, and 13. The last of these may be disregarded; it deals with "the struggle against the working class" in secret work as an agent of the Czarist or "counterrevolutionary governments during the Civil War." This paragraph was invoked against Beria because his colleagues in the Politburo considered it expedient to label him an agent of the "Mussavat party's secret police,"* for which he allegedly worked in 1918–20 in Baku. Thus, we see that while Beria and Riumin were indicted under *different* paragraphs, Abakumov was charged under *all* the paragraphs (apart from the irrelevant Paragraph 13) applied to both of them.

* The Mussavat party was an anti-Communist Moslem party in Azerbaidzhan; it was overthrown in 1920. The allegations about Beria's connection with this party were made by the former First Secretary of the Central Committee of Azerbaidzhan.—Ed.

An analysis of the materials in the Riumin case shows that by "undermining state industry" Soviet jurists at present mean the arrests and purges by the police of Soviet economic administrators in the recent past. This is fairly clear in the case of Abakumov: His fabrication of the case against the Zhdanovite managers in Leningrad is now admitted to have been just as subversive as were the actions of Riumin in the winter of 1952–53, when he attempted to carry out the purge of the managers in Moscow. The 1949 Leningrad action was indeed very brutal, and no doubt many Leningraders are now pleased to learn of the punishment being meted out to its organizers.

It looks very much as if differences on questions of economic policy really played a significant role in that purge. In any event, the letter about the arrests in Leningrad in 1949, which first brought this news to the West,* quite definitely stated that the Leningrad Zhdanovites were being accused of seeking to carry out their own economic policies. This is borne out in a recent article by Harry Schwartz, who writes in *The New York Times* of December 25, 1954, that Moscow diplomatic circles at one time had information that in 1949, Zhdanov's supporters in Leningrad were supposedly planning a large international fair in the city.

At present it is still impossible to determine whether such a plan really existed or whether accounts of such a planned move derive from the "confessions" which Abakumov and his interrogators obtained from prisoners by investigative methods supposedly prohibited by Soviet law. But it is not without interest that this idea is reminiscent of a scheme developed in the early NEP period to revitalize Leningrad (or Petrograd as it was then called), by making it a free port. Leonid Krasin,† who had a hand in working out the plan, claimed that Lenin himself regarded it favorably. The matter ended in arrests and executions; among those executed was Professor Tikhvinsky, an old friend of Krasin and Gorky. The question remains: Was there really an attempt made in 1949 to revert to this plan, or was it just another fantasy of the MGB?

* *Bulletin of the League for the Freedom of the People,* April 10, 1949.
† L. B. Krasin was an Old Bolshevik "conciliator" who occupied a most important government post in the early years of the Soviet regime.—B.N./ 1964.

The citing of another paragraph of Article 58 in the statement about the Abakumov case, namely, Paragraph 8, is more difficult to explain, yet at the same time it is more important. Paragraph 8 deals with "terroristic acts against representatives of the Soviet regime." This paragraph was not quoted in the indictment of Riumin, but it does appear in Beria's indictment.

What can Abakumov have done to have made himself liable to this charge? Just which of his actions could have been made to fit this definition? The official communiqué maintains total silence on this question. Neither are there any clues in the Soviet or the foreign press. On the whole, "terroristic acts" have in recent years been mentioned only rarely. The sole exception was in the case of the doctors' plot, when the arrested doctors were charged with causing the death of Zhdanov and Shcherbakov and with attempting to eliminate Marshals Konev, Govorov, and other members of the Ministry of Armed Forces. At the time, these alleged actions were described as "terroristic."

It should be remembered that the indictment of the doctors in 1953 under Paragraph 8, was by no means unprecedented. It was under this paragraph that the prosecution charged the doctors— Pletnyov, Levin, and others at the trial of Bukharin and Rykov, in March, 1938. Hence we see that the application of Paragraph 8 had a certain tradition in Soviet legal practice.

Under these circumstances, it is therefore natural to assume that the actions which the prosecution had in mind when it indicted Abakumov under Paragraph 8 were directly related to the doctors' plot. The doctors themselves, as we know, were freed by Beria as far back as April, 1953. The brunt of the charge at the time of their arrest, however, was directed not so much against the doctors themselves as against the state security apparatus, which "did not uncover in time" the plans of the terrorists. When *Pravda* first published the announcement on the "villainous spies and murderers masquerading as doctors," it was obvious even to the least attentive reader that the blow was aimed primarily against those who headed the MGB when Zhdanov and Shcherbakov died—in other words, against Beria, Merkulov, and Abakumov. The first two were shot in December, 1953; Paragraph 8 figures in their sentence. And now it was Abakumov's turn.

This sequence of events is hardly a matter of mere coincidence. The doctors' plot was connected with an involved struggle at the top of the dictatorship, and the fight against Beria and the other leaders of the MVD-MGB was an important part of this struggle. Abakumov was one of the main targets of the instigators of the doctors' plot; his "lack of vigilance"—which later could easily have been turned into "complicity" or even "stage-management"— was stressed rather more than that of the others. Beria, who gained his position of strength soon after Stalin's death, hastened to quash the case against the doctors, formulating the announcement of their release in such a way as to make a reopening of the case almost impossible. But it is nevertheless still quite possible to settle accounts with the MGB, which indeed is now being done.

The forces which tried to fabricate the "Jewish doctors' plot" in the winter of 1952–53 are by no means crushed. It seems they are trying to stage a comeback.

The last of the principal paragraphs under which Abakumov was accused, namely, Paragraph 1b of Article 58, dealing with treason, is the most interesting of all. Which of Abakumov's actions could have been covered by this paragraph? The official communiqué again contains no clue. The answer must be sought elsewhere.

First of all we have to establish the exact date of Abakumov's removal from the post of Minister of State Security. We know that Abakumov's last public appearance as Minister was in 1951, on November 7, the anniversary of the Revolution, when he was seen on the reviewing stand. The testimony of Vladimir Petrov,* who in 1954 defected from the Soviet Embassy in Canberra, enables us to make a more precise determination of the date of Abakumov's dismissal. It is clear from this testimony that the Intelligence Committee, in which Petrov worked, passed from the jurisdiction of the Ministry of Foreign Affairs to that of the Ministry of State Security at the end of 1951, and that at that time Ignatiev was already head of the MGB. Thus, there is no doubt that Abakumov was removed no later than the beginning of December, and most likely at the end of November, 1951.

* V. M. Petrov headed the KGB in Australia. He and his wife wrote a book about the Soviet Union in 1954, entitled *Empire of Fear* (New York: Frederick A. Praeger, 1956).—B. N./1964.

The exact date of Abakumov's dismissal is extremely important, since it can thus be established that his dismissal coincides with the arrest of Rudolf Slansky, the General Secretary of the Communist Party of Czechoslovakia (November 27, 1951), and his deputy, B. Geminder.* We know definitely that while living in the U.S.S.R., Slansky and Geminder were high-ranking officials of the MVD-MGB and that they maintained this connection later, when they held major posts in their own country. Geminder had a direct telephone line to the MGB in Moscow; those who arrested him knew this, and the first thing they did was to cut off his line to Moscow.

Thus a time relation is established between the arrests in the Slansky case and the removal of Abakumov. There are reports that initially Abakumov was removed from the Party for his alleged "corrupt way of life," but there can hardly be any doubt that this was a maneuver designed to gain time. In reality, Abakumov's removal was closely connected with the Slansky affair. As a matter of fact, the Slansky case should be seen as a reflection of the foreign-policy aspect of the struggle in Moscow for control of the MGB—between Beria and a group headed by Poskrebyshev.

Today there can hardly be any real argument over the political significance of the Slansky affair: It was connected with the great change in the general course of foreign policy which Stalin had decided to effect at about that time. Now it seems that all observers who have closely followed the policies of the U.S.S.R. in the last years of Stalin's life—from Harrison Salisbury to General Dewhurst—agree that in 1951, Stalin shifted from a policy of comparatively lengthy preparation for war to one predicated on an early war, and with the perseverance of a man possessed, he began to drive the world toward open conflict. It is probable that only his death saved humanity from the catastrophe of a world war in 1953.

* Both Slansky and Geminder were Jewish. They were accused of "cosmopolitanism," "Zionism," and other "offenses." Chief among these accusations was the charge that they had pursued an anti-Arab policy, which, in 1947–48, led to the establishment of Israel. Slansky, who without doubt acted on the instructions of Beria, made Prague the center through which all the aid to Israel passed. The trial of Slansky, Geminder, and others reflected a shift in Stalin's foreign policy to support of the Arab movement against Israel.—B. N./1964.

It was this course, headed for an early war, that determined the entire character of Stalin's policies, both domestic and foreign. Individual measures taken at that time can be properly understood only if the situation is analyzed from this angle. Only thus can one arrive at a true understanding of the Slansky case, and, consequently, of the foreign-policy aspect of the Abakumov case as well. The policy which the MGB pursued in the work of its secret apparatus abroad under Beria and Abakumov, and which, in accorddance with Stalin's original policy, was geared to a relatively extended preparation for war, was now labeled treason. Ignatiev and Riumin, as well as Poskrebyshev, who was backed by the Party Secretariat, took the place of Beria and Abakumov.

This explains the mention of Paragraph 1b in Abakumov's sentence.

Judging from everything we know, the political struggle at the top was the real reason for the disposal of Abakumov, whose decline began as far back as the end of 1951. The struggle, which revolved around the question of an early world war, was most clearly expressed in the two most important events in the final period of Stalin's life: the doctors' plot and the Slansky trial. Abakumov owes the inclusion of Article 58, Paragraph 8, in his indictment to the doctors' plot, and of Paragraph 1b to the Slansky trial. This was the core of the whole case against Abakumov.

The charge under Article 58, Paragraph 7, can be traced to the Leningrad case of 1949. This case arose at a completely different stage of the struggle among the leaders and was connected with different controversies over points of principle. But there are some threads which connect it with the struggle of 1951–53; in his fight for the restoration of the prewar role of the Party apparatus and, in particular, of the Politburo, Zhdanov was bound to clash with the "statists," who, headed by Malenkov and Beria, sought to limit the Party's influence on the governmental apparatus. It was Zhdanov who, at the end of the war, began a campaign for restricting the authority of Beria, then at the zenith of his power; it was he who succeeded in relieving the MGB of its function of gathering important political intelligence (central political espionage, in other words), a function which in 1947 was transferred to a special Intelligence Committee within the Ministry of Foreign Affairs.

In 1951–52, at the time of Abakumov's removal, the memories of the struggle against Zhdanov evidently played no appreciable role. At any rate, Suslov's article in *Pravda* of December 24, 1952, which contained the Central Committee resolution on the Voznesensky case, consolidated the anti-Zhdanovite positions in the basic controversy over principle—the controversy over the role of the Party and the state on questions of economic policy. It was also a signal for a general check on the attitudes of all Soviet economists. But now the Leningrad case—that is, the brutal purge of the Leningrad Zhdanovites—has been made the core of the Abakumov case. Why? This question is of primary importance to an understanding of present-day Soviet attitudes.

Stalin's death caused a tremendous shock throughout the country, compelling Beria to call upon the ruling group not to give way to panic. The regime was able to cope with the shock of the first days, but the feeling of psychological crisis did not pass.

Beria was the first to understand the main reason for this mood: No one in the country, no citizen, including the regime's top members, was able to stomach any longer the completely arbitrary rule to which the whole population had been subjected from the very beginning of the regime. Nobody could be sure that he would not be arrested at any moment and forced under torture into signing a false confession. However loyal a Soviet official might be, however faithfully he might carry out the orders of his superiors, he could never be certain that the mentally unbalanced dictator would not change his policy at a moment's notice and accuse of treason all those who had been instrumental in carrying out his own earlier policies.

Beria knew the country's state of mind better than many others, and he was the first, in releasing the arrested doctors, to talk about the personal inviolability guaranteed to Soviet citizens by the Constitution. Soon afterward, he carried out a partial amnesty. Shortly after that, he himself met his downfall. But the fact remains that he was responsible for the first amnesty and the present leaders are continuing his policy, although cautiously, while at the same time putting all the blame for the injustices of the recent past on him alone.

In connection with the Abakumov case it has become known that the Leningrad affair of 1949 has been reviewed and all surviving victims have had their civil rights restored. The New Year's list of people awarded medals and decorations shows that not only the victims of the Leningrad affair but Zhdanovites in general have been rehabilitated. Among the recipients listed is I. V. Shikin, who was chief of the Political Directorate of the Ministry of Armed Forces under Zhdanov and who, in 1949, suffered for his connection with Zhdanov. Still more important is the rehabilitation of other persons not connected with Zhdanov. The same list contains the name of Shakhurin, the wartime Minister of the Aviation Industry who was sent to a camp in 1945–46 by decision of the special Bulganin commission because of some irregularities in his department. Shakhurin was a faithful follower of Malenkov.

It is further known that Chief Air Marshal Novikov, who during the war was one of the main organizers of Soviet aviation in charge of long-range aircraft, has recently returned from a camp. He fell into disgrace in the early postwar years in connection with the great purge of the Army conducted by the very same Shikin under the guidance and at the direction of Zhdanov and Bulganin. It was at this same time that Marshal Zhukov, with whom Novikov was closely associated during the war, fell into disfavor.

Many more such examples could be cited, but there is hardly any need to do so. Enough has been said to show that along with the Zhdanovites now being returned from camps, supporters of Malenkov, Zhukov, and others are also being released. Doubtless a large-scale operation of releasing all members of the government, Party, military, and economic apparatuses who were victims of the purges of the postwar years is now under way, irrespective of the groups with which they were formerly allied, with one exception: the supporters and protégés of Beria.

It looks very much as if the decision to rehabilitate victims of the purge was arrived at only after a great internal struggle, when it became clear to everyone that unless they amnestied each other's followers for deeds committed under Stalin, the leadership itself would not stay in power and that its downfall would jeopardize the regime as such. This mutual amnestying naturally involved the pardoning of all their followers who had fallen victims to the internecine struggles of the recent past. The regime is now pursuing this policy systematically.

This decision of course has an important political motive: the regime is striving toward a reconciliation with the masses. Moreover, the ruling elite wishes to shift all responsibility for the crimes and misery of the recent past onto Beria, thereby exonerating all other organs of the dictatorship, particularly the Party, and hence the system as a whole. All this is clear from the handling of the Abakumov trial.

It is significant, for example, that the trial was held in Leningrad, the city in which the relatives and friends of the victims live. This must mean that some or all of the hearings were open to certain people in Leningrad—probably only the top members of the ruling stratum of Leningrad, but this would be entirely in keeping with the general policy of the regime, which seeks the support of the elite.

At this point it is hard to say whether this complicated maneuver will work. The gulf between the leaders and the mass of the population has undoubtedly grown very wide, and the fear of a powerful underground current of popular resentment is great indeed. The Abakumov case allows us to look more deeply into the behind-the-scenes struggle of the recent past; it also is a good guide to present-day developments in the U.S.S.R.

The Liquidation of Beria's "Agents" in Georgia*

O N NOVEMBER 21, 1955, the radio station of the Georgian
S.S.R. announced in Russian and Georgian that the Military
Tribunal of the Supreme Court of the U.S.S.R., which had met in
Tiflis in September, had tried eight of the most prominent Cheka
officials of Georgia and had found them guilty of "actively par-
ticipating in the anti-Soviet activities of the enemy of the people
Beria." Six of them were sentenced to death and their sentences
were carried out; two lesser defendants received long prison terms.
Among those executed two names stand out: Avksenty Narinovich
Rapava, former Deputy People's Commissar and later People's
Commissar for Internal Affairs of the Georgian S.S.R., and Nikolai
Maximovich Rukhadze, former chief of the investigation depart-
ment of the NKVD and later Georgian Minister of State Security.
This was the fourth trial aimed at eliminating the leading opera-

* This article appeared in *Novoye Russkoye Slovo*, January 8 and 9, 1956.

tors of the Stalinist terror machine, not counting the trials which were conducted secretly. The first was the trial of Beria himself and his most intimate associates (in December, 1953). The second was the trial of Riumin, Deputy Soviet Minister of State Security in the last fourteen or fifteen months of Stalin's life (in July, 1954). The third was the trial of Abakumov, Soviet Minister of State Security from 1946 to 1951, and several of his associates (in December, 1954).

The staging of the new trial in most respects repeats the pattern of the earlier ones, but it differs from them in some features important to an understanding of both the recent history of the "Cheka underground" and the struggle which is under way among the leaders of the Kremlin.

The real purpose of the Tiflis trial was to influence opinion among the Soviet elite in Georgia, and *only in Georgia.* Whereas official information about the three earlier trials of this group was carried by the press of the entire country and broadcast by *all* radio stations, news of the Tiflis trial was confined to publications of the Georgia S.S.R., and was broadcast only by the Tiflis radio. Not a line about this trial appeared in either the central Moscow or provincial newspapers. Not a word about it appeared even in such papers as the *Bakinsky Rabochy* and the Erevan *Kommunist,* which, as organs of neighboring Transcaucasian republics, usually give a lot of space to events in Tiflis. The radio stations of these republics were also silent on the matter.

It should also be pointed out that the censorship did not stop dispatches about the trial sent out by foreign correspondents in Moscow: the Soviet regime had no reason for keeping the Tiflis trial a secret from the outside world—it only wished to keep it secret from Soviet citizens.

The population of Georgia was the sole exception. It learned of the trial not only through its newspapers and radio broadcasts. The trial was public, and members of the Georgian elite were able to attend it. There is no doubt that the audience included relatives and close friends of old Bolsheviks liquidated by Beria. And as is evident from the official announcement, these liquidations were discussed in great detail at the trial. The Soviet rulers so obviously sought to win the support of these representatives of the elite that they were permitted to voice their loud approval of the sentences.

This fact was recorded in the official report, which specifically states that "the sentence met with unanimous approval from those present in the courtroom."

This is contrary to usual Soviet practice. In the early years, it is true, courtrooms were often packed with "delegates of workers' organizations," who would demand that the court mete out merciless punishment," as, for example, at the trial of Socialist Revolutionaries in 1922.* But even then, this was never recorded in official trial reports. In recent decades, the technical niceties of court procedure have been scrupulously observed, and even in the great show trials of the Purge no expressions of opinion by the audience were permitted. The Georgian trial thus sets a precedent.

There is still another important aspect to these proceedings. Officials of the government apparatus of the Georgian Republic, including ministers, were brought to trial for acts committed in their official capacities on the territory of this republic. Georgia, as well as the other Union republics, has its own Supreme Court, which has constitutional jurisdiction over all cases of this type. It was always the Supreme Court of Georgia, or special tribunals appointed by it, that tried similar cases in the past—for example, the case of Budu Mdivani and other officials of the Council of People's Commissars of Georgia in the early period;† the case of

* In 1922, the Bolsheviks tried all the members of the SR Central Committee and their most prominent sympathizers, who between them controlled more than half of the votes in the Constituent Assembly. The Bolsheviks dissolved the Constituent Assembly and thereby unleashed the Civil War.

In this trial, twelve members of the Central Committee of the Socialist Revolutionary Party were sentenced to death. The sentence was not carried out at the time, but the condemned remained in prison as hostages. After fifteen years of being shifted around from one prison to another, they were all executed during the Purge of 1936–38.

Because of their standing in the country, it was important for the Bolsheviks to discredit them at their trial; hence the audience participation.— B. N./1964.

† Budu Mdivani was the leader of the Georgian Bolsheviks in the pre-Revolutionary years. He was chief of the first Sovnarkom, created in 1921, immediately after the occupation of Georgia by the Red Army. Mdivani, like other members of the first Sovnarkom, supported a policy of greater autonomy for Georgia, opposed the persecution of other parties, etc. This group had the full support of Lenin, but in 1922–23, after Lenin fell ill, it was ousted by supporters of Stalin. In 1937, almost all its members were tried and executed.—B. N./1964.

Magaloshvili and other officials of the same Council in the mid-1930's; the case of Z. Lordkipanidze and other members of the Council of People's Commissars of the Adzhar Autonomous Republic,* etc.

So far, there does not seem to have been a single departure from this rule in the judicial practice of the Georgian Republic. It should be noted, however, that the constitution of the Georgian Republic formally does provide for handing over such cases to the Supreme Court of the U.S.S.R. This provision has now been invoked for the first time, and the trial of Rapava, Rukhadze, *et al.* was conducted by the Military Tribunal of the Supreme Court of the U.S.S.R., sitting in Tiflis. The fact that the trial was handled by the All-Union Supreme Court instead of the Georgian court is not the only important point in this connection. Perhaps it is even more significant that there was not a single Georgian among the judges. All of them were Russians—except the prosecutor Rudenko, who is Ukrainian; even the defense attorneys, to judge by their names, were Russians. The only Georgians were to be found in the dock, though there were also Russians and one Armenian among the defendants.

The composition of the court was so pointed that there can be no doubt that it was deliberately calculated. The Soviet dictatorship is no less firmly entrenched in Georgia than elsewhere in the U.S.S.R., and it could have allowed the Supreme Court of the Georgian Republic to handle the case without running any risk; the sentence would have accorded with the instructions received from the Soviet leadership. Even as it was, with the case tried by the Supreme Court of the U.S.S.R., the leaders could easily have found some compliant Georgian judges. Their failure to do so was doubtless a deliberate action. There can only be one explanation: the present leadership of the U.S.S.R. wanted to show the population of Georgia, by the very way in which this trial was conducted, that it was the *federal authority*—acting through a *Soviet army* tribunal consisting of Russians and Ukrainians—which was liberating them

---

* Magaloshvili was one of the Georgian Communists who had headed the Soviet government in Georgia at the beginning of the 1930's and who had resisted the policy of forced collectivization of the peasantry. Z. Lordkipanidze was one of those involved in the case.—B.N./1964.

from years of terror imposed by the *Georgians* Beria and his "accomplices."

This is the first conclusion to be drawn from the official report of the Tiflis trial.

But this feature of the proceeding is by no means the only peculiarity of the trial. A careful analysis of the substance of the charges is also highly revealing. The relevant passage of the official statement says that the accused are being brought to trial "for crimes covered by Article 58 (paragraphs 1b, 8, and 11) of the Criminal Code"—i.e., for high treason, terroristic acts, and membership in counterrevolutionary organizations.

These charges suggest a number of conclusions. First of all, it should be noted that Article 58, Paragraph 7, is not among the articles in the indictment. This paragraph deals with the "undermining of the economy" and was the *only* paragraph cited in the indictment of Riumin, who, it will be remembered, was shot in July, 1954, for organizing the doctors' plot and the second purge, just before Stalin's death, which was to have been directed mainly against the managers. The trial had undoubtedly been inspired by Malenkov.

Paragraph 7 later figured in the indictment at the Leningrad trial of Abakumov and his associates. It was, however, no longer the sole or even principal charge. Communist managers had also been victimized in the purge of the Leningrad Zhdanovites in 1949; yet the central charge against Abakumov was his fight against the Zhdanovites. The organizers of this Leningrad trial belonged to the Khrushchev-Bulganin camp. While striking openly at Beria, they were also striking a blow against Malenkov, who had sided with Beria against Zhdanov. In addition, however, they were trying to show that they, too, wanted to defend the managers from the arbitrary actions of the MVD-MGB.

The fact that Paragraph 7 was not invoked at the Tiflis trial proves that the above considerations no longer seem important to the organizers of the trial, that is, to the Khrushchev-Bulganin group. During the Great Purge, the period covered by the indictment of those involved in the Tiflis trial, the managers were purged on a vast scale, but the prosecution in the present trial did not find it necessary to dwell on this aspect. One can therefore conclude that the relative importance of Communist managers within the over-all apparatus of the Soviet dictatorship has diminished. They are being pushed more and more into the background.

Among the accusations brought against the defendants at Tiflis, the charge of high treason comes first. The official announcement does not offer the slightest clue to the nature of their treason, but it seems very much as if the solution to this puzzle should be sought in one of Khrushchev's most recent foreign-policy revelations, according to which Soviet relations with Turkey had deteriorated as a result of provocative acts on the part of Beria and his accomplices.

Khrushchev made this disclosure on November 1, 1955, in a conversation with the Turkish Ambassador at a banquet given in Moscow by Asian and African countries that had participated in the Bandung Conference. The significance of this declaration was emphasized by the fact that the Moscow censors allowed foreign correspondents to wire their newspapers (see the *New York Herald Tribune* of November 4).

This "private conversation" between the First Secretary of the CPSU Central Committee and the Turkish Ambassador was meant to convince Turkey of the danger inherent in her membership in NATO, since in the event of conflict she would be the first to be annihilated and, moreover, before her allies could come to her assistance. If, however, Turkey would leave the Western alliance, there would open up before her great prospects of economic well-being based on peaceful cooperation with the U.S.S.R. In the past, Soviet officials have interspersed their declarations of love for peace with threats of hydrogen bombs, but no one had yet juggled these threats with such unmitigated cynicism as Khrushchev.

It was in this context that Khrushchev mentioned Beria's role in the deterioration of Soviet-Turkish relations. The meaning is not hard to understand: Khrushchev is openly telling Turkey that the Soviet regime is ready to hold Beria personally responsible for all those actions in the Stalinist past which had transformed Turkey from a firm ally of the U.S.S.R. into an irreconcilable enemy. Khrushchev had already used this tactic in dealings with Belgrade.* Why shouldn't he try it on Ankara as well?

* Beria, of course, bore a great share of the responsibility for the break with Yugoslavia in 1948–49 and for the intrigues which Soviet agents then conducted against Yugoslav Communists. But it is noteworthy that in July,

The text of the official statement says nothing concrete about the "counterrevolutionary organization" to which the defendants were accused of belonging, but their official association with Beria in the NKVD-MVD was undoubtedly made tantamount to an affiliation. If this makes MVD men even slightly more cautious in carrying out the orders of their chiefs, then the decision of the Tiflis court might even be welcomed.

In contrast to its reticence on the first two charges, the official statement discusses in unprecedented detail the "terroristic acts" committed by the heads of the Tiflis NKVD-MVD. These sections of the report have something of the indignant fervor of Beria's comments about the behavior of the MGB in the doctors' plot which was organized by Beria's enemies—then led by Ignatiev and Riumin. Now these same enemies, though without their former leaders, Ignatiev and Riumin, have made a comeback via the MVD and are leveling similar charges against the "agents of Beria."

We read in the report of the trial:

> With the criminal aim of destroying honest cadres devoted to the cause of the Communist Party and the Soviet regime, the defendants falsified investigations, used extremely severe methods of investigation which are forbidden by Soviet law, and committed terroristic acts against honest Soviet citizens, falsely accusing them of committing counterrevolutionary crimes. [*Zaria Vostoka*, November 22, 1955.]

In support of this charge, the report cites the names of people who had been liquidated because Beria had reason to "fear exposure" by them. These people were Mamia Orakhelashvili, former secretary of the Transcaucasian Territorial Committee in 1926–31; his wife, Maria, former Georgian People's Commissar for Education; Buachidze, commander of the Georgian Division; and Bedia, di-

---

1953, in a top secret letter which the Central Committee distributed to Party organizations on the Beria case, one of the chief accusations against him concerned his attempts in April–May, 1953, to restore relations with Tito. Khrushchev became a warm defender of Tito only when this began to suit his purpose.

He made his allegations against Beria as the culprit in the break with Yugoslavia while in Belgrade in June, 1955.—B. N./1964.

rector of the Tiflis branch of the Marx-Engels-Lenin Institute. In addition, the report mentions the struggle that Beria waged "for a number of years" against an "outstanding figure in the Communist Party and the Soviet state, Sergei Ordzhonikidze," and speaks of Beria's "terroristic acts" against "members of Ordzhonikidze's family and his close friends."

The most striking feature of the list of victims mentioned in the indictment is that all of them perished in 1937–38, during the Purge, when Beria was secretary of the Central Committee of the Georgian Communist Party. The report does not mention a single act of terrorism during the subsequent period, that is, during the fifteen years from 1938 to 1953, when Beria headed the NKVD-MVD of the U.S.S.R. It should not be assumed that no acts of terror were committed in Georgia during these fifteen years. The terror machine was no less efficient there than in other parts of the country; during the war there were many arrests, deportations, and executions in Georgia. But the victims were all ordinary citizens, not members of the Communist elite, or if there were any Communists among them, they were victimized not *qua* Party members. The Tiflis trial, however, like all the other post-Stalinist trials, was concerned only with the victimization of members of the elite. In their internecine conflict, the members of the top Party leadership *vie* with each other in currying favor with the elite, and the different rival groups try to slough off onto their opponents the responsibility for all the wrongs of the past. No one thus far has raised the question of the persecution of ordinary citizens. At any rate, there has been no mention of it in the press.

The only persecution of members of the Party elite in Georgia during the whole of this fifteen-year period occurred in 1952, when Charkviani, secretary of the Georgian Central Committee from 1939 to 1952, Rapava, then Minister of Internal Affairs for the Georgian Republic, and others were removed from their posts and arrested, after being accused of nationalism at the Georgian Party conference of April, 1952. The blow was struck by Rukhadze, then Minister of State Security in Georgia and a long-time associate of Beria. At that time, Rukhadze was trying to switch over to the camp of Ignatiev, Riumin, and Poskrebyshev, who had gained control of the MGB in Moscow. This attempt failed; he was unable to gain the confidence of Poskrebyshev and Riumin, was soon dismissed from his post (June or July, 1952), and then arrested. Some of Beria's men arrested at that time, for example, Charkviani, whose name has not appeared in the newspapers since 1952, perished even before Stalin's death. But it was impossible to pin responsibility for their liquidation on Beria, since it was obvious that this was the beginning of a major campaign against Beria himself, the organizer of which was Poskrebyshev. He was aided by Khrushchev and Bulganin, who carried the struggle against Beria to a victorious end even after Poskrebyshev himself disappeared from the scene right after Stalin's death.

Thus, apart from the 1952 episode and the Purge of 1937–38, there were no reprisals against the Communist elite in Georgia during the period of Beria's ascendancy in Georgia. This was a peculiar feature of his policy.

Beria came to power in Georgia at the end of 1931—after the Central Committee of the CPSU, on October 31, 1931, had accepted his report on the existence of "political deviations" in the Communist organizations of Transcaucasia. With this report—which, along with the Central Committee resolution on it, was never made public—Beria, until then the OGPU chief of Transcaucasia, ousted the leadership of both the Transcaucasian Territorial Committee and the Central Committee of the Georgian Communist Party. He took over the post of secretary of both these centers, replacing Orakhelashvili, for whose execution in 1935 Beria has now been held responsible.

In connection with the Tiflis trial, there have been reports in the foreign press that Orakhelashvili was one of those Georgian "deviationists" who opposed Stalin's nationalities policy. This is a gross error. The fight against deviationists in Georgia was led by Ordzhonikidze, Stalin's viceroy for Transcaucasia until 1926. His methods in doing this were such that Lenin called him a "chauvinist Derzhimorda"* and demanded that he be brought to trial before a Party tribunal. Orakhelashvili, who had been associated with Ordzhonikidze before the Revolution, became particularly close

* Derzhimorda is the name of a boorish policeman in Gogol's play *Revizor* (*The Inspector General*).—Ed.

to him during the Civil War in the North Caucasus (in 1917–18, Orakhelashvili lived in Vladikavkaz), and was his close collaborator in the first years of the Bolshevization of Georgia. Ordzhonikidze made Orakhelashvili chairman of the Council of People's Commissars of the Transcaucasian Federation (1922–26); then, when Ordzhonikidze was called to Moscow, Orakhelashvili succeeded him as head of the Party apparatus in Transcaucasia and Georgia (1926–31). It is obvious from this that Orakhelashvili was no more a deviationist than Ordzhonikidze himself. Orakhelashvili was a faithful henchman of Ordzhonikidze—as were the rest of the Georgian Communists named in the report of the Tiflis trial.

From November, 1931, as secretary of the Transcaucasian Territorial Committee and the Georgian Central Committee, Beria became *de facto* boss of Transcaucasia, particularly Georgia. He quickly gained complete control over the entire Party machine, filling all the leading posts with his own men. The Party apparatus was purged not only of known oppositionists, but also of people who were suspected of insufficient devotion to Beria personally. Beria kept a firm grip on the apparatus thus created by him. He allowed oppositionists and people he considered insufficiently reliable to work only in the government apparatus—and even then only under careful control.

In 1937–38, during the Yezhovshchina, Beria of course carried out a bloody purge in Georgia, perhaps an even more ruthless and certainly a more thorough one than in other parts of the Soviet Union. Apparently, the number of show trials, and evidently the number of executions as well, were also higher than the national average. But Beria disposed of his victims according to a carefully-thought-out plan, striking at groups of the Party elite and of the population as a whole only when it was to his advantage. Consequently, the purge, rather than weakening the Party apparatus, strengthened it and enhanced Beria's authority in it even more. When Yezhov in Moscow demanded a purge of Beria's Georgian apparatus, Beria rose to its defense and in the ensuing struggle crushed Yezhov.

Beria could act this way only because he evidently knew he could count on Stalin's support, whose highly favorable opinion of Beria dated back to the early years of Soviet Georgia. At the same time,

Stalin's attitude was one of the main reasons why Yezhov, and especially Poskrebyshev—the real godfather of the Great Purge—tried to undermine Beria. They were aware that Beria was on the way toward becoming Stalin's favorite, and they knew that this spelled danger for them.

I cannot here touch upon all the twists and turns in this bitter struggle, but it seems to me that what I have said makes it clear why the organizers of the Tiflis trial, who were eager to show the Georgian Party elite that Beria had been responsible for persecuting them, were forced to reach so far into the past. Whereas Riumin was shot for acts committed in 1952–53, and Abakumov was accused of persecutions carried out in 1949, the defendants at the Tiflis trial were charged with acts committed in 1937–38. It was difficult to bring any plausible charges for the following fifteen-year period. Beria looked after his elite and there is evidence that he did in fact enjoy a certain popularity among it. It was only during the period of the Great Purge that Beria could be shown to have committed "acts of terror" against members of the Party elite in Georgia.

However, the Purge still rankles more than anything else in the minds of the Party elite of the U.S.S.R. as a whole. It shook them so severely and so depleted their ranks that even today there is hardly a top-ranking Party dignitary who does not have terrible memories of that period. Many of these officials, moreover, had personal experience of the criminal methods of investigation now mentioned in the Tiflis report. At the same time, there are people at the top level of the dictatorship who are, to a greater or lesser extent, responsible for the Purge.

All this explains not only why, in order to discredit Beria in the eyes of the Georgian Party leaders, it was necessary to conjure up the ghosts of the Purge victims; it also explains why the dictatorship had to keep the Tiflis trial secret from the rest of the U.S.S.R. The Soviet leaders have summoned up specters of which they themselves are afraid, for even the cases cited in the report of the Tiflis trial prove that Beria does not bear sole responsibility for these persecutions. A large share of the responsibility rests with the present leadership, to say nothing of Stalin himself.

This can best be demonstrated by the case of Orakhelashvili.

The fact is that he was shot not in Tiflis, which was then Beria's realm, but in Moscow, to which Beria's writ did not yet extend. Moreover, he was sentenced to death by the Military Tribunal of the Supreme Court of the U.S.S.R., that is, by the same court which has now passed the sentences in the Tiflis trial. He was not executed alone, but together with seven other prominent Communists, of whom the majority, among them Yenukidze, Karakhan, Larin, Sheboldaev, Shteiger, and others, had no connection with Georgia or Transcaucasia. (Their sentences were announced in *Pravda* on December 20, 1937.) The reasons for grouping such diverse individuals became apparent several months later; it seems that these December executions were merely the prelude for the big trial of Rykov, Bukharin, and others.

Some of the false evidence against Orakhelashvili, as well as against some of the other defendants, was undoubtedly obtained by Beria and his agents with the help of "illegal" methods of investigation. It is no less certain that evidence against all the others who were executed was obtained by similar methods. In discrediting the evidence in the Orakhelashvili affair, the report of the recent Tiflis trial acknowledges the fraudulent nature of the verdict in the case of Yenukidze,* Karakhan, and others—and consequently of the verdicts in the subsequent trial of Rykov and Bukharin.

Even more interesting conclusions emerge from an analysis of the information about the death of Ordzhonikidze. The Tiflis report states that Beria collected "slanderous material" and "intrigued" against Ordzhonikidze. This is, of course, quite probable, but it would have had no bearing on the fate of Ordzhonikidze unless his liquidation had been part of Stalin's plans. Ordzhonikidze, originally a friend and supporter of Stalin, had done much to help him gain power. But in the 1930's, Ordzhonikidze gradually began to oppose Stalin for resorting to the firing squad in the struggle against oppositionists. One fact serves as irrefutable proof of Stalin's deep irritation with Ordzhonikidze. At the end of October, 1936, Ordzhonikidze celebrated his fiftieth birthday. There were many speeches and messages, but none from Stalin. Ordzhonikidze also failed to receive the Order of Lenin, traditionally awarded to all leaders on

* See pp. 218 ff. for an extensive discussion of the Yenukidze case.—Ed.

such anniversaries. The reason will be clear if we bear in mind that not long before, the Politburo, largely on Ordzhonikidze's initiative, had reached a decision to rescind the decree of the Military Tribunal of the Supreme Court of the U.S.S.R. ordering the trial of Rykov and Bukharin. It was for this reason that Stalin was furious with Ordzhonikidze.

It is not possible here to analyze all the data on the case of Ordzhonikidze, whose liquidation is one of the most important elements in the present Kremlin struggle over the Great Purge. But the fact that the current Soviet leadership has spoken of this matter in public statements on the Beria affair, and now on the Tiflis case, can only be regarded as an indication of the keen interest in the fate of Ordzhonikidze among wide circles of the Party elite. The fact that the Soviet leaders have kept the report of the Tiflis trial from the rest of the Soviet Union will not be of much help to them. Behind the Iron Curtain, rumors circulate more widely and rapidly than is imagined abroad; and in these rumors the question of Ordzhonikidze's death will undoubtedly loom very large.

The Tiflis trial was the first of the post-Stalin trials in which the question of the Great Purge has been raised. To be sure, it was raised very cautiously and faintheartedly, but the important thing is that it has been raised at all. Now that this bloody specter of the recent past has been conjured up, it will be very difficult, if not impossible, for the regime to bury it again.

The New Committee of
State Security*

THE Supreme Soviet's ratification of its Presidium's decree (April 26, 1954) setting up a special Committee of State Security under the Council of Ministers of the U.S.S.R., has attracted relatively little attention in the Western press. This has generally been interpreted as a routine administrative reorganization, and Soviet citizens will continue to be arrested in precisely the same way as before. Such an interpretation is, I believe, both erroneous and harmful, since it prevents an understanding of the growing dangers of the situation. Of course Soviet citizens will continue to be arrested—as many of them as the authorities decree. But changes are nevertheless taking place at No. 2 Dzerzhinsky Square† in Moscow, and very important changes they are.

* This article appeared in *Sotsialistichesky Vestnik,* June, 1954.

† The address of the Lubianka, the headquarters of the Soviet secret police.—Ed.

The new Committee of State Security is not simply a refurbished model of the old Ministry of State Security (MGB). There are many indications that the new Committee will be much more active and dangerous than any of its predecessors: the Cheka, OGPU, NKVD, or MGB. In this instance, the change of name really means a change of substance and gives a clue to the correct interpretation of the changed nature of the tasks with which the new Committee is charged.

Why was it necessary to change the name? Why is the new agency not called a Ministry as hitherto, but a *committee* of State Security? To answer these questions, we have to examine the difference in status between ministries and committees under the Council of Ministers.

The creation of committees or chief administrations under the Council of Ministers (formerly the Council of People's Commissars), is not new. The practice was dictated by a proliferation of important tasks which did not somehow fit into the normal framework of government machinery. A special committee or chief administration under the Council of Ministers lent great flexibility to a new agency whose terms of reference were initially not precisely defined. At the same time, putting such a new agency *under* the Council of Ministers enabled the head of the Council to supervise the work of the new outfit and, if necessary, intervene in it.

Consequently, the number of such committees and chief administrations, always considerable, increased, particularly during the war years, when the government was faced with many new tasks. Vyshinsky, in his *Law of the Soviet State* (Moscow, Academy of Sciences Publishing House, 1938, p. 351), listed only eleven committees and chief administrations which were set up under the Council of People's Commissars in the first months after the adoption of the new Constitution (1936). Boris Meissner lists fifty-seven such agencies functioning between 1941 and 1953 (*Europa-Archiv*, Frankfurt/Main, No. 10–11, 1953). Of course, many of them were both temporary and short-lived. Nonetheless, these figures serve to illustrate the extraordinary growth of this practice.

However, the importance of these committees and their status in the machinery of the regime varies greatly. The heads of only a few of them are full members of the Council of Ministers, the one in question being specified in Article 70 of the Constitution. In the governmental machinery these committees rank no lower, and sometimes even higher, than ordinary ministries.

This has been particularly true in recent years. On the eve of the session of the Supreme Soviet, in April, 1954, the heads of only two committees were members of the Council of Ministers, and a look at the functions of the two committees in question—the State Planning Committee and the Committee for Construction Affairs— helps us to understand the general principle in accordance with which certain agencies are described as committees rather than ministries. The sphere of activities of those committees whose heads qualify for membership in the Council of Ministers is very wide and their functions are very varied. But if we try to pinpoint the feature which distinguishes them from ordinary ministries, we find it is their *supradepartmental* character. They are responsible to the Council of Ministers for the over-all planning, the coordination, and supervision of certain aspects of the work of all the other ministries. Both the State Planning Committee and the Committee for Construction Affairs have the right to intervene in the work of other ministries in all relevant matters. And all disputes are referred to the Council of Ministers as a whole.

The new Committee for State Security has been set up as an agency of this type with very wide powers. No information about the composition or the scope of this committee has as yet been published, but everything suggests that it has been set up in this form, under the Council of Ministers, because it has been given supradepartmental powers analogous to those of the State Planning Committee, i.e., it will be responsible for coordinating all intraministerial organs concerned with state security—a kind of super-MGB.

Why this change? What necessitated the creation of this supreme directorate for state security?

Of course, this change was not prompted by any change in the work of the security services inside the country. There the MGB had virtually unlimited powers. No authority, except the Communist Party Central Committee, could encroach upon its sphere, and in fact the MGB itself defined its own sphere of activity. Intervention by the MGB in the affairs of other ministries has always been common, and the ministries as well as the highest officials have always been under the strictest surveillance of the MGB. The resentment over this MGB activity was one of the major reasons for the almost solid front against Beria. And insofar as there is any change in the status of the MGB inside the country, it is a question of the diminution rather than increase in the powers of the MVD as a whole (compared with 1953, when it was still run by Beria), and of the security services in particular. Of course, these services will still find plenty to do inside the country itself, and there is no reason to think that the dictatorship will cease its terroristic activity against the population.

The functions of the MGB, however, even in the past, were not confined to the territory of the U.S.S.R. itself. Its tentacles extended far beyond the Soviet borders into every country in the world. It is here, in the MGB's activities abroad, that we must seek the reason for its recent reorganization.

The secret operations of the Soviet dictatorship outside its borders are by no means confined to mere espionage, however important that may be. The foreign press, by emphasizing espionage in writing about the work of Soviet agents, gives readers a false picture. But in fact espionage, for all its importance, occupies a secondary place in the regime's secret work abroad. Much more important is the business of *influencing public opinion abroad* in such a way as to promote the political aims of the Soviet regime.

Stalin defined the major tasks of this work as far back as thirty years ago, when he wrote that "struggle, conflicts, and wars among our enemies [and to him, all the countries of the non-Communist world were enemies]—these are our greatest allies." Stalin meant not only conflicts *among* the various non-Communist countries, but also conflicts *within* these countries. He believed that all such conflicts sowed confusion in the non-Communist world, thus reducing its capacity to resist Soviet aggression. Hence, it was quite natural to conclude that it was necessary not only to exploit already-existing conflicts, but also to provoke new ones. In short, the basic aim of Soviet undercover work abroad was the creation of fifth columns.

In essence, Soviet secret activity abroad was regarded by the Soviet leaders as the preparation and organization of social and political *subversion of the enemy's rear*. For such subversive activity, the most useful element frequently is not the Communist, whose sphere of influence in each individual country is a known quantity and whose support Moscow takes for granted. Much more important are the groups, organizations, and parties which officially profess to be non-Communist or even anti-Communist, but which, under the influence of secret Soviet agents, adopt an attitude that objectively serves the aim of Soviet policy.

The choice of personnel directing secret work abroad is governed by this primary objective. It was only in the remote pre-Stalin past that the regime recruited its agents solely among people sympathetic to Communism. During the last twenty years or so, the situation has radically changed. Today, there are only a few genuine, convinced Communists in the upper echelons of the foreign Communist parties. They are being squeezed out more and more by unscrupulous, venal but clever adventurers—"all-party scoundrels" (to use the term coined by Martov). This sort of man by his very nature has no positive ideals, never had any, and cannot have any. He is himself a product of social decay, and he corrupts everything he touches. This is what makes him so valuable to the Soviet dictatorship. The destructive nature of Soviet secret work abroad demands men of this type.

These are the troubled waters in which the Soviet Union casts its nets. The MGB has always played a leading role in this secret foreign work, though it never had a monopoly. The Soviet regime has always conducted its undercover work along diversified lines by setting up parallel networks. The MGB headed the principal one, but it had rivals, and the rivalry often led to friction which at times played havoc with the regime's secret work abroad. In the postwar years the friction was particularly great.

The two main centers of Soviet secret work abroad, apart from the MGB, are the military intelligence services and the foreign section of the Central Committee Secretariat. The foreign operations of the military intelligence units, which were reduced almost to zero during the Great Purge (all the military attachés and their staffs were apparently wiped out), were revived during and even more so after the war on a large scale. A major factor in this revival was the creation of the military police in the armies of occupation, which is still for all practical purposes in full control of the occupied countries, although, for considerations of higher policy, it is often compelled to act behind the scenes. The result has been not only a colossal growth of this police apparatus, but also a vast increase in its influence, whereas the role of its predecessor, the old Razvedupr (Intelligence Administration of the People's Commissariat for Defense), had been negligible. It is no coincidence that almost all the major posts in the Political Administration of the Ministry of Defense are now held by generals of the military police—such as Zheltov, Kuznetsov, etc. The Ministry of Defense itself is held by Bulganin, a Chekist of long standing who was mainly concerned with secret-police matters during the war and who was closely connected with the organization of the military police, doing everything in his power to give it a position of strength and influence. From the Soviet-occupied areas, this military police has extended its power into the western areas of Germany and Austria, as well as into the countries of the Western democracies—France, Italy, Switzerland, Scandinavia, etc.

A substantial role in Soviet undercover work is also played by the Foreign Section of the Central Committee Secretariat of the CPSU. This section had always influenced the activities of the vast secret network of the Comintern, and has, since the dissolution of the Comintern in 1943, formally taken over its activities. Foreign Communists and the top leaders in Moscow refer to this former Comintern network simply as the *apparat;* everyone understands what is meant.

The construction of this vast and complex network began in the early days of the Comintern. By now it has a long and even more complex history; and to understand it one has to be something of a sociologist or criminologist. At first, the *apparat* depended on foreign Communists, and it was Moscow's "eye," watching the internal affairs of foreign Communist parties in order to prevent the emergence of anti-Moscow sentiments. But later it became an organization gathering in and around itself the very flower of the "all-party scoundrels."

Beria tried very hard to bring this *apparat* under his aegis, and once Malenkov lost control of the Secretariat of the Central Committee and it came under the control of Zhdanov (late in 1946), Beria achieved his goal: jurisdiction over the *apparat* was transferred from the Foreign Section of the Central Committee Secretariat to the MGB. But Beria's victory was not permanent, and even he, try as he might, could not keep the *apparat* in his hands once Malenkov returned to a dominant position in the Central Committee and began to step up the "peace movement." The help of a network of international "all-party scoundrels" was vital for this work, and control of it reverted to the hands of the Central Committee Secretariat.

Space does not permit a full account of the events of 1951–53, which is essential to an understanding of the recently formed Committee of State Security. I can only give the main outline.

The struggle among various Soviet secret networks outside the U.S.S.R. ended in victory for the military police—which had the support of the Foreign Section of the Party Central Committee—over the MGB. Abakumov, Minister of State Security and one of Beria's men, disappeared in the winter of 1951–52. He was replaced by Ignatiev, a stooge of the Party apparatus. The trial of Slansky and other Czech Communists directly linked with Beria and the fabrication of the doctors' plot were typical expressions of Ignatiev's policy. These developments were a direct threat to Beria himself.

The death of Stalin, who had evidently supported Beria's opponents, altered the situation, but only temporarily. During the first months, Beria was at the pinnacle of power and he began to purge his enemies. The doctors' plot was exposed for what it was, the doctors themselves were solemnly rehabilitated, and some of the instigators of the affair were ousted. But in June, Beria was arrested and his henchmen in the security apparatus were given short shrift.

Other issues also played a major role in this fight, but all evidence seems to indicate that the decisive factors were those connected with the secret work abroad. The Committee of State Security has been entrusted with coordination of this secret work. The Committee is supposed to put an end to interdepartmental strife and to establish a uniform policy. In this context, the person of the chairman, Ivan Alexandrovich Serov, Colonel General of State Security, takes on special interest.

Serov has been called an old Chekist. This is quite true, of course, since Serov has been connected with the regime's terror machine for the last thirty years. The description is inadequate, however. Serov is not simply a Chekist, he is one of the most important figures in the group of Chekists that made its career while working in Stalin's personal secretariat under Poskrebyshev and Malenkov (who, in the 1930's, was Poskrebyshev's closest collaborator). Tokaev says in his memoirs* that Serov was chiefly responsible for the execution of Tukhachevsky and his co-defendants. This is quite true; it was Serov, on the instructions of Poskrebyshev, who prepared and carried out the bloody purge of the Army in 1937–38.†

Serov's active part in the Great Purge was by no means limited to the Tukhachevsky affair. He headed the "special sector" of the NKVD, which, working on direct instructions from Stalin's personal secretariat, was given the most responsible assignments connected with the liquidation of Stalin's major adversaries. But his role in the Tukhachevsky affair, and the purge of the Army in general, are

---

* Grigory Tokaev, *Betrayal of an Ideal* (Bloomington, Ind.: Indiana University Press, 1955).

† Marshal Tukhachevsky was tried in 1937, along with a number of other Army commanders, on trumped-up charges that he was plotting against the Soviet regime. He was accused of being in league with the Germans. The case was based on faked documents given to the Russians by the Nazis and on the false testimony of a double agent, one General Skoblin. Stalin seized on this evidence to do away with potential Army opposition to his foreign policy. Between 1937 to 1939, seven deputies of the People's Commissar for Defense disappeared. Of the fourteen commanders of the military districts listed for May, 1937, only one—Budyonny—was left by the end of 1938. Of the fifteen Army commanders of the first and second rank whose appointments were announced in 1935, only two died natural deaths: Shaposhnikov and Kamenev. (Kamenev was posthumously accused and his remains were removed from the Kremlin wall; he has since been rehabilitated.) The other thirteen were denounced as "mad dogs." In all military and naval establishments, in all departments and sections of the People's Commissariat of Defense, etc., there were at least two complete changes of high-ranking personnel during these two years of purge. The number of middle- and lower-rank commanders who disappeared in those years must be counted in the *tens* of thousands.

Marshal Tukhachevsky was rehabilitated in 1957. This became known via the publication of the supplementary volume of the *Large Soviet Encyclopedia*. It was only in 1962–63, however, that true accounts about Tukhachevsky and his associates began to appear in the Soviet press.—B. N./1964.

especially important. Simultaneously with the Purge, new personnel was selected to take the place of the victims, and Serov, who played such a large part in the destruction not only of the military personnel of the old Soviet Army, but also of its political and police machinery, was one of the creators of the political and police sectors of the post-Yezhov army. And this post-Yezhov apparatus still exists.

Serov's work during the war as deputy chief of SMERSH, and then as political aide to the commander of the occupation armies in Germany, helped to strengthen the ties between Serov and the top officials of the military police. On the other hand, Serov has always maintained the closest ties with the leaders of the Party apparatus around Poskrebyshev. Stalin himself trusted him and personally gave him very responsible assignments. (Tokaev's memoirs provide interesting information on this subject also.)

Since Beria knew about Serov's ties, it is probable that he treated him with reserve and tried to keep him as far from Moscow as possible while at the same time entrusting him with responsible work (Washington, Berlin). That is why after the war, Serov was not assigned to the MGB but was given the post of First Deputy Minister of Internal Affairs. This was the post of deputy for political matters, but the Ministry itself was in charge of the nonpolitical departments of the old, unified NKVD. Serov was decorated in September, 1952, for his role in the building of the Volga-Don Canal, though there is little doubt that his interests were not limited to construction problems.

In view of what we know of Serov's past behavior, it should be clear that one cannot make any simple appraisal of his present attitude in the quarrels now raging among the Soviet leaders, especially since in the past he had worked closely both with Malenkov and with Khrushchev. New disputes always lead to new alliances. All we know for sure is that in the recent past, Serov was not in Beria's camp, and that he has had extremely close ties to the present heads of the military police.

This latter factor unquestionably influenced his selection for the chairmanship of a committee charged with coordinating and supervising the work of all Soviet bodies connected with security work outside the Soviet Union. In this, he has doubtless been invested with tremendous powers, particularly for coordinating the three main networks charged with sowing dissension in non-Communist countries.

What the *policy* of this work will be in the immediate future can easily be determined by anyone able to solve a political equation with one unknown factor. The newspapers provide the necessary data literally every day. In April and May, 1954, Pătrăscanu, the founder of the Romanian Communist Party and leader of its right wing, was executed in Romania, the case against Ana Pauker was reopened, and a series of trials against the leaders of Zionist organizations is in progress; in Hungary, P. Gabor, former Minister of Internal Affairs and a Beria man, has been brought to trial; in Czechoslovakia, trials are under way against Communists connected with Slansky, Clementis, etc. All these events are connected with the struggle among the various secret networks which ultimately led to the execution of Slansky and the liquidation of Abakumov. All were started in 1951–52, and all were suspended after the death of Stalin. Their resumption indicates a return to the reckless course pursued during the last months of Stalin's life—to the policy behind the Slansky trial and the doctors' plot.

The return to this policy does not yet signify a return to the *tactics* of the earlier period. Reports on these recent trials indicate that they are being conducted in a more restrained manner than the Slansky trial. If my appraisal of the present situation is correct, we may conclude that the regime is pursuing its aims more cautiously than in the period preceding Stalin's death. But the basic policy remains the same.

The creation of the Committee of State Security means that the dictatorship has decided to take the offensive against the non-Communist world.

FOUR

The Process of
De-Stalinization

Khrushchev's "Secret Speech"*

THE publication by the State Department of Khrushchev's "secret speech" on the crimes of Stalin at a closed session of the Twentieth Congress of the CPSU on February 24–25, is an event of tremendous importance.

The authenticity of the document is indisputable; even Moscow does not deny it. True, there is reason to believe that the text as circulated is not complete, that it omits a number of passages dealing with aspects of Stalin's activities about which his present heirs are particularly touchy. It is more than likely that this is so, since the State Department got the text from Communists outside the Soviet Union in a version prepared by the Secretariat of the CPSU's Central Committee for the information of the leaders of the "frater-

* This article appeared in *Sotsialistichesky Vestnik,* June, 1956. The author also wrote some detailed notes on Khrushchev's secret speech. These were published in *The New Leader* supplement "The Crimes of the Stalin Era," 1962.—Ed.

nal" parties, in whom, as we know, Moscow does not place boundless trust. For this reason it is certain that the document sent abroad was subjected to strict censorship.

It is likely that a particularly large number of cuts was made in the section dealing with Soviet foreign policy, into the secrets of which Moscow is highly reluctant to initiate foreigners, even if they are Communists. That would explain the lack of details about Stalin's relations both with Mao's China and Tito's Yugoslavia, although Khrushchev cannot possibly have ignored this question altogether in his speech. It would also explain the report's complete silence about Stalin's bloody purges of non-Soviet Comintern *apparatchiks,* although Khrushchev was speaking at the very moment when it had been decided to rehabilitate the Polish, Hungarian, and other Communists liquidated during the Great Purge. But there must also have been cuts in sections of the speech dealing with internal affairs. For instance, in talking about the purges in the Army, Khrushchev cannot have failed to mention, if not Tukhachevsky,* then at least Bluecher and Yegorov, who have now, according to *Voprosy Istorii,* been rehabilitated. A close study of the text as published reveals clear traces of the blue pencil.

In short, the version we have of what Khrushchev told the Twentieth Congress is not complete, but what there is is more than sufficient to justify the tremendous impact it has made abroad, and particularly, in Russia itself. It is extremely important not only for the Stalinist past, but, since today's rulers are all "disciples and close comrades-in-arms" of the fallen idol—of whom Khrushchev himself was by no means the least prominent—it is also of the highest importance for an understanding of the Soviet present. In describing Stalin's activity in the past, Khrushchev, even when he names no other names, throws light on the part played by some of his closest associates in certain of his actions in which they are known to have been involved. One only has to collate what Khrushchev now says with facts known from other sources. This is, of course, difficult, since Khrushchev often speaks of events which remain very obscure or have never even been mentioned in public

---

* At the time this article was written, Tukhachevsky had not yet been rehabilitated. See also "The New Committee of State Security," pp. 188 ff.—Ed.

before. The style of the speech is also typical of Khrushchev. To the uninitiated he gives an impression of great candor. He appears to be unburdening himself completely, even bringing out facts which are unfavorable to him personally. But in fact this is not so. The mask of candor and simplicity conceals the shrewd calculation of a man who knows his audience and knows how to sway it by playing on its susceptibilities, manipulating the facts to his own best advantage, and hence trying to mold public opinion for his own specific purpose.

In his speech about Stalin, however, Khrushchev's task is by no means easy, mainly because he is pursuing mutually incompatible aims. He is trying to put *all* the blame for past crimes and blunders on Stalin alone, and simultaneously he is trying to vindicate all the major policies pursued by Stalin for decades. The trouble with Stalin, to listen to Khrushchev, was not so much the criminal nature of his policies, nor indeed the criminal methods which he used in pursuit of them, but only the defects of his personality, which in the last twenty years of his life had taken on paranoiac and megalo-manic proportions. It was these traits which, according to Khrush-chev, changed Stalin from a man with an outstanding record of service to the Party and the cause of revolution into a half-mad despot who rode roughshod over the opinion of his associates and began to destroy loyal Party members, accusing them of all kinds of imaginary plots and assassination attempts.

This contradiction in Khrushchev's aims is a striking feature of his secret speech. Khrushchev does not say one word about the atrocities perpetrated by Stalin against non-Communists and the nation as a whole. He is concerned with the terror only insofar as it involved Communists, and in Khrushchev's eyes Stalin's chief crime, the one at the root of all the others, was his flouting of the "Leninist principles" of "collective leadership." Khrushchev com-pletely ignores the indisputable fact that it was the unbridled terror against the population in the years of collectivization (1929–33) and the destruction of millions of completely innocent people from all walks of life which created the atmosphere in the country, and particularly in the Party, without which there could have been no purge. Khrushchev closes his eyes to the fact that the trials of "wreckers," Mensheviks, and others, in 1930–31 paved the way for the big show trials of the Yezhovshchina, just as the torture by the Cheka of large groups of non-Party specialists and professional people was an essential prelude to Stalin's liquidation of the "Leningrad center" of Bukharinites, of the Sverdlovsk "insurrectionary staff" of Kabakov, and of similar cases mentioned by Khrushchev.

All the facts cited by Khrushchev concern Stalin's persecution of Communists only (with the sole exception of the doctors' plot framed in 1952, and although the doctors may not have been Communists they had Communist leaders as their patients). And this is the key to Khrushchev's whole position: He would like to turn the political downgrading of Stalin into an internal Party affair, excluding all "outsiders." To judge from reports from Moscow, Khrushchev's attempt seems doomed to failure; his revelations have already gone beyond the ranks of Communist Party organizations and have become common knowledge—at least in Moscow. And the facts Khrushchev cites are so telling that no amount of commentary by Party propagandists can stop the people from drawing their own conclusions. Khrushchev's intention was to indict Stalin only for what he had done to Communists, but in fact he has struck a blow at the very basis of the terrorist practices of the Communist regime. In trying to prove that the remedy for past evils is to be found in the principle of "collective leadership," he has actually given grounds for concluding that there must be an end to Party dictatorship, which is the real root of the evil, and that true democracy based on elementary political freedom should be introduced.

The most important part of Khrushchev's speech is, of course, his recital of facts about Stalin's crimes. But here, too, one has to be cautious, since not everything can be taken at face value: There are many distortions, and the general picture which Krushchev tries to draw is not only inaccurate but often mendacious. Nevertheless, he offers much material that can, if properly interpreted, provide the basis for a serious history of the Stalin era.

Khrushchev touches on various periods of Stalin's career, beginning with 1922–23, the time of his sharp clashes with the ailing Lenin, and ending with 1953, when the Kremlin doctors were arrested on Stalin's order and made to give false confessions under torture. But most of all, Khrushchev concentrates on the period of the Great Purge. In my opinion, the most important revelation concerns the telegram sent by Stalin and Zhdanov from Sochi ordering the dismissal of Yagoda because of his incompetence in "unmasking the Trotskyite-Zinovievite bloc," and his replacement by Yezhov as head of the NKVD. The telegram stressed that the NKVD *"is four years behind in this matter"* (my italics) and added that "this is noted by all Party workers and the majority of the representatives of the NKVD."* Because this document is so important for an understanding of the Purge, I shall comment on it in some detail.

The Stalin-Zhdanov telegram was sent from Sochi on September 25, 1936. The following day, Yezhov's appointment was officially announced by the Presidium of the Soviet Central Executive Committee; and this, reported in *Pravda* and *Izvestia* on September 27 was the signal for the beginning of the Purge. Even more important than this confirmation of Stalin's direct part in the Yezhovshchina are the words of the telegram saying that the NKVD was four years behind in the matter. This shows that Stalin felt that a major purge was overdue. But why exactly by *four* years?

We can find the answer by looking at what had happened four years before the dispatch of the telegram—i.e., in October, 1932. From September 28 to October 2, 1932, a Central Committee Plenum was in session. The official communiqué issued at the end of this meeting spoke only of discussions on Soviet trade, production of consumer goods, and the development of heavy industry. But in actual fact, these issues were not central to the Plenum. The main question, about which there was a stormy debate was *whether or not the death penalty should be applied to the leaders of the Riutin opposition group,* who had been arrested shortly before. (For details, see the *Letter of an Old Bolshevik,* pp. 26 ff, and the chapters on Stalin and Kirov, pp. 69 ff.) The Riutin group was accused of drawing up a strongly anti-Stalin memorandum.

* The full telegram, as quoted by Khrushchev, reads: "We deem it absolutely necessary and urgent that Comrade Yezhov be nominated to the post of the People's Commissar for Internal Affairs. Yagoda has definitely proved himself to be incapable of unmasking the Trotskyite-Zinovievite bloc. The OGPU is four years behind in this matter. This is noted by all party workers and by the majority of the representatives of the NKVD." ("The Crimes of the Stalin Era," p. 23.)—Ed.

Stalin denounced this document as a call for his assassination and demanded the execution of Riutin and other leaders of the group as terrorists. But Stalin was thwarted, both in the NKVD, which claimed that it had no authority to take such action, and in the Politburo, where Kirov and Ordzhonikidze were particularly vehement in opposing execution. Finally, at the September 28– October 2 Plenum, Stalin's request was thrown out. On October 9, the Presidium of the Party's Central Control Commission (then headed by Rudzutak, also an opponent of execution) decreed the expulsion from the Party of all the leaders of the Riutin group and others close to it (among them Zinoviev and Kamenev) and their imprisonment.

Stalin continued to fight this decision vigorously, and at the next Plenum (January 7–12, 1933), he again raised the issue of the death penalty in cases involving opposition groups within the Party, this time in connection with the case of Eismont, Smirnov, and others.* Again, both in the Politburo and at the Plenum, Stalin was defeated by a solid majority. His main opponents were Kirov, Ord-zhonikidze, and Kuibyshev, who were supported by Kalinin and Kossior; Andreyev, Voroshilov, and even Molotov vacillated. Only Kaganovich stanchly supported Stalin throughout.

Thus we see that beyond any doubt Stalin and Zhdanov, in speaking of a four-year delay, were thinking back to the grand debate of the winter of 1932–33 between Stalin and Kaganovich (Zhdanov at that time was not in the Politburo), and Kirov, Ord-zhonikidze, and other members of the Politburo. Stalin demanded that measures be taken immediately to make up for lost time and that executions of his opponents in the Party begin at once.

Of course, during these four years—October, 1932, to October, 1936—Stalin had by no means been idle; he had been busily pre-paring his bloodbath since the summer, perhaps even the spring, of 1933, when he set up the special "Secret Commission of State

* A. P. Smirnov's underground group, with which Eismont and others were connected, opposed extensive industrialization, urged changes in the OGPU and the removal of Stalin from the Central Committee, and pressed other demands similar to those of the Bukharin group. The Smirnov group was uncovered at the end of 1932 and Smirnov, Eismont, and others were accused of having established an anti-Party faction.—Ed.

Security" in his personal secretariat. This commisison, kept secret even from members of the Politburo, was headed by the same Poskrebyshev whom Khrushchev fleetingly refers to as Stalin's faithful "shield-bearer," but whose real role was very much greater. At first, the commission included Yezhov, Agranov, and others, but its composition changed from time to time. Its actual chief was always Stalin. Kaganovich, it seems, was not in the commission, but he closely advised Stalin in all matters connected with it, and it was also he who under Stalin's direction drafted the new Party Rules for the Seventeenth Congress. The new rules (Khrushchev cites several of their hitherto secret clauses) eliminated the Central Control Commission, which had special rights and was nominally independent of the Central Committee. The new rules further helped clear the way for the Purge by providing for a new "Special Department" in the Central Committee, thus giving official status in the Party machinery, if not to the "Secret Commission of State Security" itself, then at least to certain of its functions.

In these same years, however, in which Stalin was preparing the Purge there was a rapidly growing mood in the Party—not least because of the famine of 1932–33 and Hitler's triumph in Germany (for which Stalin also bore great responsibility)—that it was time for a change both of Stalin's conduct of Party affairs and of his over-all policy as it had developed since 1928–29. At the Seventeenth Congress, the advocates of a change enjoyed the support of the great majority of the delegates, and this was reflected in the composition of the new Central Committee. The reforms of 1934–35 (the abolition of rationing, of the political departments of the Machine Tractor Stations, and then the new Constitution, whose real author was Bukharin) give a good idea of the policy of this new majority, which was led by Kirov.

This group had a majority at Central Committee Plenums and in the Politburo, but it was hamstrung by its fear of inner-Party strife, and many of them were convinced that a split in the Party would lead to a crisis the Soviet regime could not survive. Their strategy therefore was to work for a peaceful transfer of power in the Party apparatus to themselves. Kirov was to play a key role in this design by moving from Leningrad to Moscow and taking control of crucial departments of the Party apparatus.

All this was ended by Nikolaev's assassination of Kirov, organized by Stalin's Secret Commission of State Security just as Kirov was preparing to leave for Moscow.

Khrushchev adds little new to what we know of Kirov's assassination; what matters is not *what* he says but that it is *he* who says it. He confirms a previous account of the mysterious circumstances surrounding the death of Borisov, Kirov's bodyguard, and has set up a special commission to investigate the affair. There is no doubt that the Presidium of the Central Committee holds Stalin responsible for Kirov's assassination.

It is difficult at this point—twenty-one years after the event—to get reliable and legally valid evidence on the guilt of Stalin. But even before Khrushchev's speech there was sufficient evidence for the historian. But the fact that Khrushchev has now confirmed it greatly strengthens conclusions already drawn. It can now be definitely stated that Stalin, finding himself in a minority and with no hope of obtaining a majority in the Central Committee and in the Politburo, organized a plot against the Party majority. The assassination of Kirov, carried out on his orders, eliminated his most powerful opponents. The subsequent Great Purge, the Yezhovshchina, swept away anyone connected, however remotely, with those who proposed a radical change of policy. Stalin reaped his vengeance mercilessly and despicably, visiting his wrath even on descendants of the victims.

The Stalin Myth Exposed*

L ONG before its start, it was apparent that the Twentieth Congress of the CPSU—its first since Stalin's death—would be an
event of major historical significance. By the time it was over, it
had opened a new chapter in the history of the ruling party and of
the country as a whole.

The preparations for the Congress made it clear that it would not
only give its formal backing to the Khrushchev-Bulganin line in
foreign and domestic policy, but that it would also demonstrate
to the world that the Khrushchev-Bulganin bloc was, for the time
being, firmly in the saddle.

In the year preceding the Congress, Khrushchev, after getting
rid of Shatalin, Malenkov's man in the Central Committee Secretariat, had carried out a major, though apparently bloodless, purge,

* This version of the original article which appeared in the *Sotsialistichesky Vestnik,* April, 1956, is based on the one published in *The New Leader,*
April 23, 1956.—Ed.

down to the smallest units of the Party apparatus. According to G. P. Moroz of the Munich Institute for the Study of the U.S.S.R., in the last months before the Congress, 9,500 new secretaries, about 20 per cent of the total of all such secretaries, were appointed to primary Party organizations in the Ukraine; in Uzbekistan, the percentage was 36. The further up one went in the Party hierarchy, the greater the percentage of new appointments; in a number of provinces (*oblasts*), the secretaries of almost every district committee (*raikom*) were replaced.

Khrushchev appeared to have revamped the Party so thoroughly that the victory of his ruling faction at the Congress seemed a foregone conclusion. According to the data of the Congress Credentials Commission, 500 out of 1,355 delegates (37 per cent) had been promoted during the "Khrushchev period," and thus could be regarded as Khrushchev supporters.

But in the event, things turned out very differently. The Congress delegates displayed greater independence than anyone had expected, thus clearly showing that knowledge of the Stalinist past is insufficient for an understanding of post-Stalin developments. Furthermore, the Congress revealed that there are groups at the top which can successfully challenge the leaders of the Party apparatus.

Although information is still scanty, we know enough to see that instead of consolidating the Khrushchev-Bulganin bloc, the Congress saw the first signs of a rift. In fact, we may well ask whether the Khrushchev-Bulganin bloc still exists, or whether we are now faced with a completely new alignment of forces in the Kremlin.

The immediate cause of the rift was the issue of exposing Stalin and the form of the revelations, but this issue was as much a symptom as a cause.

Beria, as we know, had begun the de-Stalinization process right after Stalin's death, and the issue has plagued the regime ever since. The basic argument among the leaders, who were all agreed on the desirability of doing away with the excessive cult of Stalin and were concerned to show the country that they could rule without him, was about the *extent* to which Stalin should be reduced in stature. The changing attitude of the collective leadership during the last three years is reflected in the Soviet press by the frequency of references to Stalin, which increase in number when the leaders think it better to stick to the "tested traditions" of Stalin's policy, and decrease when they find it wiser to depart from them. Without going into detail, it is important for our present purposes to stress that in the year before the Congress, during which Khrushchev and Bulganin have been on top, there had been a sharp growth of such pro-Stalin sentiments. This was conspicuously so after the July, 1955, Plenum of the Central Committee, at which it was decided to convene the Twentieth Congress.

The fall and winter months of 1955–56 were taken up by two complementary campaigns: the Personnel Department of the Central Committee (headed then as now by A. B. Aristov) carried out a drastic purge of the local Party apparatus, replacing insufficiently reliable secretaries, and the Agitprop Department (then headed by P. N. Pospelov) started a massive drive in all propaganda media to "rehabilitate" Stalin. This, of course, was also an effort to strengthen Stalinist "traditions." On every conceivable occasion, the press referred to the Communist Party as "the Party of Marx, Engels, Lenin, and Stalin." Since the Central Committee Secretariat was headed by First Secretary Khrushchev, he was probably the guiding force behind this "creeping Stalinism."

The Congress, however, manifested a different spirit. To understand the about-face, we must trace its first indications. At the end of January, 1956, Stalin's name disappeared from the columns of *Pravda*. The last time it appeared in a lead article was on January 16. After that, it appeared once more—in a speech by Alexei Kirichenko at the Ukrainian Party Congress on January 19, reported in *Pravda* of January 23.

This was the last such mention of Stalin in *Pravda,* but not in the rest of the Soviet press. In other publications, especially in provincial papers, the glorification of Stalin went on right up to the opening of the Congress on February 14. In other words, the provincial press had received no instructions on a change in line from Pospelov, whereas in Moscow, Dmitri Shepilov, editor of *Pravda* and a Secretary of the Central Committee, who knew which way the wind was blowing, had halted the publication of pro-Stalin material.

These signs of a radical shift in the latter part of January must have been caused by two different factors: (1) developments in the regime's relations with the satellite countries, and (2) changed relations in the regime itself between military leaders and the police apparatus.

The situation of the Communist parties in the satellites is always precarious. There is scarcely a satellite regime that could stay in power without Soviet military might. The maintenance of the Soviet armed forces is a heavy burden for the people of the U.S.S.R., and the day when pro-Soviet governments in the people's democracies might stay in power on their own is not in sight. Attempts to lighten the burden of this military commitment were major aspects of the policies of Beria and, later, Malenkov, but they came to nothing. The political and police apparatus of the Soviet occupation armies gave major support to Bulganin and Khrushchev in their struggle for power, just as Khrushchev backed them in the winter of 1952–53, when they supported Stalin's reckless foreign-policy plans.

The problem of the satellites had another facet. As a condition for an agreement, Tito, at the Belgrade meeting with Khrushchev, Bulganin, and Mikoyan, demanded that the Kremlin openly admit the trumped-up nature of the charges brought at the trials of "Titoist traitors" in Hungary, Poland, Romania, and other countries. Tito would not accept a *sub rosa* rehabilitation of the victims of the trials of 1948–52. He wanted public rehabilitation and an admission of the guilt of those who organized the trials. This demand was reiterated when Mikoyan revisited Yugoslavia in the spring of 1955, and again in Moscow through the Yugoslav Ambassador at the beginning of 1956.

At this moment, Tito's influence in Moscow is very great, and every effort is made to secure his favor. Tito's conditions could not be brushed off, and they were discussed by the Presidium shortly before the Congress. The result was not merely the publication of a document rehabilitating the prewar leaders of the Communist Party of Poland,* but also a request to the Communist parties of Hungary, Romania, Bulgaria, Albania, and other countries for the immediate rehabilitation of the "Titoists" condemned in various trials.

* This document is not dated, but it was first published in *Trybuna Ludu* of February 19, 1956, which would indicate that it must have been approved on the eve of the Twentieth Congress.—B. N.

Complete rehabilitation of the victims of these 1948–52 frame-ups is impossible without revealing the part played in them by Stalin personally.

The pro-Stalin attitude of the Khrushchev-Bulganin bloc also came under attack just before the Twentieth Congress over a second issue—that of relations between the Party and the army. On this subject, there has been a lot of nonsense in the foreign press, in which Zhukov and Bulganin are described as old comrades-in-arms and personal friends. In fact, they are long-standing personal enemies and also, to some extent, "class enemies," insofar as there is now great tension in the Soviet Army between the military commanders and their police and political watchdogs. In 1942, under pressure from the former, Stalin was forced to abolish the system of political commissars, who had been so hated in the Army that many of them were killed in battle by their own men. The commissars were replaced by "political aides," who performed the same tasks, though during the war their authority was restricted. After the war, their authority increased, and with their and Bulganin's help, Stalin in 1945–48 carried out a brutal purge, which Army circles sardonically called "the purge of the heroes," since many of its victims were battle-scarred veterans who found it difficult to adjust to postwar life in the Army and were therefore the special object of political indoctrination. The Army, according to Stalin and Bulganin, had suffered a loss of ideological integrity during the war.

The "purge of the heroes" cost the Army dear. Former inmates of Soviet concentration camps now in the West say that this purge was much greater as far as number of victims is concerned than the Army purge of the 1930's, although it did not affect the top ranks as spectacularly.

As a result, relations between the Army commanders and the members of its political administration are as strained today as at the beginning of the war, and the bitter personal conflict between Bulganin and Zhukov typifies the general situation of the Army (see pp. 236 ff.). Zhukov's tremendous popularity throughout the country and in the Army, plus the intercession of several Politburo members (including Malenkov and, perhaps, Beria), saved his life. Such things are not forgotten.

In the summer of 1952, even before Stalin's death, however, Zhukov was recalled to Moscow, where—according to German sources —he occupied the relatively minor post of Defense Ministry representative to the cabinet of the Russian Soviet Republic (R.S.F.S.R.). When Stalin died, he became one of Bulganin's two Deputy Defense Ministers, and when the latter became Premier, he had to make Zhukov his Defense Minister. But for a whole year, Bulganin dealt badly with him at this post, not making him a Deputy Premier and excluding him from discussions of major political questions. Even within his Ministry, Zhukov found himself surrounded by Bulganin's appointees to the political and police apparatus, over which Zhukov could have no control.

Zhukov, whom postwar experience had made more cautious but who retained his great organizational talents and forceful personality, could not long endure this situation. He took advantage of the preparations for the Twentieth Congress to strike out against the Bulganinist political administration of his Ministry.

Pre-Congress Party conferences in the Army and Navy started in the first part of December. On December 16, *Krasnaya Zvezda,* the Defense Ministry paper, published a cautious editorial which referred sympathetically to the delegates who had already "sharply criticized the defects in Party-political work." All subsequent reports on the conferences underscored critical speeches of this type. There was only one report, given by Marshal Chuikov, occupation commander in East Germany before Stalin's death, which commented favorably on the work of the political administration.

The tenor of the criticism was that political propaganda was not specific enough, not sufficiently relevant to military training, and not coordinated with the work of the officers. This series of meetings culminated in the conference of the Moscow Military District, at which Zhukov himself spoke with unmistakable sympathy of the various critics of the political administration.

These reports on the eve of the Twentieth Congress dealt a severe blow to the political administration in the armed forces. The elections to the new Central Committee constituted a major concession to the military: Not a single member of the Army political administration was elected either a member or a candidate member of the Central Committee, an unprecedented event in the history of the Party. On the other hand, Zhukov was not only elected a member of the Central Committee, but also became first alternate member of the Presidium. This represented a complete victory for Zhukov over the political apparatus of the Army, the first such victory in Party history.

Zhukov's struggle against the Bulganinist political representatives was also directed against Bulganin as the guardian of "Stalinist traditions" in the political Army administration. This assault on Stalin was the most determined; as early as 1953, a new edition of the *Short Philosophical Dictionary* dropped all the passages of a previous edition in which Stalin's military role had been glorified. Zhukov and his colleagues knew better than anybody Stalin's worth as a military figure. They knew only too well how he had claimed the glory that rightfully belonged to others. As regards "Marshal" Bulganin, they only knew him as the one who had carried out the most sordid assignments of the late dictator, and it is this knowledge that underlies Zhukov's attitude toward Bulganin.

Although many other matters were doubtless involved when the Party Presidium considered the Stalin problem prior to the Congress, the position as regards Tito and the satellites and the Army situation were crucial in weighting the balance against the late despot—and against the initial resistance of the Khrushchev-Bulganin bloc. It was necessary to break with the dead Stalin in order to win Tito's friendship, vital for bettering the situation in the satellite countries, and in order to improve relations with the high command of the Soviet Army. Khrushchev and Bulganin obviously resisted all this, but undoubtedly suffered a defeat on both scores.

The most intransigent opponent of the policy was Bulganin; neither at the Congress nor after did he utter a single anti-Stalinist word or make a single gesture to indicate that he favored the campaign to expose Stalin. This is all the more understandable in that the issue of Stalin's military record directly involves Bulganin himself and that phase of his career which is central to his political biography.

Khrushchev's position was somewhat different. He, too, of course, did not particularly approve of the move to unmask Stalin, for he had an important role in the Purge. He is said to have talked about the precariousness of his own position at that time, but this claim does not stand up to examination. It is true that during the Purge the police arrested people almost indiscriminately, but by then Khrushchev already occupied a special position: As Secretary of the Moscow Regional Party Committee (*obkom*) he was therefore the chief organizer of the Purge in the Moscow region. It is true that even *obkom* secretaries were arrested at that time, but Khrushchev was not. He, Beria, and Zhdanov were the three *obkom* secretaries who not only did not fall victim to the Purge but made their careers because of it. Khrushchev was appointed Ukrainian Party Secretary in March, 1938, as a reward for two years of devoted service to Stalin in the merciless conduct of the Purge in Moscow.

Nevertheless, Khrushchev's behavior before and during the Congress shows that he was more flexible than Bulganin. It was only after Mikoyan's speech which precipitated the anti-Stalin mood of the Congress that Khrushchev went over to the anti-Stalinist camp and made his famous indictment of Stalin at a closed session.

It was this that split his alliance with Bulganin, and the rift will continue to widen. In fact, an alliance with Bulganin is probably no longer in Khrushchev's interest. Zhukov's successful campaign against the political administration shows how thoroughly detested Bulganin is in the Army. The "purge of the heroes" which he carried out less than ten years ago is still fresh in the memory of the Army commanders. Concentration-camp prisoners who have been released under recent amnesties serve as a constant reminder of the fate of those still in the camps. Since Bulganin has consistently sought to prevent a general amnesty, his unpopularity is bound to grow, and he is bound to become more and more of a liability to the collective leadership.

At the same time, as a result of the fierce controversy about Stalin, there must have arisen a group within the leadership which would like to carry the unmasking of Stalin to its logical conclusion —as a guarantee against any return to Stalinist practices. Mikoyan's statements in Pakistan show that the pre-Congress activity of Khrushchev and Bulganin aroused fears among some of the Soviet leaders of just such a return to Stalinism. Having learned from experience, they are inclined to regard an appeal to the entire Party and the people as the surest means of preventing such attempts in the future. Khrushchev's attack on Stalin has made them confident that he will not try any return to Stalinism. Their distrust of Bulganin, who has not committed himself on the subject of Stalin at all, must be all the greater.

There is another side to the whole question: Revelations about Stalin's crimes could well lead to an outbreak of indignation not only within the Party but among the people. Never enamored of the regime, the population has been kept in check by brutal terror, but the ever more bitter struggle within the Party organization with its 7 million members is obviously affecting the Komsomol with its 18.5 million members, through whom it will inevitably reach the whole population. The ferment has now been going on for three years, and the disclosure of Stalin's crimes is bound to be a powerful stimulus to the antiregime mood of the population, especially the youth, to which, significantly, a number of speakers at the Congress devoted particular attention.

The *Pravda* editorials of April 5 and 6 indicate there has already been a strong reaction throughout the country, which the Party leaders are trying to control. We shall see how successful they will be. A new page may well be opening in the tragic history of the peoples of the U.S.S.R.

The Rehabilitation of Yenukidze*

O N May 19, 1962, *Pravda* published a long article about A. S. Yenukidze, an Old Bolshevik who had served as the chief secretary of the Presidium of the Central Executive Committee of the Congress of Soviets from 1918 to 1935, and was later liquidated by Stalin as "an obvious enemy of the Soviet regime" and an agent of foreign imperialism. The *Pravda* article does not merely rehabilitate Yenukidze: It is an outright eulogy. After giving a rather detailed biographical sketch—in which Yenukidze incidentally is called a "charming person"—the author of the article notes with satisfaction that the "good name of the stanch Bolshevik" Yenukidze has now been completely restored. He goes on to assure his readers that "the Communist Party and the Soviet people profoundly revere his bright memory." Up to now, no Soviet paper has ever written in such glowing terms about any of the rehabilitated victims of the Stalinist terror.

* This article appeared in *Sotsialistichesky Vestnik*, May–June, 1962.

The unusual tone of the article is partially to be explained by the fact that it was written by L. S. Shaumian. This is the grandson of S. G. Shaumian, the head of the first Soviet government in Baku, who was shot by the English in 1918. Until his liquidation, Yenukidze was a close friend of the Shaumian family, and there is no doubt that this strongly influenced the young Shaumian. However, this article could not have appeared in *Pravda* without editorial approval. Hence the importance of the article as a document that not only throws light on the recent Stalinist past, but also helps us to understand the Khrushchevian present.

The influence of the Khrushchevian present makes itself felt in the way in which Yenukidze's "crime" of a quarter of a century ago has been defined. The *Pravda* article does its best to put all of Yenukidze's misfortunes at the door of the notorious "personality cult," the creation of which demanded among other things that Stalin, not Yenukidze, be credited with the setting-up of the Leninist Iskra organizations in Transcaucasia and Baku. This particular fraud was perpetrated by Beria, the "notorious faker and provocateur" whose first step was inevitably "the removal of the man who had really been responsible for organizing the first revolutionary Marxist circles in Baku," i.e., Yenukidze. "This is why," *Pravda* concludes, "at the beginning of 1935, Avel Yenukidze was vilified, removed from his government and Party posts, and later arrested and convicted."

From the point of view of strict historical truth, it is, of course, wrong to call Yenukidze the organizer of the first Marxist circles in Baku, let alone the creator of the first Iskra organizations in Transcaucasia. The creation of the first Social Democratic organizations in Baku, and in Transcaucasia as a whole, came about in a way different from that recounted—even now, when they are no longer obliged to reproduce hackneyed Stalinist clichés—by the official Communist historians. Social Democracy was introduced to Transcaucasia by means both more complicated and interesting than would appear from the publications of the Moscow Institute of Marxism and its Tiflis and Baku branches. Nevertheless, Yenukidze was indeed one of the early pioneers of the Social Democratic movement in Tiflis and Baku, though he was not one of its original founders. He worked for it with great devotion, soon coming to the fore as a good and energetic organizer. At any rate, his role during the years in question—the end of the 1890's and the beginning of the 1900's—was incomparably greater than Stalin's, who, being almost three years younger, played a very minor role indeed and was distinguished only by his passion for petty intrigues and troublemaking.

This is why, in the 1930's, people who wished to make a career under Stalin began to rewrite the whole history of the Bolshevik movement, especially those phases in which Stalin had any part whatsoever. This is also why Yenukidze's memoirs came under fire. But it is sheer nonsense to reduce the whole question of the nature of Yenukidze's "crime," as *Pravda* is now doing, to a dispute about the respective roles of Yenukidze and Stalin in the founding of the "Leninist Iskra organizations" in 1901–2. And although Beria was undoubtedly a faker and provocateur, he made his bow as an authority on historical matters for the first time only on July 21, 1935,* whereas the first action had been taken against Yenukidze on March 4, four and a half months earlier. Furthermore, Beria's first excursion into the historical field was directed not so much against Yenukidze as against Philip Makharadze and other moderate Bolsheviks,† and also, of course, against N. N. Zhordania and the Mensheviks in general—the real pioneers of the Georgian Social Democratic movement.

The charges against Yenukidze by Beria and others for his alleged historical mistake played a minor part, if any at all, in Yenukidze's downfall. The real reasons as well as the reasons given at that time in the press and at public meetings were of a completely different order. I do not claim that everything then said in public statements was true or that anything like the whole truth was told about Yenukidze's ouster. But I maintain that earlier accounts were

---

* The text of this report was first published in *Pravda*, July 29–August 5, 1935. This text differs somewhat from the one which was issued as a separate book in 1935 by the Party Publishing House of the Central Committee of of the CPSU. There were fewer quotations from Yenukidze's memoirs; subsequent editions contained fewer still, and the last—the ninth edition, published in 1952—did not contain a single quotation from Yenukidze.—B. N.

† They had been prominent in the movement for greater autonomy for Georgia. All except Makharadze, who was spared because of his advanced age, were tried and executed in the summer of 1937.—Ed.

closer to the truth than the recent article in *Pravda*. For example, *Pravda's* editorial of June 8, 1935—the issue that published the decision of the Central Committee to expel Yenukidze from the Party —called Yenukidze a "typical specimen of a corrupted, degenerate, Menshevik-like Communist," who "in both his political and personal behavior has shown himself to be in the thrall of the sworn enemies of the Party and the Soviet regime." In particular, *Pravda* accused him of "wanting to play the kind uncle to the enemies of the working class," of "rotten liberalism," of "totally ignoring the interests of the Party and the Revolution," and so forth. Khrushchev, then Secretary of the Moscow Party Committee, in reporting to the local Party activists on the Yenukidze affair, not only repeated *Pravda's* accusation that Yenukidze had wanted to help the enemies of the Party and that he had admitted enemies of the working class to the Secretariat of the Central Executive Committee, but he also charged that Yenukidze had "betrayed the cause of the Revolution" (*Pravda*, June 13, 1935). The reports of foreign correspondents, who at that time were much better informed about what was going on at the Kremlin, linked the downfall of Yenukidze directly to the disbanding of the Society of Old Bolsheviks and the Society of Former Political Prisoners. They also mentioned the "oppositional conspiracy" which had allegedly been organized by Yenukidze together with Krupskaya and others, Yenukidze's supposed contacts with oppositionists abroad, and so on.

We now know for certain that the Society of Old Bolsheviks and the Society of Former Political Prisoners were in fact dissolved because they protested against the trials of Kamenev, Zinoviev, and the others who were convicted of being morally and politically responsible for the assassination of Kirov, and that this protest was supported not only by Krupskaya but by Gorky as well.

At the time, the Soviet authorities scarcely made any secret of the fact that Yenukidze was gotten rid of because of his opposition to the wave of terror launched by Stalin after Kirov's assassination. There is much more truth in this than in the recent *Pravda* article in which the grandson of Yenukidze's old friend showers praise on him in order to obscure the reason for his death.

The real reasons for Yenukidze's downfall are bound up with

the dispute then raging over basic policy. I have had occasion to write about the grand policy promoted by Kirov during the last years of his life.* I shall not repeat myself except to note that Yenukidze not only supported Kirov's proposed policy, but also very actively assisted its author. This support was of extreme importance to Kirov, since Yenukidze, particularly in his last years, wielded enormous power.

In general, Yenukidze occupied a rather special position. When Lenin (and Sverdlov) made him Secretary of the Presidium of the Soviet Central Executive Committee in 1918, he entrusted him at the same time with the day-to-day administration of the Kremlin. This was an extremely tricky job. The Kremlin was then being transformed into the main residence of the top government and Party leaders, and its administration had to cater to all the needs of these leaders, from the provision of apartments and cars to food and entertainment. In his capacity of Kremlin comptroller, Yenukidze disposed of vast material resources and had virtually unlimited control over them, but at the same time he had to meet the most varied and sometimes extraordinary claims on them. In the midst of almost total chaos, he set up an enormous service-and-supply organization. As he was not only a good organizer but also a superb diplomat, his functions gradually grew until they included looking after scientists, writers, and artists, the main Moscow theaters, the entire Party hierarchy, and so on. Later he was also made responsible for the Kremlin security guards. In the end, he came to have unlimited control of a vast and highly diverse apparatus. While he himself was dependent on no one, he had some hold on large numbers of people at all levels of the Party and government who were dependent on him.

As I have already stated, he supported Kirov's policy up to the hilt. One episode graphically illustrates Yenukidze's mood in the fall of 1934. He had gone to Paris on a brief visit, and there met a young Georgian actress who had managed, with his help, to get abroad shortly before. Now Yenukidze tried to persuade her to return to Russia, promising her, among other things, a great career

* See "The Letter of an Old Bolshevik" (pp. 26 ff.) and the chapter on Kirov (pp. 69 ff.).

in the theater. He told her that the policy of the Soviet government would be greatly changed in the months ahead, that the economic situation would improve and the regime would become more liberal. The actress was doubtful. She was tempted by the possibilities which offered themselves outside the Soviet Union. Eventually she said she would think about it for a few months and wait for a letter from Yenukidze which he was to send her by the end of the year in a prearranged code. Instead, she received in December a postcard written in a disguised hand which told her to forget their conversation in Paris and not to return to Moscow at any price.

Yenukidze had asked the Georgian actress not to talk about their meeting to anybody. But when she had almost made up her mind to go (before she got the card), she decided to consult I. G. Tsereteli, a close friend of her late father and told him in detail of her conversations with Yenukidze. She was completely unpolitical and the question of her return had no political significance; Tsereteli nevertheless advised her, just as a matter of elementary caution, to put off her return for several months. And then, in December, 1935, she came to him with the postcard. Tsereteli told me all this at the time, and not long before his death, we talked about this episode again. I can vouch for the complete accuracy of this account.

From a political point of view, Yenukidze's hopes were entirely justified. Kirov's line seemed bound to triumph and the Central Committee Plenum of November, 1934, actually approved it. But Yenukidze failed to take Stalin's plans into account: Stalin had no intention of abandoning the weapon of terror; on the contrary, he was then preparing the Purge. Kirov's assassination was his first move against the adherents of liberalism; his elimination of Yenukidze was the second. He had to be eliminated because his Secretariat of the Central Executive Committee was too powerful. At that time, the Kremlin security forces were under the command of an old Latvian, Peterson, who with his Latvian sense of loyalty stood firmly by Yenukidze. (He was in the same barracks in Vorkuta as Yenukidze's nephew, whom he took under his wing. He used to go about in his long Latvian overcoat, to the end maintaining military discipline and calling himself a faithful Communist. He did not like to talk about his past, and if asked he kept silent. Only rarely did he say that he had been wrongly condemned; he had been tried in connection with the "second Kamenev trial," or in connection with the case involving the attempt on Stalin's life in the library of the Central Executive Committee. In Ciliga's memoirs about the Kerkha-Uralsk "isolator" there is an account of how Kamenev was brought to this trial. The main character was supposed to be the young Countess Orlova-Davydova, who had allegedly prepared the attempt on Stalin's life. She did not live to be tried; she was shot immediately after being arrested, apparently on Stalin's personal order. She was evidently the same "princess in the Kremlin" whom Alexander Orlov mentions in *The Secret History of Stalin's Crimes*.) It was not easy to get rid of Yenukidze: He had too many friends. But Stalin managed it.

Peterson was replaced as commandant by Tabachkov-Trenin, a creature of Yezhov, and with his assistance, the Kremlin became the main base for the shady activities of the hoodlums in Stalin's personal secretariat. Tabachkov-Trenin lasted until the beginning of 1939, when Beria took over the NKVD and sent all of Yezhov's men to the firing squad or to Karaganda.*

These facts and many others are, of course, well known in Moscow, and hence available to the commission which decided on the formal rehabilitation of Yenukidze and asked the young historian Shaumian to write a eulogy of his famous grandfather's friend. In particular, they know perfectly well at what point Yenukidze became close to Kirov and in what connection. The inclusion of Kirov's name in the list of Yenukidze's seven intimate friends was obviously deliberate. So why does *Pravda* publish absurdities about the "notorious faker of the history of the Party" Beria as the chief culprit in Yenukidze's liquidation? Why this myth about the supposed omnipotence of Beria, who, in 1935, was far away in his Party post in Tiflis and therefore could not have stage-managed a fake attempt on Stalin's life in the Kremlin library as a means of

* Karaganda, a region in Soviet Central Asia, had a number of forced-labor camps. During the Great Purge, a number of East European Communists, along with Volga Germans, Finns, and other groups regarded at one time or another as being politically suspect, were shipped to camps in this Virgin Land area. For a detailed treatment of this forced-labor area, see D. Dallin and B. Nicolaevsky, *Forced Labor in Soviet Russia.*—Ed.

toppling Yenukidze and thus clearing the way for the coming operations of Poskrebyshev and Yezhov? Beria is guilty of enough crimes as it is without being made responsible for the crimes of others.

Yenukidze's murder was a direct sequel to Kirov's murder, and the same people are responsible for both. In his speeches about Stalin's crimes, Khrushchev dwells so much on the Kirov assassination that it is all too obvious that the people investigating Stalin's terror in Moscow are aware that the Kirov affair is the key to everything that followed. It is also obvious that they know who organized this typical Stalin crime, which was conceived and carried out in such a way as to throw the blame on someone else who himself was marked for liquidation. It is true, Beria was a provocateur, but he was only a humble pupil of Stalin. The real organizer of Kirov's murder was Stalin, and the liquidation of Yenukidze was also his handiwork.

FIVE

Three Political Biographies

N. A. Bulganin*

Aⁿᵒᵗʰᵉʳ round in the fight over the succession of Stalin has
ended. Malenkov has been defeated and Bulganin has been
made head of the government. Up to now, Bulganin had been completely unknown not only in the West, but also among the Russian
émigré community. In recent weeks, the American press has frequently called him the "dark horse" in Moscow's political "steeple-
chase." Very little official biographical material about him exists.†
There is, of course, the brief entry in the new edition of the *Large
Soviet Encyclopedia,* though it says nothing about him as a political
figure. Nevertheless, both Soviet and foreign journals contain many

* This article appeared in *Sotsialistichesky Vestnik,* February–March,
1955.
† Several biographies have been published on Bulganin in the Soviet
Union. But the most interesting of these appeared in the *Politichesky Slovar,*
1958 edition, after the ouster of Bulganin as Chairman of the Council of
Ministers.—Ed.

229

scattered and fragmentary mentions from which one can piece together the outlines of the political biography of this man who has played an important role in Soviet life during the last fifteen years and who seems destined for an even greater role in the near future.

Official sources are very sparing of details concerning Bulganin's early years. We learn only that he was born in 1895, in Nizhny Novgorod, that he studied in a *gymnasium* (it is not said whether he graduated), and that he joined the Communist Party in 1917, after the February Revolution. This information is too skimpy to give a clear picture of his background; Soviet biographies used to say that he was the son of a "worker's family"; they no longer do. From this it can be concluded that this part of Bulganin's life does not come up to official Communist standards. It is also not at all clear why the future marshal was not in the army in 1917. He did not work in a factory, for this would have been mentioned in his biography with pride—and his age-group was called up as far back as 1915.

It is also quite interesting that Bulganin joined the Communist movement only in 1917, after the Revolution. He was then twenty-one, a grown man. In those years, people joined the movement at the age of seventeen or eighteen—the age at which almost all of Bulganin's colleagues in the present Presidium of the Central Committee joined. Bulganin and Khrushchev, his present sponsor, are the sole exceptions. Khrushchev joined only in 1918, at the age of twenty-four.

On the other hand, Bulganin, after entering the Communist Party, immediately found work to his taste. The official biography states that "soon after the victory" of the Bolsheviks, Bulganin went to work in the Cheka, and he now rightfully wears the badge of an Old Chekist. From its very inception, the Cheka in Nizhny Novgorod has been linked with Bulganin's name. In the summer of 1918, he played the leading role in the crushing of all non-Bolshevik workers' and peasants' organizations in the city itself and in the adjoining working-class centers of Sormovo, Karnavino, Belakhna, and others.* He was instrumental in the dispersal of the

* Some extremely interesting facts on the personal part of Bulganin in the development of the Red terror in the first years after the Soviet Revolution are given in the account of "Professor Johann Wenzel," published by

regional non-Party workers' conference and in the forcible seizure of the Sormovo workers' cooperative. Somewhat later, in August of that year, Bulganin became the chief organizer of the Red terror in the Nizhny Novgorod region. He also headed the detachment of Nizhny Novgorod Chekists sent to put down the uprising in Yaroslavl and played an important part in the reprisals that followed.

---

the author in *Sotsialistichesky Vestnik,* May, 1959. Wenzel, whose real name is not known, was for many years an important member of the German Communist underground, and during World War II was one of the chief Soviet intelligence agents inside Nazi Germany. Some details of his work are given in David Dallin's *Soviet Espionage* (New Haven, Conn.: Yale University Press, 1955). After his arrest by the Nazis, Wenzel told them all he knew and evidently rendered them some important services in general. This earned him both his freedom and provided him with the means to live comfortably for the rest of his life. He died in West Germany in 1957 or 1958. He left behind papers which included a note evidently written after the appointment of Bulganin as chairman of the Council of Ministers. This note was first published in the *Sotsialistichesky Vestnik,* and is here given in full:

It was in 1926—the beginning of Stalinism. In Tomsk, that "Siberian Athens," most students were having a hard time. True, they studied diligently, but they had to work hard to keep their stomachs even half full and just barely existed. Only Mishka Kataev and a few other students did not have to worry. Mishka was always neatly dressed, well-fed, and often slightly high. He was plump, always smiling, and in high spirits. Mishka was not especially studious, nor did he earn very good grades, but to everyone's surprise, he was not expelled from the university. He was a good listener and always ready with a joke. Among themselves, some students said that Mishka was an agent of the OGPU.

Once six or seven students threw a small party in which three foreign students also took part. True, there was not enough to eat, but on the other hand there was plenty to drink. It was a real gay students' party. Mishka showed up at the party too, although no one had invited him. He drank a lot of vodka. He told many jokes and laughed at them like a child. About two hours went by like this, and then something very unusual happened: Mishka began (who knows whether it was intentional or not) to talk about his life in Sormovo.

"I've got a right to be lazy," he said. "I put in a lot of work in Sormovo. Listen, comrades," he shouted in a drunken voice. "Already in the last century, various secret socialist organizations began to spring up in Sormovo—Socialist Revolutionaries, People's Socialists, Social Democrats. . . . The Czarist police seized these people and sent them to Siberia and

Three Biographies

To some extent, I am able to speak of all this as a witness, since I had occasion to visit Nizhny Novgorod twice, in July and August, 1918, in connection with the movement of non-Party workers' conferences, and I well remember the expression "Bulganin's goons," applied to the detachment formed by Bulganin to break up meetings and carry out arrests. Many details, of course, have faded from my memory, particularly since I had occasion to

---

Central Asia. But still their ranks grew. They sprang from the ground like mushrooms after a warm rain, like the bacteria in an epidemic. The Czar acted like a rotten liberal in this affair. But our leaders headed by Stalin had to put in hard work in Sormovo. Ha-ha-ha! Others did too. But our chief, Nikolai Aleksandrovich Bulganin, did the most work. With his own hand he finished off at least three hundred. It was a real record. Ha-ha-ha!"

Mishka said this with complete equanimity, and to those present it seemed that his eyes, glazed from drink, were carefully watching the impression his words had made on the listeners.

In the fall of 1918, after the attempt on Lenin's life, the Soviet government launched the "Red terror," which was on such a scale and took such forms that it aroused the indignation even of many Bolsheviks. As a result, there arose a storm of protest not only in the closed sessions of the Soviet and of Communist caucuses, but also openly in the Party press. In the All-Union Central Executive Committee in Moscow, as well as in a number of provincial cities, in local soviets, commissions for the investigation of the activity of the Cheka grew up.

Nizhny Novgorod, near which there were big industrial centers such as Sormovo, was among those places where the terror was particularly violent because of resistance by the workers; indignation against the terror was correspondingly strong.

At the head of the provincial Cheka there was a certain Yakov Vorobiev, who had not been involved in the revolutionary movement of previous years. His most active assistant was Bulganin, who was even less involved than Vorobiev in the workers' and socialist movement of the pre-Revolutionary period. Indignation about the activities of the Cheka in Nizhny Novgorod was particularly great, and in January, 1918, Vorobiev was forced to resign from his post, declaring that he had been "insulted" and "the Cheka and Chekists persecuted." This is taken from Illarionov (ed.), *Materials on the History of the Revolutionary Movement in Nizhny*, 1922, vol. 1, p. 25. Along with Vorobiev, his close assistants, including Bulganin, also left.

But soon after the beginning of the advance of Kolchak, in order to mobilize former Chekists, the Central Committee restored them all to their jobs and sent them to the front.—B. N./1964.

visit a great number of workers' centers, and Bolshevik practice was essentially the same everywhere. But I do remember one meeting of our party's Nizhny Novgorod committe, already greatly depleted as a result of persecution, at which there was much talk about the actions of Bulganin's goons and about Bulganin himself as a man who had nothing to do with the working-class movement. This meeting has become etched in my memory because it took place in the apartment of Grinevetsky, a cousin of Ignaty Grinevetsky, who threw the bomb that killed Alexander II. I spent the night there, and my conversation with Grinevetsky lasted until morning. It is necessary to point out that Bulganin at that time was only a secondary figure in the Red terror. His political mentor in Nizhny Novgorod was Kaganovich, who had been sent there in June, 1918, by the Bolshevik Central Committee with special instructions for organizing the defense of the city. This was the time when the Samara Committee of the Members of the Constituent Assembly, with the aid of the Czechoslovak Legion, captured Kazan, and everyone expected them to advance further up the Volga. The close relationship of Bulganin and Kaganovich, both political and personal, dates back to this time. Kaganovich did much to help Bulganin's advance up the ladder of the Soviet hierarchy.

Bulganin left Nizhny Novgorod comparatively early in his career. He transferred to the All-Russian Cheka, where he worked in the Special Sections which supervised the Red Army and the frontline areas. By then, he had already made a very thorough study of this work on all levels. This knowledge proved very useful to him later on, during World War II and after. His personal contacts among the military also proved useful. He had worked in the Special Section of the cavalry of Budyonny and Voroshilov, and he was well connected in these circles, too. After the Civil War, when the Special Sections were greatly reduced as a result of the general demobilization of the Red Army, Bulganin went to work in the economic sector. From 1922 to 1927, he worked in the Supreme Economic Council (VTsNkh), and from 1927 to 1930, he was director of the Moscow Electrical Works. It is important to note that this work was only nominally of an economic nature, since Bulganin specialized mainly in the selection of personnel, work which involved contact between the VTsNkh and the Economic Directorate of the OGPU. Bulganin undoubtedly showed shrewdness and executive ability, and during these years, he built up a reputation as one of the Party's most promising economic administrators.

All this, however, was only a prelude to a really important career. Here again Kaganovich was instrumental. In the summer of 1930, Stalin appointed Kaganovich Secretary of the Moscow Regional Committee, with the special task of radically purging Moscow's Party and government apparatus, which at that time was a hotbed of "Rightist" deviationists. Kaganovich chose Malenkov as his assistant, making him head of the personnel section of the Moscow Regional Committee. At the same time, Kaganovich found a post for Bulganin: he got him elected chairman of the Moscow Soviet in January, 1931, and it became Bulganin's task to purge that body. Bulganin performed his job with a zeal that completely satisfied his employers, so that later, during the Yezhovshchina, the purge of the Moscow Soviet apparatus was comparatively mild. The principal work had already been done—though without bloodshed.

It was not, however, only through this work that Bulganin, the Chekist economic administrator, was promoted to the post of Lord Mayor of Moscow, as he was then called in the Soviet press. In those years, the reconstruction of Moscow was begun—the subway was started, a vast plan was worked out for rebuilding the entire city, for widening streets, and so forth. Bulganin took an active part in this, not just as a figurehead, but as an active organizer. It was in this post that he attracted the particular attention of Stalin, who took great interest in such projects and personally sat in on many planning meetings. Stalin was the nominal chairman of such conferences, while Bulganin was the actual organizer.

No doubt, Bulganin's acquaintance with Khrushchev also dates back to this time. In January, 1931, Kaganovich installed Khrushchev as Secretary of the Bauman District Party Committee. This was the same district in which Bulganin had done Party work in the summer of 1930, and it was from here that he went as a delegate to the Seventeenth Party Congress in 1934.

Bulganin's subsequent ascent up the ladder of the Soviet hierarchy dates from the Yezhovshchina period. To Bulganin, the Great Purge brought new advancement, eloquent testimony as to his allegiance in those days. In July, 1937, after the execution of Tukhachevsky *et al.*, when a large number of People's Commissars and other prominent officials were arrested, Bulganin was named to fill the vacancy as Chairman of the Council of People's Commissars of the R.S.F.S.R. In the fall of 1938, he became Molotov's deputy as Chairman of the Council of People's Commissars of the U.S.S.R. and simultaneously head of the board of the State Bank. This latter post, in particular, testifies to Stalin's high opinion of Bulganin's managerial and organizational abilities; it put Bulganin very close to the exchequer of the regime, which was vigilantly watched over by Stalin himself.

Always very well dressed, and clean-shaven except for a trim goatee, Bulganin seems amiable, self-possessed, and cautious. He gives the impression of being open and benevolent. He consciously tries to maintain this pose, but it is merely a mask, not his real self. The fact of the matter is that Bulganin is a callous and shrewd careerist, a good judge of people who exploits their weaknesses in order to get what he wants.

In 1947, the present writer had occasion to meet among a group of former Soviet prisoners of war a field officer who had served on the staff of Budyonny's cavalry during the Civil War and afterward had been on good terms with Bulganin. He told me many interesting stories about Bulganin. The friendly relations between Bulganin and Kaganovich were personal as well as official. Bulganin's sister, Nadezhda, had studied with Kaganovich's sister, Rosa, and the two were friends. They saw each other often, and by means of this ladies' grapevine (to use my informant's expression) Bulganin was kept informed of Stalin's moods; Rosa M. Kaganovich, a doctor by training and an intelligent and observant woman, was then married to Stalin. Bulganin told my informant that he knew about the tense struggle among the leadership in the mid-1930's, had a premonition that it would not end well, and, having decided to cast his lot with Stalin, had long since made it a rule not to accept any post unless it were offered to him by Stalin himself.

Bulganin moved confidently but cautiously toward his goal: to become directly associated with Stalin and to have no other master but him.

The war proved to be a new and important stage along this path. Moscow was taken by surprise and a mood of panic reigned in government circles. At this time, Bulganin made a decision that predetermined his subsequent role: he appeared before the Party Central Committee and asked to be transferred to the front.* The story has it that he was almost the first to make such a request. Malenkov, who was then in charge of personnel in the Central Committee and was trying to organize the home front, eagerly accepted Bulganin's offer.

Bulganin was appointed a member of the Military Council for the Western Front, which was responsible for organizing the defense of Moscow, and he was given special missions connected with the city's defense. When the Germans were approaching Moscow, in October, 1941, and its military command was handed over to the future Marshal Zhukov (October 21), Bulganin acted as the eyes of the Central Committee in Zhukov's command. During these weeks, Bulganin and Zhukov began to work together, and they did not get on very well. They disagreed on the selection of commanders and the role of political commissars. Zhukov insisted on concentrating all military affairs in the hands of the commanders, while Bulganin, as watchdog of the Central Committee, upheld the importance of the commissars. Rumor has it that the two men clashed sharply. Some say that as a result of these clashes, Bulganin asked to be transferred to another post; according to other sources, Zhukov demanded that Stalin dismiss Bulganin. Most likely, there is some truth in both these versions. But since the military situation was so critical and the time not auspicious for a conflict with Zhukov, Bulganin resigned. But the incident, of course, rankled with him. Bulganin had naturally acted with the agreement or rather on the instructions of Stalin, who was strengthened in his

* Wenzel says that the feeling against the leaders of the Red terror of 1918 was so acute in the Sormovo area that in August and September— three months after resigning from the Cheka and after the Central Committee restored them to their jobs—Vorobiev, Bulganin, and others of the Nizhny Novgorod Cheka found its advisable to "volunteer" for work at the front.—B. N./1964.

favorable opinion of Bulganin by this affair and appointed him to other fronts. The most important assignment was to the Military Council for the First Belorussian Front, which was under the command of Rokossovsky.

Rokossovsky was a different type of general from Zhukov. Although a good soldier, he was not exceptionally brilliant. A former volunteer cavalryman, Rokossovsky rose to the position of division commander somewhere in Trans-Baikalia and probably would not have advanced beyond this had it not been for the Great Purge. After the removal of the top commanders chosen by Tukhachevsky and his friends in the summer of 1937, Rokossovsky became corps commander in Leningrad. There he fell victim to the second or third purge wave and served a brief sentence in a camp. Released after the Finnish campaign, he convalesced in a sanatorium, was given dentures to replace the teeth knocked out during interrogations, and resolved to be more careful in future. He decided on a policy of blind loyalty to the regime. During the war he fought well, but he was inclined to become overconfident and as a result he would suffer defeats. Bulganin spotted his weaknesses—a fondness for the "good things of life," especially women—and took him in hand. With Stalin's encouragement, Bulganin began to promote Rokossovsky's career.

The headquarters of the First Belorussian Front was made into the operations base for the capture of Poland. A Communist government set up in Russia in preparation for the takeover accompanied the army. From the very moment they set foot on Polish territory, the Soviet army and especially the NKVD organs dealt viciously with the non-Communist Polish underground resistance movement. In Lutsk, Polish workers who had approached the Soviet command as delegates of non-Communist organizations fighting the Germans were shot; in Lublin, the Polish Communist government was formally installed. Then came the infamous and criminal betrayal of the Warsaw uprising, which had been largely provoked by Soviet appeals. These appeals promised help by the Soviet armies camped on the opposite shore of the Vistula, but when the uprising began, the Soviet authorities calmly allowed the Germans to drown the revolt in blood.

The plan for this monstrous provocation was Stalin's, but it was put into effect by Bulganin, who was extremely adept at anticipating Stalin's wishes.

Stalin had exceptionally strong nerves and remarkably good health, but even he was worn out by the war. In the early spring of 1944, he suffered a serious heart attack. He was found unconscious at his desk and was in critical condition for several days. These were the very days when a portrait of Stalin—with gray hair —was displayed in the window of a bookstore on Kuznetsky Most. The Muscovites who crowded around the window looked closely but were afraid to comment. The next day, the portrait was taken down. Foreign correspondents, however, had spotted it, and word got into the foreign press. Stalin recovered and heard about the portrait. He also learned that Beria and Malenkov were responsible for its display but he held his peace. Basically, they were right: public opinion had to be prepared for the possibility of his death. But it was not a very pleasant thought, and Stalin did not forget the matter. Perhaps it was this episode that was responsible for the rift between Stalin and Malenkov and Beria, which played such an important role in later relations among the Kremlin leaders.

Knowing his past and his methods, it is not hard to understand Stalin's attitude. During the war, all power in the country was concentrated in the hands of a small group of men who were members of the State Committee for Defense. In addition to Stalin himself, the Committee comprised Molotov, Voroshilov, Beria, and Malenkov; later Kaganovich and Mikoyan were added. Molotov, however, was kept busy with foreign policy, Voroshilov was attached to Stalin for special assignments, and Kaganovich and Mikoyan were occupied with economic matters. In addition to running certain industrial ministries, Malenkov and Beria were responsible for the entire domestic policy of the Soviet Union and for the Party apparatus. Tremendous power was concentrated in their hands, but it was not in Stalin's nature to tolerate strong power centers around him, regardless of who headed them.

In this situation, the steady, self-possessed, and, at the same time adroit and quick-witted Bulganin was a godsend to Stalin. Stalin sized him up, giving him various missions and having him draw up all kinds of memoranda. On November 21, 1944, *Izvestia* announced the appointment of Bulganin as Stalin's deputy in the People's Commissariat for Defense, and, on November 22, the "release" of Voroshilov from his duties as a member of the State Committee for Defense and his replacement by Bulganin.

It very soon became clear that Bulganin had also been given special tasks by Stalin: acting on Stalin's personal instructions and invested with special powers, he prepared the ground for a postwar purge of the army and of many other agencies as well, especially those connected with defense work.

Preparing his blows cautiously and painstakingly, Bulganin worked with Stalin's encouragement, undoubtedly maintaining contact with Poskrebyshev, whose influence had weakened after the Great Purge and the rise of Beria, but who nevertheless remained a force to be reckoned with. In these circumstances, the blows dealt by Bulganin were bound to be very telling. In a very interesting passage in his memoirs, Tokaev tells how Malenkov's face became covered with beads of sweat when he learned that his old associate Shakhurin, whom he had made Minister of Aviation Industry, had been sent to a concentration camp by a commission headed by Bulganin. Shakhurin was not the only one. At the same time, this commission meted out the same fate to Chief Air Marshal Novikov, commander of the entire air force, as well as to a number of other prominent military leaders who were careless enough, in the course of fighting the war, to step on the toes of the army's political apparatus headed by Bulganin.

The time had also come for the squaring of accounts with Zhukov. Zhukov being Zhukov, it was especially difficult for Bulganin to deal with him. Zhukov's military talents were exceptional and disposing of him was not an easy matter. But through the joint efforts of the political apparatus in the army, then headed by Shikin, and with the help of Stalin personally, who was envious of Zhukov's military fame, he was ousted. To be sure, they did not put him in a concentration camp—the scandal would have been too great—but he was exiled to the provinces—first to Odessa, then to Sverdlovsk.

This is how Bulganin achieved his power. In March, 1946, a

Central Committee Plenum elected him an alternate member of the Politburo, and in March, 1948, he was made a full member. In 1947, when Stalin relinquished the post of Minister of Armed Forces, he gave it to Bulganin. At that point begins Bulganin's later career, which is better known to the outside world.

Marshal I. S. Konev*

O N August 11, 1961, Radio Moscow announced that Marshal Ivan Stepanovich Konev had been named to replace Yaku-bovsky, an experienced but little-known soldier, as head of the Soviet armed forces in East Germany. Konev's appointment is an event of great importance, and not only from a purely military point of view. Of course, major policy decisions about Berlin are determined by the top leaders, primarily Khrushchev. It is they who decide how far they can go in playing the atomic game. But Marshal Konev is by no means merely a figurehead. He is a personality in his own right, not merely a man who carries out other people's orders. He is a soldier as well as a military politician, the leader of an influential group among the top-level political figures in the Soviet government. In the recent past, he has more than once made his influence felt on Soviet policy. It was in fact his attempts

* This article appeared in *Sotsialistichesky Vestnik,* August–September, 1961.

to exercise his influence that resulted about a year ago in his removal from the highest military and political post: commander-in-chief of all Soviet-bloc armed forces. At the time, he was fighting the reduction of the Soviet army undertaken by Khrushchev, but there is no doubt that he has now been appointed to his new and important post in order to carry out a policy to his taste. It is no coincidence of course that his appointment came at the same time as the reversal of the decision to reduce the strength of the Army. At the top level of the regime, the name Konev stands for a quite distinct policy, and Konev is now returning to active duty not as the vanquished but as the victor.

Marshal Konev is frequently compared to Marshal Zhukov. The Soviet press has often referred to Konev in a manner clearly suggesting that as a military figure he is second only to Zhukov. This is scarcely true as regards their respective military talents. None of Konev's campaigns ranks on the same level with Zhukov's, and Konev knows this only too well. Hence the hatred rooted in envy so apparent in everything he says and writes about Zhukov. But despite his inferiority as a soldier, Konev undoubtedly heads that group of Communist marshals which is now most influential in the top reaches of the dictatorship. It was Konev who fought Zhukov for a number of years in these circles, and eventually he came out on top.

Konev's present role can be correctly understood only against the background of his past, about which unfortunately, very little is known. The *Large Soviet Encyclopedia* (2d ed.) devotes a total of thirty-two lines to him; this is disproportionately little considering the long way traveled by the poor peasant boy from his village in Vologda to his present exalted position of military-political leader in the Soviet army. Local Vologda publications provide a little more information, but they, too, are extremely deficient when it comes to hard facts. The sources used in the present study, in addition to published material—statements in the Soviet and foreign press—are the unpublished accounts of people who have had personal contact with Konev and have served under him. Of course, such accounts are always highly subjective, but in our troubled times there is no such thing as an impartial reporter.

Konev was born in 1897, the son of a poor peasant in the village of Ladeino, in the backwoods between the Vologda and Vyatka provinces. Official sources say nothing about Konev's early years. In effect, they begin his biography in August, 1918, when he joined the Communist Party. But even these bare official biographical entries bear out by implication reports published abroad (e.g., *Osteuropa,* 1955, p. 182), that prior to his official Communist past, Konev went through a Populist period, when he was active in the Socialist Revolutionary Party and had contacts with their underground organization. The same sources say further that in 1917–18, Konev went over to the Left Socialist Revolutionaries and so found himself, during the July, 1918, uprising, taking up arms against his former comrades.

Konev's Populist period began in 1913–14, when, at the age of sixteen or seventeen, having finished the local school, he left home, to seek a living in Archangel. At that time there was a strong upsurge of revolutionary and working-class activity, in which the Populists (Socialist Revolutionaries) played a considerable role.

Nikolsk, in Vologda Province, where Konev worked before the Revolution,* was an important center of agricultural cooperatives. It was there that Konev, as a Left Socialist Revolutionary, was promoted to the post of district military commissar; there he first showed his energy and drive in suppressing peasant uprisings; and it was also from there, now as a Communist,† that he went to the front to fight Kolchak in June, 1919. At that time, he was constantly involved in military-political work, which was then in effect largely Cheka work. At the front he began his career as commis-

---

* In 1946, an exhibition about Konev was held in Nikolsk, and later it was evidently converted into a small museum (see *Vologzhane—geroi Sovetskogo Soiuza,* Vologod. Knizh. Izd., 1959, p. 341).—B. N.

† As far as can be determined, Konev joined the Communist Party during the Second Vologda Province Special Congress of Communists, which was held on August 15–17, 1918, in Vologda. At this Congress, according to the report of the official Party paper, there were 112 delegates, a "large part" of whom had been "sent by the soviets." Among the delegates were "three or four Left Socialist Revolutionaries who broke with their mad Central Committee and are working in contact with the Communists." (*Borba za vlast sovetov v Vologodskoi gubernii* [1917–1919]; *Sbornik dokumentov,* Vologda, Obl. Knizh. Redaksya, 1957, p. 165.) At this Congress, these Left Socialist Revolutionary delegates were formally admitted to the Communist Party.—B. N.

sar of Armored Train No. 102, and he went all the way to Vladivostok with this train. After the Civil War, Konev continued in his military-political work. He stayed in the Far East, where he rose rapidly, becoming corps commissar fairly early in his career. He is undoubtedly an extremely able person.

Thus, two important aspects of Konev's past must be kept in mind: first, that he began his political activity not in the Bolshevik but in the Populist, Socialist Revolutionary ranks, joining the Bolsheviks only after October; and second, that the early years of his career among the Bolsheviks were spent in military-political and Cheka work. Although the son of a peasant, he was conspicuous for the zeal with which he helped to suppress peasant uprisings. Inevitably, these two aspects of his early career affected Konev's status as a Party member.

As a rule, the Old Bolsheviks had little respect for or trust in defectors from other parties who joined their ranks after October. They tended to regard them as opportunists. This was especially true of their attitude toward former Populists. During the Civil War, when the Soviet regime was in jeopardy, these feelings were muted: the help of defectors was needed—even outsiders were welcomed. But the situation changed when the NEP was introduced and the regime's position became stronger. The competition for jobs among Party members was intensified, but the number of places in the apparatus was reduced, while the number of candidates for them grew. The old Communists began packing the apparatus with their own people. This was the beginning of the practice of periodic checks and purges, especially in those bodies which had anything to do with ideological work. Ideological workers were constantly being weeded out in the Red Army in particular. A former Populist, even one who had shown total loyalty to the regime, could not count on holding on to any position of responsibility, since a Populist past was considered a hindrance to the acceptance of true Leninism, and therefore it was thought unlikely that he could become an ideologically reliable Bolshevik.

Things became even worse with the emergence of the first oppositionist groups. Defectors from other parties were blocked on two fronts: if they got mixed up in opposition politics, they were penalized more severely than others, and if they fought against the oppositionists, they found themselves in the position of semi-outcasts.

Oppositionist sentiments cropped up early on among Red Army political functionaries. This was an early manifestation of Trotskyism, which was as yet by no means hostile to the regime. The Tolmachev (later Lenin) Military-Political Academy, taken over by Trotskyites in 1922–23, became the center of this opposition.

It is not completely clear how and why Konev turned up in Moscow at the very height of this struggle. His connection with this academy is not mentioned in his biographical entries, but reliable informants assert categorically that in 1924 he was either at the academy or tried to get into it, and that in the battle in and around it, he quite definitely sided with the enemies of the oppositionists. Konev's relations with colleagues at the academy became intolerable, and he decided to leave the political sphere and devote himself to purely military work. Just at that time, Frunze, in an attempt to increase the number of Communists among his commanding officers, appealed to political personnel in the army to become ordinary serving officers. Frunze's appeal met with some response, but the practical effect was not great. At any rate, of all the political functionaries who turned officers at this time, only one—Konev—became a marshal. The path by which he eventually reached this position was very unusual. In 1926, he completed the advanced course for senior officers at the Frunze Academy. Then, for seven years, he remained in the rank of regimental commander. Not until 1934, after again attending the Frunze Academy and graduating from its "Special Faculty," did Konev begin to move ahead rapidly; in February, 1939, he was promoted to the rank of army commander second grade (equivalent to lieutenant general).

The significance of this acceleration in his career is to be explained by the fact that the "Special Faculty" prepared trained people for special intelligence work and for military Cheka work in general. In 1934–35, this department, as well as similar establishments in other academies and institutes, came under the direct supervision of Stalin's personal secretariat, then already busy recruiting people to carry out the coming Great Purge, which was being quietly prepared in Party offices under the guise of a check on Party dossiers. The fact that Konev, a former Socialist Revolutionary, safely came through all the shoals of the Great Purge although the whole Far Eastern command of the Red Army was particularly hard hit, and the fact that he advanced so rapidly at this time, can be taken as sure proof of his connection with the instigators of the Great Purge—i.e., the heads of Stalin's personal secretariat.

The exact details of this connection must be left to future historians; at the moment it is sufficient to note the existence of his connection as a stepping-stone in Konev's career.

Konev's promotion to the rank of army commander was announced on February 8, 1939, and he was named second in command to Stern, the commander of the Second Far Eastern Army, which had been carved out of Bluecher's old Far Eastern Army after Bluecher's liquidation, in September, 1938. Stern himself did not last long. He disappeared at the end of 1939, and to this day his case remains one of the most obscure affairs of that tail end of the Yezhovshchina which came after the downfall of Yezhov himself.* Stern's fate has been linked to the setbacks suffered by the Second Far Eastern Army in the spring of 1939 in military engagements against the Japanese attack on Mongolia. For the time being, no one knows whether this is true, since Stern's case thus far has not been reviewed and he has not been rehabilitated.† As to Konev, who from February to July, 1939, was directly in charge of the military operations against the Japanese, not only did he not suffer, but, on the contrary, his stock rose even higher and he took over Stern's post.

Konev was not very successful in his operations against the Japanese. The Japanese launched their well-prepared offensive in the beginning of May, 1939, and advanced into Mongolia in a brief and hard-hitting campaign. The counterattacks led by Konev ended in failure. Since the situation in the West was deteriorating (Hitler was about to attack Poland), Stalin had to wind up the campaign in the Far East. Konev, therefore, was relieved of his post and

---

* We now know, from the memoirs of Ilya Ehrenburg among others, that Stern was shot a few weeks before the war started.—Ed.

† Apparently he has been rehabilitated, but not formally—that is to say, he is mentioned in military histories and in the *History of the Great Patriotic War* without any sort of commentary.—Ed.

Zhukov, assistant commander of the forces of the Belorussian Military District who had made his mark during the maneuvers of 1938, was put in charge of the operation. He was hastily transferred to the Far East and given only a short time to complete his assignment. In this he was successful: he quickly mobilized his forces and won the engagement at Nomonhan with a brilliance that took both the Japanese and Moscow by surprise.

This battle was the beginning of Zhukov's great military career, but it also marks the beginning of Konev's burning hatred toward Zhukov, a hatred which has not abated over the years. With his great talent for exploiting human weakness, Stalin quickly sized up Konev and cleverly used his feelings toward Zhukov. This is an intriguing subject on which a great deal remains to be written. At the moment I am concerned with only one thing—i.e., to show that, if we trace the history of Stalin's treatment of these two soldiers, the chronology of their promotions and awards, we shall see that as early as the end of 1941, Stalin was grooming Konev, the politician, as a rival, whom he could play off against the real soldier, Zhukov. This was typical of Stalin's foresight and bears all the marks of his style. He conferred honors on Zhukov only when he had no choice, but on Konev he bestowed them even when there was no particular reason for doing so. This was necessary in order to maintain the balance between the indispensable "organizer of victory" and the even more indispensable political counterweight to him.

After the war, Zhukov remained a short time—about three or four months—in a position of supreme responsibility as Stalin's deputy in charge of the armed forces. He was then sent to an obscure province as head of a minor military district. The actual control of the Ministry of Armed Forces passed into the hands of that crafty courtier Bulganin, though nominally it went to a political marshal, Konev. From the summer of 1946 to the summer of 1952, Konev was commander-in-chief of Soviet ground forces and he was privy to all major policy decisions. It was only at the beginning of this period that the regime's foreign policy was not yet actively aggressive. Nineteen forty-seven marks the return to the old Leninist method of indirect aggression through support of revolutionary movements in the West (this was the policy of Zhdanov and the

Cominform). In 1950, however, the regime embarked once more on the Stalinist method of fanning open international conflicts. The North Korean invasion of South Korea was the first such move. In 1951–52, a closely knit group formed in the Kremlin and began to look for the key to the defeat of the West.

The central figure in this group was Stalin himself. He felt death approaching and did not want to die without consolidating the victory of the world revolution "à la Stalin." He outlined his program to this effect in his closing address to the Nineteenth Congress. The man he had chosen as his chief lieutenant in the implementation of this program was Poskrebyshev, with Khrushchev, Suslov, Bulganin, and Pospelov eagerly casting themselves in the roles of his assistants.

Stalin was sure that once again he would be able to drive a wedge between the Western countries, and he hoped to provoke hostilities over the Arab-Israeli conflict. The Slansky affair and the doctors' plot were only preliminary skirmishes. Some of the Soviet marshals, particularly Konev, were made party to his plans. Konev was given command of the Transcarpathian Military District, which in actual fact was designed as the jumping-off point for a blitzkrieg in the Balkans and, in particular, against Tito's "revisionist" Yugoslavia.

This malignant design on world peace was thwarted by other Soviet Marshals, chiefly by Zhukov, whose position oddly enough had somewhat improved as a result of the Nineteenth Party Congress. It is true that on the whole this Congress was a victory for the worst elements of the Party apparatus, but in their struggle against the government and the managerial forces, these same elements were compelled to pay lip service to inner-Party democracy. Zhukov, then in disfavor, enjoyed enormous and ever-growing popularity, especially among the younger generation of army officers. For instance, his lectures at the Frunze Academy always drew exceptionally large audiences. There was no option but to invite him to give his expert opinion on the purely military aspect of the grand strategy devised by the then chief of staff, General Shtemenko, by Konev, and by their associates. Zhukov's devastating criticism of these plans made a great impression on the military specialists present. This made Shtemenko's position almost intolerable, since his answer to Zhukov was extremely weak. Many of the marshals demanded his removal.

Stalin, who had inspired the aggressive plans of Shtemenko, Konev, and the others, was furious. The story told by the then Indian Ambassador Krishna Menon about his visit to Stalin around this time (February 17, 1953) is perhaps significant in this connection. Menon reports that Stalin was well and in a talkative mood, but during the whole of the meeting, he doodled with a red pencil on a pad lying in front of him. Looking closely, Menon saw that Stalin was drawing wolves: he kept drawing them and then crossing them out, over and over again. Noticing that Menon could see his doodles, he explained that the Russian peasants had learned to fight wolves, that they knew how to kill them. It was clear that he had in mind some particular "wolves." But of course he gave no clue as to who they were. It was learned later that a battle royal was then being waged about the post of chief of staff. Stalin was against the dismissal of Shtemenko, which was being demanded by a number of marshals. But he had to give way, and at a reception on Soviet Army Day, February 22, it became known that Shtemenko was out and had been replaced by Marshal Sokolovsky, who had served as Zhukov's chief of staff at crucial moments during the war.

As though on signal, the tone of the press changed overnight, whereas until February 22 it had been calling for blood. After Stalin's death, it was widely rumored that the "wolves" Stalin had designated for slaughter were the opponents of the reckless plans of Konev and Shtemenko, but that Stalin lost his nerve, or, as others maintain, somebody had the courage to stay his hand.

At any rate, there is no doubt that the death of Stalin was directly connected with his plans for aggression abroad and that Konev was his chosen instrument for their implementation.

The conflict over the last foreign adventure planned by Stalin and the consequent battle among the top army commanders were not the only issues in the waning days of the Stalinist era. In the madness of the last months of his life, Stalin had created a large number of hopeless imbroglios which his successors could not easily disentangle, even by the most drastic means.

Stalin's death, of course, put an end to plans of foreign aggression. Shtemenko disappeared from the scene, but Konev remained.

He returned to Moscow from his Transcarpathian Military District and took an active part in the "war of succession." It is common knowledge that Konev chaired the secret tribunal which sent Beria and his henchmen to the firing squad. Khrushchev, who was the prime mover in the action against Beria, had always trusted Konev. There were stories in Moscow at that time according to which Konev's part in getting rid of Beria went beyond his chairmanship of the secret tribunal, and that it was he who personally commanded the tanks which surrounded Beria's country house at the moment of his arrest and wiped out the detachment of Beria's Georgian bodyguards who had seized the premises of Stalin's personal secretariat while the dictator lay dying. He is also believed to have disposed of Poskrebyshev and seized the secret files of Stalin's secretariat.

From this moment on, although he held no official position in the hierarchy, Konev became a close associate of Khrushchev, particularly as a restraining influence on Zhukov. It was Konev, for example, who thwarted Zhukov's attempts to rehabilitate Tukhachevsky and the other Red Army leaders executed in the Great Purge. Again it was Konev who is credited with holding up the re-examination of the case of Stern, who had been Konev's chief in the Far East in 1939. And, needless to say, Konev played a major part in the downfall of Zhukov in October, 1957.

But Konev was not only a force in domestic matters; he also played a large part in the creation of the Warsaw Pact and in the direction of foreign affairs. It is known that he is a stanch opponent of a moratorium on atomic tests and that he firmly opposed Khrushchev's plans for cuts in the army (January, 1960). Indeed, on this issue he clashed violently with Khrushchev and as a result was removed from his post as commander-in-chief of the Warsaw Pact forces.

This demotion, and particularly his quarrel with Khrushchev, have considerably undermined Konev's position. Yet by all accounts it would seem that he has continued to head that military faction which favors a more aggressive Soviet foreign policy.

Of course, in talking of a military faction in Soviet conditions, we must be careful not to oversimplify by applying Western concepts to the vastly different context of the Soviet Union. A military faction in Moscow consists of course of *Communists* holding responsible posts in the hierarchy who nevertheless remain high-ranking *military men*. They are military specialists, not politicians. This point cannot be stressed too strongly. However, the Party network in the Soviet army is now evidently quite subservient to the heads of the over-all Party machinery—i.e., the heads of the Central Committee Secretariat. A conference of secretaries of the Party cells in the army was convened by the Central Committee Secretariat in May, 1960, at a moment of acute conflict between Khrushchev and the Soviet army commanders, or, rather, those of them who opposed Khrushchev's proposed cuts in the military establishment. At this meeting, Brezhnev, a Khrushchev man, briefed the Party apparatus of the army and spoke out against those in the military who opposed cuts in the military budget.

Even under Stalin, the Soviet high command was able to exert some influence on policy in so far as specifically military matters were concerned, as witness the opposition to Shtemenko and Konev at the beginning of 1953. After Stalin's death, the situation of the military improved. Their influence in the Ministry of Armed Forces and in the general staff increased, but after Zhukov's dismissal, this influence became that of Konev and his minions. Though we have no detailed knowledge of it, there is certainly some kind of permanent council of representatives of the high command in the Ministry of Armed Forces. All the marshals are probably members of it, and there is evidence that there has been a struggle, begun already under Stalin, for their right to take part in any discussion of major military matters. The council deals with such issues only from a strictly military point of view and the marshals give expert opinion, but opinions on major military problems are bound to affect political decision-making, and thus all of foreign policy.

It is more than likely that there are differences of opinion in the meetings of this council and that there are various factions among its members. It would seem that Konev, who was against stopping atomic tests in 1959 and against cuts in the Soviet army in the beginning of 1960, had powerful opponents and found himself in a minority even in this council.

To all appearances, Konev continued to take part in this council even after his dismissal as commander of the Warsaw Pact forces in the summer of 1960. His name still figures in the lists of participants at all kinds of military conferences—a sure indication that he has not been denied the right to express his point of view at meetings of military experts. In this respect his position is very different from that of Zhukov, whose name ceased to figure in such lists immediately after his dismissal as Minister of the Armed Forces in October, 1957; though theoretically he remains a member of the Supreme Soviet of the U.S.S.R., Zhukov's name is not mentioned in the public reports of its sessions. But Konev has certainly been able to defend his views. The very fact of his appointment as Soviet commander in East Germany at a moment when Khrushchev went back on his decision to make cuts in the army clearly suggests that the appointment represented a victory for Konev's policy. Even more conclusive evidence for the victory of his position was the resumption of atomic tests just three weeks after his new appointment.

Although Konev takes over his new post as a victor, this does not necessarily mean a complete triumph for his political line. There are many reasons to believe that the controversy over his policy continues. In this respect, the recent appearance of Zhukov at the French exhibition in Moscow was not without significance. This was his first public appearance since his dismissal in 1957, and it seems unlikely that he came to Moscow merely to sign the guest book at the exhibition. He went there to make sure that his arrival in Moscow did not go unnoticed, and hence that there was more to his presence than met the eye. But however that may be, Konev's appointment is an important gauge of the present state of relations between the Soviet army and the country's political leaders.

M. A. Suslov*

IN recent months, in view of the striking inconsistencies in Soviet foreign policy, the world press has begun to take an interest in M. A. Suslov. Much has already been written on his role in the government in general and on his influence on Khrushchev's foreign policy, and widely different interpretations and conclusions have been offered. It must be admitted that the problem of Suslov is a difficult one. The Stalinist era produced a type of leader who almost never appeared before the outside world, who published almost nothing, and whose activities were carried on behind the scenes. During the post-Stalin years, the tendency has changed. We now have a new type of leader, one prolific both on paper and in speech. Suslov remains faithful to the old tradition. On the whole, very little is known about him; the best available summary of his career

* This article appeared in the *Sotsialistichesky Vestnik,* November, 1960, and January, 1961.

has appeared in the June, 1960, issue of the German journal *Osteu-ropa*. But we know enough to give us a general picture of Suslov's Party career in the context of the power struggle that has been going on in the Kremlin during the last few decades.

The son of a poor Saratov peasant, Suslov began his political career as a completely green youth of sixteen or seventeen, taking part in the movement of the Committees of the Village Poor in 1918–19.* This movement was started by Lenin with the deliberate purpose of "intensifying the class struggle in the countryside"; the fact that Suslov's political career began there is almost symbolic: his whole life has been marked by an intensification of the class struggle in the countryside.

In 1921, at the very beginning of the NEP (New Economic Policy), Suslov was sent to Moscow by the Komsomol. There he attended the newly established *rabfak*.† Later, he graduated from the Plekhanov Institute of National Economy (1928) and the Red Professors' Institute, and in 1930, he was appointed a lecturer at Moscow University. Thus, he was among the first wave of young workers and peasants who were to break into the universities without the traditional diplomas, and who, as Trotsky said, began "to gnaw the granite of learning" with their young teeth. These were the young people whom Trotsky tried to win over when, in 1923–24, he made his first attempt to fight the Bolshevik old guard. Suslov, however, was not among the young people who greeted Trotsky's lectures with ovations. At any rate, current entries in official encyclopedias say that even then, Suslov took part in the fight against Trotskyites and other deviationists, "firmly upholding and spreading the general Party line." For these services, he was, in 1931, promoted to a "responsible post" in the Central Control Commission, combining it with work in the People's Commissariat of Workers' and Peasants' Inspectorate (*Narkomrabkrin*). He obviously preferred the career of a Party Chekist to that of a Party scholar—for

* Established June 11, 1918, these Committees were designed to fight the *kulaks* and to acquire the grain needed to feed the cities. The requisitioning was often carried out by Communists from the city, thus serving to embitter the poor peasants, and the program ended in failure. In November, 1918, the Committees were abandoned.—Ed.

† The *rabfak,* or "workers' faculty," prepared students for the university within a couple of years.—Ed.

that was what a "responsible position" in the Central Control Commission, especially in 1931, meant.

At that time, after the Sixteenth Congress, the Central Control Commission, formerly the relatively impartial arbiter in inner-Party conflicts it was intended to be, was turned into a militant tool of narrow Stalinist policy. The work of its apparatus was directed by Yezhov centrally and by Malenkov in Moscow; Malenkov's activities were guided by Stalin himself, either directly or through Poskrebyshev. This apparatus was charged with purging "errant" Communists, especially those in responsible government posts. After Rykov was removed as Chairman of the Council of People's Commissars (in January, 1931), the government apparatus was completely ravaged. It was at this time, and probably for this purpose, that Suslov assumed his post in the Central Control Commission.

We know very little about his specific part in this purge, and it is not of great interest anyway. The main thing is that he moved along his path smoothly and successfully. He worked in the Central Control Commission until 1937, that is, until the height of the Great Purge. In 1937, he was named Secretary of the Provincial Party Committee in Rostov—no doubt after Sheboldaev and his entire apparatus were arrested there, and no doubt also in order to finish that purge.* From 1939 to 1944, he was First Secretary of the Regional Committee in Stavropol and a member of the Military Council of the North Caucasian Front. In this connection, it was undoubtedly Suslov who carried out the liquidation of the Autonomous Kalmyk Republic and the deportation of its population to Central Asia.† As a reward, he was made chairman of the Party

* B. P. Sheboldaev (1895–1939), was caught in Stalin's onslaught on the Party which lasted from 1936 to 1938. He had previously been one of the provincial secretaries on whom Stalin relied to put through his policy.—Ed.

† The Soviets had established the Kalmyk Autonomous Province in November, 1920. This was transformed into an Autonomous Republic after the elimination of the Kalmyk national leadership in 1933. In the early stages of World War II, Soviet propaganda referred favorably to the Kalmyks, stressing their patriotism, and the regime allowed them to reopen their schools, etc. But sometime between 1943 and 1945, the government changed its policy. Along with the Volga German and Crimean Autonomous Republics, the Kalmyk Republic was destroyed in 1944 and its population deported. The peoples of these areas were charged with having cooperated with the Germans. (See in this connection Walter Kolarz, *Russia and her Colonies* [New York: Frederick A. Praeger, 1952], pp. 81–87.)—Ed.

Central Committee's Bureau for the Lithuanian S.S.R. at the end of 1944. For eighteen months, he directed the mass executions and deportations in Lithuania, as well as the forced collectivization, which was carried out with unusual speed and ruthlessness. The individual-farm economy of the region was denounced as having been the social basis of German military rule. There is enough material about the conduct of this operation in the Lithuanian S.S.R. to give us an idea of Suslov's character as a cold and ruthless automaton.

The work of leading Party figures was always closely watched by the top men in the Kremlin, a number of whom personally knew Suslov from his past activities. It therefore came as no surprise when, in March, 1946, the first postwar Plenum of the Central Committee rewarded his services by making him a member of the Central Committee's new Orgburo.

The Plenum of March, 1946, was in general an important event, an understanding of which is essential to an insight into both the history of the CPSU and Suslov's career in particular. From all outward signs, the Plenum looked like a victory for Malenkov, whose name appeared immediately after Stalin's in the lists of all bodies set up at the Plenum. Undoubtedly, this Plenum also made the decisions by which the Supreme Soviet, which met right after it, reorganized the government apparatus, renaming the Council of People's Commissars the Council of Ministers. This reorganization was connected with major changes in the relations of the government and the Party apparatus. There was a definite tendency to increase the power of the government at the expense of the Party. Of course, Stalin quite openly sought to concentrate all the power in his own hands irrespective its source—state or government. Yet it has now become clear that at the same time, both in the Plenum and outside it, there was a move to mobilize the forces opposed to Malenkov, the real author of the policy of strengthening the government. The principal part in this anti-Malenkov move was played by Zhdanov and his Leningrad group, who wished to broaden the role of the Party.

Zhdanov's struggle against Malenkov continued for three years, but the duel between the Zhdanovites and the Malenkovites was not the main bout being fought within the Politburo. The situation was considerably more complex and, in trying to understand it, the historian must take note of the existence of at least two other influential groupings which pursued their own political lines and whose influence was at times very considerable.

The first of these was Beria's, backed by the power of the political police, to which Stalin, after the Purge, had left its dual function of exercising surveillance over the Party apparatus and purging it when necessary. Of course, the police apparatus had always been under Stalin's personal control and all major purges were carried out by Beria on Stalin's instructions, but the power of the police, and hence the power concentrated in Beria's hands, was so enormous, that even if he had been completely loyal to Stalin (and there is room for doubt), Beria could not help but create a personal following. By its very nature, this following was antagonistic to Zhdanov's group and tended to gravitate toward Malenkov, all the while, however, maintaining its independence.

Finally, it is possible to assume the existence of one other force in the postwar Stalin era. This group sided with the supporters of the Party but did not join with the Zhdanov group. The emergence within the Kremlin leadership of men who moved into very responsible posts without being connected with the other groups mentioned seems to argue for the existence of this other force. These men could not have remained in such posts without very influential support; a study of their roles leads to the conclusion that such support could only come from Poskrebyshev, the *éminence grise* of the Stalin era. Poskrebyshev's role is dealt with in greater detail elsewhere (see pp. 105 ff.). Here I wish merely to point out that at all times he could have played this role only with the knowledge and encouragement of Stalin himself. Stalin kept Poskrebyshev in reserve, so to speak, in the event that he might have to intervene covertly on his own behalf in the struggle among the leaders. Poskrebyshev was Stalin's hidden trump card. For this reason, Poskrebyshev secretly picked out men suitable for his purposes.

Only in this light is it possible to understand the make-up of the Orgburo created at the March, 1946, Plenum. This Orgburo was unusually large (fifteen members; the Orgburo set up after the Eighteenth Congress, in March, 1939, had had only nine members). The inclusion in it of some secretaries of provincial regional committees who had come up during the war was an entirely new departure. In addition to the secretaries of the Moscow and Leningrad regional committees, the new Orgburo included Andrianov from Sverdlovsk, Patolichev from Cheliabinsk, Radionov from Gorky, and Suslov. The future was to prove that there was not a single Malenkovite among them. This, of course, was not accidental; during the ten years in which he controlled the cadres at the center of the Party, Malenkov had established close ties at the upper levels, whereas the regional secretaries whom he had appointed did not regard themselves as his adherents. Most of them were Zhdanovites. In addition to A. A. Kuznetsov (Leningrad) and Radionov (Gorky), who were liquidated in 1950,* Patolichev undoubtedly also was a Zhdanovite; in the spring of 1947, he had been sent to the Ukraine with Kaganovich in an anti-Khrushchev move, but soon got into hot water there and had some difficulty extricating himself.† Andrianov, no doubt, was one of Beria's men; he was liquidated in September, 1953, following Beria's downfall,

* M. Radionov, Chairman of the Council of Ministers of the R.S.F.S.R., A. A. Kuznetsov, Secretary of the CPSU Central Committee, and other close collaborators of Zhdanov—whose arrests began in March, 1949—were executed in 1950.—B. N./1964.

† N. S. Patolichev, until then Secretary of the Chelyabinsk *obkom*, was assigned to the central Party apparatus in April, 1946, and elected Secretary of the Central Committee of the CPSU. He was there caught up in the struggle between Zhdanov and Malenkov. At the beginning of 1947, he was appointed Secretary of the Central Committee of the Ukrainian Communist Party, the post formerly occupied by Khrushchev. This appointment was connected with Kaganovich's transfer to the Ukraine; he was charged with the supervision of Khrushchev, who in turn had been demoted during the war years from the post of First Secretary of the Ukrainian Party to Chairman of the Ukrainian Council of Ministers.

At the time, Malenkov supported Khrushchev and sabotaged Kaganovich's assignment. Kaganovich was subsequently recalled to Moscow, and Patolichev, who had been sent to help Kaganovich, was taken from the Ukraine and appointed *obkom* Secretary in Rostov-on-Don, which was in effect a demotion. Evidently, Patolichev did not show special fervor in his work against Khrushchev, for he suffered relatively little later on; even before 1950, he was appointed Secretary of the Central Committee of Belorussia, and at the present time he is Minister of Foreign Trade of the U.S.S.R.—B. N./1964.

in the same purge in which two other Beria men, the Azerbaidzhani Bagirov and the Armenian Arutiunov, were also caught.

Suslov was the only "provincial" in the Orgburo in March, 1946, who not only maintained himself at the summit but who, despite all ups and downs, became a star of the first magnitude. In part, his rise is due to his personal qualities: caution, self-control, and flexibility. But these alone would not have sufficed. He also needed influential support, and all available information leads to the conclusion that Suslov received his support from Poskrebyshev. In the postwar years, the role of Stalin's personal secretariat was not so great as during the 1930's. After Stalin had, via Beria, disposed of the organizers of the Great Purge, many of the secretariat's functions were transferred to relevant departments of Beria's far-flung apparatus. But Poskrebyshev himself was retained by Stalin and even allowed to continue his work.

In 1946–48, a major conflict unfolded between Zhdanov and Malenkov. Zhdanov, for whom ideological questions were paramount, took the offensive against Malenkov personally as well as against his followers. In August, 1946, Malenkov was deposed as First Secretary of the Central Committee. He was charged mainly with having shown leniency toward the "bourgeois West" in wartime propaganda and of glorifying Russia's national past. Stalin, far from agreeing with Zhdanov, did not permit Zhdanov to finish off his opponent; instead, he took Malenkov into the Council of Ministers and in effect made him its chief. But Stalin did allow Zhdanov to "correct" the Party's ideological line, and Zhdanov launched an attack against G. F. Aleksandrov, then head of Agitprop. The resultant "philosophical discussion" led to a slump in Aleksandrov's fortunes.*

In October, 1947, Aleksandrov was replaced by Suslov, who continued the basic "tightening up" of the ideological front. It is known that he was the one who implemented the Central Committee's resolution of February 10, 1948, against Muradeli and other

---

* Aleksandrov was caught in the series of attacks launched by Zhdanov between 1946 and 1948 against intellectuals, with the aim of tightening the control which had been allowed to slacken during the war. Aleksandrov was removed from his post, but in 1954 he became Minister of Culture, falling into complete disgrace only after Malenkov's downfall.—Ed.

composers,* in line with Zhdanov's policy. He was no doubt concerned to demonstrate to Zhdanov his disapproval of Malenkov. Yet Suslov was not an orthodox Zhdanovite, and in the summer of 1948, at the meeting of the Cominform in Sinaia (Romania), he played an active role in exacerbating relations with Tito. He is said to be the author of the measure adopted at this meeting which played a decisive role in Tito's break with Moscow.† This conflict with Tito was a hard blow indeed for Zhdanov, who did not recover from it either politically (he was ousted from the Cominform) or personally (he died on August 31, 1948, officially from heart failure).

Regaining power over the Central Committee apparatus in July, 1948, Malenkov began a brutal purge of the Zhdanovites, in which he had Beria's complete support and Stalin's blessing. The purge reached its height in March, 1949, with the arrest of thousands of Zhdanovites, headed by Voznesensky, A. A. Kuznetsov, and Radionov. In this period Suslov, too, had his difficulties. At the end of 1948, he lost his post as head of Agitprop; and it was Pospelov, not he, who delivered the traditional speech on the anniversary of Lenin's death in January, 1949, a sure sign that the Agitprop was now headed by Pospelov. The *Large Soviet Encyclopedia* states that in 1949–50, Suslov was editor-in-chief of *Pravda,* and also that during this time he remained a Central Committee Secretary. No doubt this is formally correct, since Suslov headed the delegation of the CPSU at the meeting of the Cominform in November, 1949, although the report of the meeting does not call him Secretary of the Central Committee and, what is more, the entire CPSU delegation consisted of only Suslov and Yudin. But

---

* Vano Muradeli, a Georgian composer whose work had always been impeccably conformist, was accused of having "formalist" sympathies. His opera "The Great Friendship" was condemned in a resolution of the CPSU Central Committee of February 14, 1948. This resolution also criticized a number of other composers. Its author was Suslov, who then headed the Agitprop. On May 28, 1958, Khrushchev, at the height of a bitter conflict with Suslov (who opposed Khrushchev on domestic policy, relations with China, and particularly relations with Tito), got the Central Committee to rescind its resolution of February 14, 1948.—B. N./1964.

† This concerned plans for the political and economic consolidation of Eastern Europe under Soviet control in the Cominform.—Ed.

essentially, the title of Central Committee secretary could have been only a nominal one at that time. Suslov's *Pravda* job must have taken up a great deal of his time, and he could not have devoted himself fully to his secretaryship. The Cominform and relations with foreign Communist parties remained under his jurisdiction, but Malenkov attached very litle importance to that aspect of the Central Committee's work.

There can be only one explanation for Suslov's diminished status: during the years of Zhdanov's dominance, Suslov had incurred Malenkov's enmity, and Malenkov had become almost omnipotent in the Central Committee after the break with Tito. However, Suslov was not directly connected with the Zhdanovites and therefore was not caught in the purge. He also had influential support, and Malenkov had to reckon with that. All that happened, therefore, is that Suslov lost his leading position in the Secretariat and fell into semidisgrace.

This situation lasted until the beginning of 1951, when, according to *Osteuropa,* the press began to mention Suslov's name more frequently and more prominently. If his position was now very much stronger, this was because of his role in a new phase in the power struggle among Stalin's henchmen.

The dispute about amalgamating kolkhozes and creating *agrogorods* came into the open. Khrushchev, who in December, 1949, had been transferred to Moscow to the post of Central Committee Secretary, was the author of this scheme. In February, 1950, he had won a victory over Andreev, who until then had directed the Party's collective-farm policy, and had taken over his post. But Khrushchev ran afoul of Beria, and in March, 1951, Beria dealt him a serious blow. The most detailed account of this setback for Khrushchev was given at the time in speeches by Bagirov and Arutiunov, secretaries of the Azerbaidzhan and Armenian Central Committees, published in the official papers of these two republics.

But Khrushchev had no intention of giving in. Stalin was on his side and he had the full support of Poskrebyshev. The question of the *agrogorods* was a detail; in actuality, the point at issue was a radical change of line in support of a more aggressive foreign policy. The amalgamation of the kolkhozes had as its purpose the strengthening of the home front for the coming period of war and revolution. In the last analysis, the theoretical disputes over the various roads to Communism were also concerned with this issue, as were the plans for a new purge and the deportation of the Jews to Siberia. The drive to increase the role of the Party in the general machinery of the dictatorship was also geared to this aim; the implementation of Stalin's new policy hinged on such a reorganization of the Party.

Little is known about Suslov's standing in the bloc that was formed to carry out the new program. The history of this final period of Stalin's life has, on the whole, been kept secret, although quite a bit of reliable information is beginning to come to light. But there is no doubt whatever that Suslov was part of this new alignment of forces and that his was a significant role. His attack on Fedoseev in *Pravda* (December, 1952), and his speech at a meeting of the Soviet Academy of Sciences (January, 1953), show that Stalin had entrusted the forthcoming purge of the scientific and ideological front to him, and great importance was then attached to this front. Suslov's role, however, was undoubtedly not limited to this. His long tenure as director of the foreign section of the Central Committee of the CPSU and his membership in the Supreme Soviet's commission on foreign affairs leave no doubt that he had a hand in working out Stalin's new foreign policy. The fact that in 1954, Suslov was elected Chairman of the Supreme Soviet foreign-affairs commission is further evidence of his importance.

Although we do not know exactly what Suslov's role was in the grisly plot against the peace of the world organized by Poskrebyshev on instruction of Stalin in 1952–53, we know enough to say that he was one of the chief architects of the plot.

One more fact must be noted: in this plot, Suslov worked hand in hand with Khrushchev. It was at that time that the close contact of these two partners in a common cause was established.

Hans-Jürgen Eitner, the author of the *Osteuropa* article on Suslov, writes that after Stalin's death, the ground was cut from under Suslov's feet and that for a whole week he was virtually without a job. He managed to extricate himself only with great difficulty.

The first post-Stalin days—from the moment of Stalin's death (the official time given is 9:50 P.M., March 5; there are reliable reports that he actually died earlier) until the meeting of the first Plenum of the CPSU Central Committee (March 12–14)—were perhaps, the most "fateful" days in the entire history of the dictatorship, particularly if we include the days during which Stalin, having suffered a stroke (officially on the night of March 1–2), lay on his deathbed. What actually took place in those days behind the high walls of the Kremlin is not yet known, and one would have to sift through mountains of contradictory information in search of a grain of truth. Two events, however, must be noted, since they left their imprint on what followed: during the very hours when Stalin lay dying, Poskrebyshev, the head of his personal secretariat and keeper of all his secrets, disappeared from the political scene. And during these same hours, Beria took command of the MGB building.

These two events were just two facets of the great palace revolution. Beria, who had been marked down as the chief victim of the carefully prepared new purge, forestalled his enemies at the last minute and, after getting Poskrebyshev out of the way, he seized the MGB. This shake-up within the regime, coinciding with Stalin's death—and perhaps hastening it—finished an important chapter in the history of the dictatorship, a chapter that involved Stalin's master plan for a new purge at home and aggression abroad. It also opened a new chapter in the history of the Soviet regime.

This backstage coup was followed and even consolidated by an overt one. On March 6, 1953, a meeting was held—officially called a "joint session of the Plenum of the Central Committee of the CPSU, the Council of Ministers of the U.S.S.R., and the Presidium of the Supreme Soviet of the U.S.S.R." There is no provision for this type of meeting either in the statutes of the CPSU, the Constitution of the U.S.S.R., or any other Soviet law. Though it had no formal right to make decisions of any kind it did do so, and these decisions provided the quasi-constitutional sanction for the activities of the Party and the government in this new post-Stalin phase of their history. These decisions virtually nullified the resolutions of the Nineteenth Party Congress, particularly those dealing with the structure of the central Party bodies, as well as the relevant sections of the Party statutes. They also made nonsense of that section of the Constitution of the U.S.S.R. dealing with the central government structure.

This joint session introduced by decree a radical change in the whole structure of the government machinery, thus formalizing the political *coup de main* carried out by Beria. Now that Beria had gotten rid of Poskrebyshev, the joint session rescinded all the major structural changes in the Party and government institutions carried out by Poskrebyshev during the preceding six months.

Poskrebyshev had been associated with Stalin for more than thirty years and was greatly trusted by him. He kept nearly all of Stalin's secrets and was privy to nearly all his plans. I say "nearly" because it is inconceivable that Stalin trusted any one person completely. Nevertheless, there is no doubt that Stalin's trust in Poskrebyshev was enormous. Poskrebyshev's position in relation to Stalin varied at different stages of Stalin's rule, but there can be no doubt that on at least two important occasions he played his own hand; in 1933–34, when he was head of the secret commission responsible for preparing the Great Purge, and in 1951–53, when he prepared and started to carry out a second mass purge. He was a murderer by nature, or perhaps it would be more accurate to say that he was a machine for the mass annihilation of people. On the first occasion his "operation" was carried out "successfully"; in the second instance it failed, though through no fault of his.

The process of winding up the abortive second purge included the smashing of Poskrebyshev's network. The removal of people who were mere tools of Poskrebyshev in a technical sense was not recorded at all in the press, and neither their names nor the numbers involved are known to us. We know about liquidations only in so far as more prominent people were affected. One must bear in mind that in those days there was a general truce among the feuding leaders and they all found it in their interest to keep reprisals to a minimum. This makes any reprisals that were actually carried out all the more notable, and there can be no doubt that all such cases concerned relations with Poskrebyshev—relations, moreover, that went beyond the official dealings with a man occupying such a key position in the regime's apparatus.

Hence we see the significance of Suslov's temporary eclipse. Although I have not been able to find confirmation of Herr Eitner's report that Suslov was for a time removed from his post, he doubtless did have some troubles. The reorganization of the Party's central apparatus then taking place was in effect a return to the political arrangements existing prior to the Nineteenth Congress. The enlarged Presidium of the Central Committee set up at the Nineteenth Congress was dissolved and replaced by a small Presidium, which was almost identical in its composition with the Politburo existing in the years before the Nineteenth Congress. All the Central Committee secretaries of that period were now promoted, except Suslov. (Even Ponomarenko, who had just been brought into the Secretariat, became an alternate member of the Presidium.) Apart from Malenkov, Suslov had been a Secretary longer than any of the others—since 1947. But now he was passed over for membership in the Presidium. This "discrimination" can only be interpreted as a sign that he had fallen into some disgrace.

It is also pertinent to note that Frol Kozlov as well was in difficulties at that time. Before Stalin's death he was First Secretary (this title was not in use then, but the post itself already existed) of the Leningrad Regional Committee; on March 6—the day after Stalin's death—Andrianov was sent to Leningrad to take over his post. This action against Kozlov was certainly due to the part he played in preparing the new purge. He was the author of an article —the only one of its kind—actually arguing in favor of a new purge (*Kommunist,* No. 1, January, 1953).

The changes in government and Party organization carried out on March 6 looked like a complete defeat for the Poskrebyshev forces which had managed to reorganize the central Party apparatus at the Nineteenth Congress. On the other hand, there was little internal unity among those responsible for bringing about this reversal of the decisions on the Nineteenth Congress. The new Presidium announced on March 6 was, as I have said, nearly identical with the old Politburo. But this body, even under Stalin, was so rent by internal dissension that it could scarcely function at all. Thus, in carrying out his palace revolution, Beria settled his personal score with Poskrebyshev, but the major problems were left unsolved and there was still no basis for harmonious collaboration between members of the Presidium.

Basically, this was a power struggle between the Party and the government, especially the industrial sector of the latter—a struggle between the Party *apparatchiki* and the Party technocrats. The millions of rank-and-file Party members are responsible for the day-to-day management of all the country's affairs. Almost all members of the Party occupy posts in some sector or another of the apparatus. The function of coordinating this work is shared by the central government and central Party organizations. These two sectors of the ruling apparatus compete with each other and fight each other for power. The rivalry was at the basis of the conflict which Poskrebyshev hoped to resolve by the second mass purge. Stalin's death and the consequent removal of Poskrebyshev did not put an end to this rivalry. On the contrary, they only exacerbated the conflict which now flared up with a vengeance.

The decisions of March 6 were a hastily improvised compromise between the two contending forces. At that moment, Malenkov appeared to be dominant. His position can best be described as that of a leading Party *apparatchik* siding with the Party technocrats. This is like Lenin's definition of a revolutionary Social Democrat as a Jacobin who had adopted the attitude of the proletariat. All the parties to the compromise of March 6, 1953, hence found a natural focus in Malenkov, and he formally became Stalin's successor in all the posts which Stalin had held. He was elected Chairman of the Council of Ministers, he headed both the Presidium and the Secretariat of the Central Committee of the CPSU.

But appearances were deceptive. Malenkov had no real power, and none of the forces around him gave him unqualified support. He lacked Beria's dynamic quality. The collapse of the alliance was inevitable; the only question was who would open hostilities and when. They were in fact started by the Party apparatus headed by Khrushchev. Khrushchev had harbored a grudge from the very beginning, and at the first opportunity he came out against Malenkov's monopoly of the top posts. The first full Plenum of the Party Central Committee opened on March 12 (not all members of the Central Committee had been present on March 6). This was the last time that Malenkov was described as a Central Committee Secretary in the press. He was replaced in this capacity by Khrushchev, who selected a Secretariat of his own. Only one of its members, Shatalin, was a definite Malenkov supporter, and he left the scene when Malenkov was ousted as Chairman of the Council of Ministers. The rest—Suslov, Pospelov, and Ignatiev—were allies of Khrushchev.

The appointment of Ignatiev as a Central Committee Secretary was an open challenge to all who believed that Stalin's death would put an end to the terror. Between December, 1951, and March 6, 1953, Ignatiev had been Minister of State Security and as such he was thought of by the general public as the chief organizer of the second mass purge. Of course, he only carried out orders coming from Stalin and Poskrebyshev, but the same might be said of Himmler in Hitler's Germany. Later, in defending Ignatiev, Khrushchev said that Stalin had forced Ignatiev to use torture, threatening otherwise "to shorten his body by a whole head."* But all the others who carried out Stalin's orders, including minor interrogators, were in the same position. Yet this did not prevent Khrushchev from using strong language about them and inflicting penalties on them.

Only after Beria quashed the Jewish doctors' plot and publicly revealed the part played in it by Ignatiev (who, according to *Pravda,* had exhibited "political blindness and gullibility") was Khrushchev forced to remove the newly appointed Ignatiev from his post. Even so, Khrushchev has continued to stand up for him, giving him an important Party post in the provinces. Ignatiev is now First Secretary of the Central Committee of the Tatar Republic.

It is important to be clear about these facts in view of recent attempts to present Khrushchev and the whole group centering on the Secretariat of the Central Committee as de-Stalinizers doing everything in their power to fight the "Stalinists" (a term applied above all to the "anti-Party group" of Malenkov, Molotov, Kaganovich, etc.). In reality, in the three years before the Twentieth Congress, the body which most stubbornly resisted de-Stalinization and the revelation of the truth about Stalin's crimes was the Secretariat of the Central Committee, headed by Khrushchev. The fact is that in this period, the only attempts to expose Stalin's crimes were made by Beria, the head of the MVD.

* "The Crimes of the Stalin Era," p. 49. See also "Russia Purges the Purgers" in this volume, pp. 120 ff.—Ed.

Three Biographies

This situation, which at first glance seems completely improbable, can be explained by reference to the relations among Stalin's heirs. The first point to remember is that everybody around Stalin was willy-nilly an accomplice to Stalin's crimes. To gain Stalin's trust one had to be prepared to carry out any of his orders. Of course, this did not apply to Old Bolsheviks like Molotov or Voroshilov, who were tested by Stalin in other ways. But younger Communists who wished to earn Stalin's confidence had to take part in the persecution of others, demonstrating their readiness to perpetrate the most terrible crimes for the sake of the cause.

The people at the top were grouped not according to the *number* of crimes they had committed (in this respect they were all on a par), but according to the *period* in which they had carried them out. Khrushchev and Suslov were particularly afraid of revelations about their activities during the last two years of Stalin's life, when Ignatiev was Minister of State Security (the purge in Georgia, the doctors' plot, and other crimes of the second purge), whereas Malenkov and Beria were more worried by their personal responsibility for the liquidation of Zhdanovites in 1949–50, the mass deportations of whole ethnic groups in 1944–46,* the Great Purge, etc.

It would be wrong to whitewash Beria, but he deserves credit for making the first move to break the conspiracy of silence in which the regime tried to envelop the crimes of Stalin. His exposure of the doctors' plot was of revolutionary importance. He had been authorized by the Presidium of the Central Committee to close the case against the doctors, but he went far beyond the bounds of his instructions by publishing a long article in *Pravda* of April 6, 1953, in which the accusations against the doctors were called a "vile slander of honest and respected citizens of the Soviet state"; it was reported that torture was used in the investigation and that the

---

* In 1944–45, immediately after the defeat of Hitler's armies, the Soviet government carried out a cruel purge in all areas formerly under German occupation. There were mass executions, arrests, and deportations of everybody accused of sympathy or collaboration with the Germans. Whole ethnic groups (Crimean Tatars, Chechens, Ingush, Kalmyks, Adyge, Kabarinians, Balkhars) were deported to Siberia and Central Asia. Great Russians suffered no less than the other ethnic groups.—B. N./1964.

guilty persons were under arrest and being brought to trial. Since Khrushchev's "secret speech" at the Twentieth Congress was never published in the Soviet press, this *Pravda* article is so far the only document on record which not only rehabilitates a large group of arrested persons, but also denounces the criminal conduct of the people responsible for the case. It was, furthermore, particularly significant in that it concerned the rehabilitation not of Party members, but of "non-Party specialists," who as a class only began to be rehabilitated later.

It is now known that this action of Beria's provoked strong indignation in Party circles and was largely responsible for the downfall of Beria, which was engineered by Khrushchev. At that time and until his speech at the Twentieth Congress, Khrushchev opposed any revelations about terrorist activities of the Stalinist regime and did everything possible to prevent them. When Malenkov, in June or July, 1954, mounted the trial against Riumin, Ignatiev's deputy and the chief organizer of the Jewish doctors' affair, Khrushchev, in December of that same year, retaliated by bringing up the so-called Leningrad affair of 1949, when the Zhdanovites were liquidated at the instigation of Beria and Malenkov. In so doing, Khrushchev was making the point that he would not allow emphasis to be placed only on those crimes committed in the last period of Stalin's life.

Thus, the initiative in disclosing the truth about the crimes of the Stalinist period clearly did not come from the Central Committee —i.e., Khrushchev's group.

One word of caution: the exposure of Stalin's crimes must not be confused with the campaign against the personality cult or with the simultaneous propaganda for the necessity of collective leadership. The origins of the latter go back to the time of the Nineteenth Congress and the fight to prevent the transformation of the Party into a mere adjunct of an all-powerful government as the sole policy- and decision-making force. One can speak of an absence of collective leadership only during the four-year period (1948–52) when not a single Plenum of the Central Committee was convened. These were the years when Malenkov ruled the government and the Party by Stalin's authority and when he did everything in his power to boost the authority of the government, where the industrial ministries were becoming increasingly dominant. The campaign of April, 1953, in favor of collective leadership, which culminated in a pamphlet by Slepov,* was nothing less than a struggle against the authoritarian attitude of Malenkov, and particularly Beria, and for "Leninist democratic centralism" in the Party. This call for "democratic centralism" had nothing to do with democracy; it was simply the battle cry of the influential captains of Soviet industry who wanted to subordinate the Party cells in Soviet industrial enterprises to the managers.

This was the reason for the stepping-up of the campaign for "collective leadership" in the period just preceding the Twentieth Congress, when it overlapped with the general political campaign then being waged by the Secretariat of the Central Committee under the slogan "Raise up high the banner of the Party of Marx, Engels, Lenin, and Stalin." This slogan was to provide the keynote of the Twentieth Congress, at which Stalin was to have been "rehabilitated" and glorified. It was by no means coincidental that the last volume of Stalin's works was planned for publication in time for the Congress; it had been announced in *Literaturnaya gazeta* in January, 1956. The extent to which the Central Committee Secretariat was prepared to glorify Stalin is indicated by the fact that the volume was to have contained Stalin's speeches between the Seventeenth and Eighteenth Congresses—i.e., for the period of the Yezhovshchina, a time when there had also been much talk about "Leninist principles of leadership" and when Yezhov and Poskrebyshev had given many demonstrations of what was meant by the practical application of these principles.

This campaign for collective leadership owed much to the energetic work of Aristov, the new head of the personnel department of the Central Committee, who was now brought back from exile in the Far East, where he had been sent after the disappearance of

* L. Slepov, then editor of the Party-affairs department of *Pravda,* in April, 1953, published under his own name an article in *Pravda* on "collective leadership," at the instance of the Central Committee Secretariat. The gist of it later appeared as a pamphlet, in which form it was used for the guidance of local organizations.—B. N./1964.

Poskrebyshev.* He carried out a radical purge of the Party apparatus at the secretarial level; in the Ukraine, no less than 20 per cent of the secretaries of primary organizations—i.e., the smallest unit of the Party organization—were removed. It was confidently expected that the Twentieth Congress would be a tame affair, obedient to the dictates of the Secretariat. But the Secretariat made a number of miscalculations and its apparently well-articulated plan for a campaign in favor of collective leadership and the rehabilitation of Stalin had to be hastily altered.

The original plan broke down on several points, and the Communist parties of the satellite countries played a very important part in this. In Hungary and Poland particularly, there was a rapid growth of that mood which was to explode so violently in the summer and fall of 1956. In an attempt to damp it down, the Hungarian and Polish Party leaders came to Moscow with demands for the

---

* A. B. Aristov, born in 1903, was a metallurgical engineer and lecturer at the Leningrad Metallurgical Institute. According to his official biography, he held a responsible position in the Party apparatus from 1940 on. Elected to the Central Committee in 1952 at the Nineteenth Congress, he immediately was assigned to work with personnel, and he played a very active role in the preparations of Stalin's final purge. We can infer this from the fact that after Stalin's death, when Beria and Malenkov began to purge the purgers, Aristov lost his post as Central Committee Secretary and was unemployed for a number of months. Then, after the fall of Beria, there must have been a decision to send him to the Far East. At first, he was appointed chairman of a local soviet, i.e., a non-Party post. Only in 1955, after the fall of Malenkov, did he return to Moscow; thereupon he took up the post of Secretary of the Central Committee, heading the personnel department.

In view of these facts, Aristov may with certainty be regarded as one of the chief organizers of the new purge. His own background as a technician suggests that he might have been entrusted with the purge of the technocrats, who were the main target.

After the Twentieth Congress, Aristov's department was chiefly responsible for sabotaging all attempts to revise Stalinist historiography by Burdzhalov and other historians who had tried in *Voprosy Istorii,* a journal of the Academy of Sciences, to begin a critical reassessment of Stalin's career. Later, Aristov sponsored attacks by *Partinaya Zhizn* on the Department of Social Sciences of the Academy. This led to a great crisis in the Academy and the dismissal of its president, Nesmeyanov. It was certainly as a result of his part in these campaigns that Aristov, sometime in April or May, 1961, lost his job in the Central Committee and was "demoted" to the ambassadorship in Warsaw.—B. N./1964.

rehabilitation of the *émigré* Polish and Hungarian Communists executed by Stalin during the Great Purge. In the final weeks before the opening of the Congress, all kinds of conferences and committee meetings were held in Moscow. The "collective leadership" of Khrushchev and Suslov had to yield to the demands of the "fraternal parties." The decision to rehabilitate the Polish and Hungarian Communists who had died in the Lubianka was made on the eve of the Congress, and the public announcement of it appeared after the Congress was already under way.

The issue of rehabilitations was raised not only by foreign Communists but by Soviet Party members as well. Thousands of written statements by individual Party members were addressed to the Congress. Of even greater significance were the group requests, especially those from the non-Russian republics of the U.S.S.R. Stalin had dealt even more mercilessly with Latvian, Estonian, Central Asian, and Siberian Communists than with the Poles and Hungarians. It was psychologically impossible for the Soviet leadership to make concessions to the satellites and not to the Latvians and Uzbeks. Finally, it was impossible to ignore similar statements from Russians and Ukrainians. As more and more delegates flocked to Moscow, it became obvious that it would be difficult to talk of Stalin in laudatory terms at the Congress. The sentiments in local Party organizations were very similar to those in Party groups in the army, where a series of regional army conferences was marked by opposition to the political directorate of the Ministry of Defense.* This made a strong impression, and it is scarcely a coincidence that the phrase launched by the Central Committee Secretariat about "the great Party of Marx, Engels, Lenin, and Stalin" made its last appearance in *Pravda* on the very day when the conference of the Moscow Military District, in the presence of Marshal Zhukov and after his speech, adopted a restrained but clearly critical resolution concerning political work in the army.

The organizers of the campaign leading up to the Congress had to change their tack abruptly. The fourteenth volume of Stalin's

* As required by regulations, Party conferences were held in the armed forces as part of the pre-Congress campaign.—Ed.

works, which was supposed to exalt his role in the period of the Great Purge, was not published; it is not known whether it is still being held in warehouses or whether it has already been pulped. The last time Stalin's name was linked with Marx's and Lenin's in a *Pravda* editorial was on January 16. This was at the very time when the Presidium of the Central Committee finally got around to listen to the stories of the police officials who had tortured Eikhe,* Chubar,† and other Politburo members. "I thought," one of the Chekists said, "that I was carrying out the will of the Party." Khrushchev indignantly attacked this Chekist. But what had he himself been doing at that time? He claimed on a later occasion that he was not responsible for such crimes because he was not then a member of the Politburo and had no part in decisions which he merely carried out. This was the same answer given by the Chekist who tortured Chubar.

In this article on Suslov I have mentioned his name only rarely. On the whole, as I said earlier, he is one of the Party secretaries of the old school who write and say little and whose activity we can only judge from that of the group to which they belong. At the time of the Twentieth Congress, Suslov headed all ideological divisions of the Secretariat. This means that he was the leading light in the campaign to revive the Stalin cult. His whole career in the Party has

---

* Robert I. Eikhe, a Latvian who was Secretary of the Western Siberian Provincial Committee from 1929 to 1934, became an alternate member of the Politburo in 1938. He seems to have gone out of his mind in 1938 after being tortured and cried out that he was guilty "of belonging to a criminal organization which goes by the name of the Central Committee of the Communist Party of the Soviet Union." Khrushchev went into the Eikhe case at some length in his secret speech.—B. N./1964.

† Vlas Y. Chubar, a worker and son of a peasant, was Chairman of the Ukrainian Council of People's Commissars from 1923 to 1932. He was removed from his post for refusing to requisition grain from the Ukrainian peasants in 1932 on the scale demanded by Stalin, on the grounds that obeying Stalin's demands would cause a famine, a justified fear, since the winter of 1932–33 was a period of frightful famine in the Ukraine and elsewhere. Later Chubar became Deputy Chairman of the Council of People's Commissars of the U.S.S.R. and an alternate member of the Politburo. He was arrested in 1938, on charges which, as Khrushchev admitted in his secret speech, were fabricated.—B. N./1964.

been that of backstage ideologue who, though totally lacking in ideas of his own is a past master at adjusting other people's theories to the Party line. On the rare occasions when he appears in public, he is adept at putting across a hodgepodge of smoothly formulated ideas. And it was he who worked out this pre-Congress campaign, which could not stand the test of contact with reality. His speech at the Congress also was filled with hackneyed phrases.

All his utterances are based on the primitive manipulation of a few concepts. The term "personality cult" was used at this time as a euphemism for Stalinist despotism, and this was the specific meaning then attached to it. To Suslov, however, "personality cult" meant simply any nonviolent deviation from "democracy" within the Party. There is no element of de-Stalinization in his speeches, because they do not deal with the essence of historic Stalinism. It is significant that he spoke only of the period preceding the Nineteenth Congress but not of events preceding Stalin's death, since he was not concerned with Stalin's subjugation of the Party, government, and Soviet society through the application of universal terror, but rather with the policy, associated with Malenkov, of not convening Central Committee Plenums for years on end, of subordinating the interests of the Party to the interests of the government apparatus—in short, of demoting the Party to the status of an auxiliary agency of the regime, whereas for Suslov and his like, the Party was supposed to be the supreme arbiter of the regime.

This is a tricky distinction, and it was part of Suslov's task to mislead his audience, to allay their misgivings, and to confuse them by his ambiguous use of terminology. In this Suslov is often successful. (I was misled by his choice of language and thought for a time that he was trying to assume a position somewhere between Malenkov and Khrushchev.) Suslov's words have to be studied carefully and compared to those of other Communist speakers who, when they use the expression "personality cult," are thinking specifically of Stalin's practices. Mikoyan, speaking almost immediately after Suslov at the Twentieth Congress, made a strong impression not because his words were in themselves more pointed or more vivid, but because he was attacking Stalin even though he did not mention him by name. Suslov, on the other hand, tried to sidetrack

the issue of Stalin by mouthing empty phrases. He did this quite deliberately for the simple reason that he was and is a Stalinist, a colorless one perhaps, but nonetheless distinctly so. In Moscow such Communists from the *apparat* used to be called *"poskrebyshi."**
Suslov is a *poskrebysh* who has survived the Poskrebyshev period.

* A pun on Poskrebyshev's name, which is derived from a word meaning "scraping." It suggests some rather unappetizing leftover.—Ed.

Selected Ann Arbor Paperbacks
Works of enduring merit

For a complete list of Ann Arbor Paperback titles write:
THE UNIVERSITY OF MICHIGAN PRESS ANN ARBOR